Book 12

THE CAUSE OF JAPAN

by

TŌGŌ SHIGENORI

*Foreign Minister of Japan
at the Time of Pearl Harbor and
Again at the End of the Pacific War*

*Translated and Edited by
Tōgō Fumihiko and Ben Bruce Blakeney*

19 — 56

SIMON AND SCHUSTER · NEW YORK

PUBLISHED IN JAPAN IN 1952
AS *JIDAI NO ICHIMEN*

FIRST PRINTING
LIBRARY OF CONGRESS CATALOG CARD NUMBER: 56–9916
MANUFACTURED IN THE UNITED STATES OF AMERICA
BY AMERICAN BOOK–STRATFORD PRESS, INC., NEW YORK

THE AUTHOR
WHEN AMBASSADOR TO GERMANY
1938

CONTENTS

Translators' Introduction

THE LIFETIME OF the author of this book, Tōgō Shigenori,[1] spanned an era which saw Japan emerge from international nonentity, attain position first as a Power in the Far East and then as one of the Great Powers of the world, challenge half that world in war and achieve rapid and brilliant mastery of much of the Pacific and Asia, and at last go down in defeat and ruin. In the later acts of this drama the author, as a professional diplomatist, played a role of growing importance, until in the denouement he dominated the stage.

Shortly after the Second World War was brought to an end by Japan's surrender, Mr. Tōgō was taken into custody, by order of the Supreme Commander for the Allied Powers, as a "war-crimes" suspect. In the spring following he was put on trial at the International Military Tribunal for the Far East,[2] charged with "conspiracy to wage aggressive war" and with responsibility for atrocities committed during the war by Japanese military forces. The interminable proceedings of this "tribunal"—it sat continuously from 3 May 1946 to 12 November 1948—resulted in a judgment convicting Mr. Tōgō of conspiracy, while acquitting

[1] Oriental names are given in this book in the Oriental manner, the surname first.
[2] The abbreviation "IMTFE" is used throughout the book for the tribunal when it is referred to or its proceedings cited.

1

him on the atrocities charge. The sentence passed upon him was to serve twenty years' imprisonment; and this was singular. This tribunal had dutifully convicted, impartially, all defendants haled before it by the prosecutors, condemning seven to hang, sixteen to serve life imprisonment, and two only to shorter terms. Despite the prosecution's obsession that Mr. Tōgō, as Foreign Minister at the commencement of the Pacific War, must have been a ringleader of the "conspiracy" which they had invented, he alone of those convicted of "crimes against peace" received less than the standard life sentence. The reasons for the tribunal's imposing a sentence so inconsistent with its verdict of Mr. Tōgō's guilt of crimes of aggression may be left to the discernment of the reader of this record of the climactic epoch of his lifelong fight for justice and peace.

By the time Mr. Tōgō was incarcerated in Sugamo Prison at the beginning of his trial, his health—not good for some years past—had been shattered by the strain of his struggle as Foreign Minister in the Suzuki Cabinet of 1945 to put an end to the war. More than half of his prison life was passed in American military hospitals in Tokyo. One day in the middle of July 1950, when his wife and daughter visited him at the hospital for one of the semimonthly half hours permitted them, he handed to them a package of notebooks, laboriously filled with penciled writing, asking their perusal of and comments on it. The comments were never given; the meeting proved to be the last, the next news to the family being notice from the hospital of Mr. Tōgō's death in the early-morning hours of 23 July. The notebooks constituted the manuscript of this book.

Concerning these last years and his trial, Mr. Tōgō has not written in his book. His purpose was, as he stated it in the foreword to his manuscript, "neither autobiographical, nor the writ-

2

ing of an apologia for actions of mine nor yet justification of the policies pursued by the Japanese government; it is intended herein to describe the movement of the times as I have seen them and to consider as cultural and historical phenomena the events which I have observed and participated in." He obviously felt that upon him, as a statesman once charged with heavy responsibilities in the conduct of his nation's foreign affairs, a duty rested to leave for posterity a factual account of the part played by him in the most eventful days in the history of Japan. This task he undertook in prison, and—knowing that he could not live long—for the last few months of his life he literally poured into his manuscript all his remaining vital force, in the effort to complete his record. His hold on life was too tenuous to permit him to finish his book as he would have wished—he had intended to amplify it, to polish its expression, to have searched out and inserted the many references to source materials to which in prison he had no access. Thanks, however, to his powerful memory, he has been able from it alone to give us this invaluable firsthand account of the momentous period of Far Eastern history in which he lived and worked.[3]

Mr. Tōgō was born, in 1882, scion of a family of *samurai* of the province of Satsuma, in southern Japan, into a time of ferment. The American Commodore Perry, coming with his "Black Ships" a short three decades earlier, had peremptorily awakened Japan from medieval slumber, had taught her the lesson that

[3] The book as published in Japanese was divided into three parts: the first (omitted in this translation, except as use is made of it in this Introduction) covering events from the author's entry into the foreign service to the formation of the Tōjō Cabinet; the second and third, Parts I and II of this edition. In the editing, the translators have added to the few references which Mr. Tōgō was able to supply (all attributed to "T. S.") a number of citations to works which, though the author did not cite them, he is known to have used in preparing his manuscript. In addition, a few biographical and other notes have been given in the hope that they will be useful in orienting the Western reader in a milieu which may be unfamiliar.

3

even an island empire was part of the world and must embrace the world's thought and the world's machines if it would survive. Japan's egocentric feudalism crumbled under the onslaught of the nineteenth century, and she entered the world; Japan adopted a modern system of government and administration, modern finance and modern arms; railroads were built; the telegraph came; diplomatic relations were opened with foreign countries. Japan became a member—probationary, and not fully accepted, as yet—of the community of nations.

Japan learned from the world not only the world's forms of speech, not alone the power of its fleets and its battalions, its power of steam; she learned, too, its power politics. Japan saw that success, not to say survival, in that nineteenth-century world meant empire, and forthwith she set about attaining one. By the nineties she had equipped herself with the paraphernalia of a modern state—Prussia, in the main, was her model, and she had her Prussian-trained Army, her Prussian-inspired Constitution and administration. In 1894 quarrels with the great continental neighbor, China, led to blows; and in a short and easy war the new Japanese forces routed those of the decayed, corrupt and *fainéant* Ch'ing bureaucracy, and Japan emerged as the new Power of Asia.

But as the aftermath of the Sino-Japanese War, Japan received an advanced course of instruction in power politics. The war had had its origin in controversy over control of Korea, the peninsula which from protohistoric times the Japanese had observed to be "a dagger pointed at the heart of Japan" and therefore at all costs to be kept from falling into unfriendly hands. The international status of the peninsula had for centuries been equivocal, and in the nineteenth century China was still maintaining pretensions to suzerainty over it; but in 1876 Japan—employing a faithful

4

replica of Perry's tactics—had "opened" Korea, and obtained for herself recognition of a special sphere of interest there. China was not content to acknowledge that Korea was no longer in any realistic sense her tributary, and the immediate *casus belli* in 1894 had been Chinese efforts to reassert and strengthen her shadowy dominion over it. The Treaty of Shimonoseki which ended the war awarded to Japan as the victor's spoils an indemnity—recognition of the independence of Korea, of course—and cession not only of Formosa and the adjacent Pescadores Islands but as well of the Liaotung Peninsula at the southern tip of the Chinese province of Manchuria. A glance at the map of northeast Asia shows Liaotung standing a gateway open to Manchuria, a barrier athwart Chinese access to Korea, its occupant in strategic dominance of the whole of North China, with its historical capital, Peking.

But there were uninvited guests at the peace conference of 1895. The European Powers did not welcome the participation of a newcomer in the "cutting of the Chinese melon" which during the second half of the century had yielded them many succulent morsels; and even before the meeting of the plenipotentiaries at Shimonoseki the Japanese government had become aware that there was in the offing an unfriendly tripartite intervention to influence the peace terms. On 23 April 1895, hard on the signing of the peace, the Ministers of Russia, France and Germany called at the Foreign Ministry in Tokyo and delivered notes stating that the possession by Japan of the Liaotung Peninsula "would render illusory the independence of Korea" and would be "a perpetual obstacle to the peace of the Far East," and "advising" that it be retroceded to China. Faced with overwhelming force, Japan could only bow to this "advice," and relinquished the coveted foothold in Manchuria in return for an added indemnity. She had

5

followed the most approved patterns of imperialism of the day, but she had come on the scene too late; the empires were already pre-empted.

That the Tripartite Intervention had been conceived and managed by Russia, Japan well knew. That an active Russian imperialism in northeast Asia would bring Japan to conflict, soon or late, with the Tsarist Empire was manifest—would, unless Japan was content to waive all claim to that share in exploitation of the continent to which geographical propinquity and the international mores of the day entitled her. The conflict was not long delayed. The Sino-Japanese War had demonstrated how much more debilitated was China than the European Powers had comprehended, and its prompt sequel was an accelerated "scramble" by them for concessions, leases, spheres of interest in China. The "breakup of China" was freely spoken of, and plans for the actual, formal partitioning were drawn in the chancelleries of Europe. In the forefront of the scramble was Imperial Russia. First, lending to China the gold for payment of the Japanese indemnity, she procured for herself in 1898 a twenty-five-year lease on the southern part of the same Liaotung Peninsula Japan's control of which she had a few short years earlier viewed with such pious apprehension. With this leasehold went the right to extend the Trans-Siberian Railway across northern Manchuria to Vladivostok, to connect it with the Liaotung territory by a new line, and to police and administer the railway zones. American concern over the impending partition of China prompted Secretary of State Hay in 1899 to postulate the doctrine of the "Open Door" and equality of commercial opportunity in China; but the scramble went on, and soon a pretext was given for a more elaborate Russian imperialistic venture. The Boxer Rebellion brought about, in 1900, a joint foreign intervention in North China to rescue the missions and nationals and protect the interests of the treaty Powers from the xenophobic Boxers. Under guise of thus protecting its interests, Russia overran the whole of Manchuria, established itself as *de facto* sovereign, and gave every indication of intending to remain without term. Tsarist penetration of Korea as well had been vigorous and determined since 1895, and by the turn of the century it was an open secret that the Autocrat of all the Russias was dreaming dreams of a new Oriental empire which should join to his Siberian possessions earlier wrested from China Korea, all of Manchuria and Mongolia, and Peking with half a million square miles of North China.

Japan observed with dismay the unfolding of these events. A Russia established and ascendent in Manchuria was an obstacle to Japan's legitimate continental aspirations; but a Russia regnant in Korea—grasping the dagger—was a deadly menace to the very existence of Japan as an independent nation. As Russia developed her Far Eastern rail net, as her military and naval fortifications in Manchuria proliferated, and as her political encroachments not only in China but in Korea became ever more widespread and more insolent, Japan watched—and prudently armed. During those years Japan endeavored unremittingly to reach a *modus vivendi* effecting recognition of a sphere of interest for Japan in Korea and for Russia in Manchuria, but all efforts were unavailing. At last in late summer of 1903 Japan instituted formal Russo-Japanese negotiations to try to find a solution, but half a year of parleying was equally barren of result, and at last, frustrated by Muscovite evasion and obstinacy, the Japanese government on 6 February 1904 broke off the negotiations and severed diplomatic relations with St. Petersburg, reserving the right "to take such independent action as they may deem best to consolidate and defend their menaced position."

7

The Russo-Japanese War began on 8 February, with the devastating torpedo attack on the Russian Pacific Squadron lying in the Port Arthur roadstead.

Japan had been forehanded, this time, to obviate any contretemps which should again deprive her of the fruits of a victory fairly won. In 1902 had been executed the Anglo-Japanese Alliance, by which England had abandoned her historic policy of "splendid isolation" to ally the greatest naval Powers of West and East for mutual defense of their interests in China and Korea respectively. By the alliance—which provided that if either signatory, at war with another, should be attacked by a third, the other signatory would come to its aid—Japan was assured of being able to deal with Russia with no repetition of the intervention of 1895.

If the Sino-Japanese War had been won on the enemy's weakness, the Russo-Japanese was another story. Here Japan engaged a modern military power; but in the eighteen months following the attack on Port Arthur, the Japanese arms were ever-victorious, and in battle after battle the Tsarist forces were driven from their strongholds in southern Manchuria and from the seas. The chronicle of the war is of the gradual, inexorable crushing out of the Russian power in the Far East: the forcing of the Yalu and the march down Liaotung; the grim siege of Port Arthur, "the most impregnable fortress in the world," to its fall on New Year's Day of 1905; the Battle of Mukden in March, with a hundred thousand Russian casualties; the culminant sea battle in the Tsushima Strait in which on 27–28 May the Russians' Baltic Fleet met the doom of total annihilation to which it had sailed half around the world. This war was not fought without cost, material and human, to both belligerents; and both were content to accept President Theodore Roosevelt's invitation to meet at

Portsmouth, New Hampshire, in August 1905, to make peace. By the Treaty of Portsmouth Japan obtained a quitclaim to the lease of southern Liaotung—now known as Kwantung—and to the Russian railroads and other interests in southern Manchuria, together with recognition of a virtual protectorate over Korea (which she went on to annex formally, in 1910) and cession of the southern half of the island of Sakhalin, lying north of Japan's own islands. For the ensuing forty years, until her ruin in the Pacific War, Japan's history was the tale of the vicissitudes of her continental enterprise.

By the issue of the Russo-Japanese War, Japan sprang, a scant half century after her awakening from feudalism, to rank as a world Power. It was as one of the Allied Powers that she joined in the First World War, drove Germany from Asia and the Pacific, then, one of the Five Great Powers, redesigned the world at Versailles and took her seat as a permanent member of the Council of the League of Nations. In becoming a world Power, however, Japan had come into conflict with the Western nations who possessed or aspired to special interests in Asia. Following the Russo-Japanese War, those Powers had begun to feel suspicion—not entirely unmixed with envy—of the burgeoning Japanese ascendency in Manchuria and China. Britain—although, it is true, renewing and extending the alliance—grew perceptibly cool to Japan's foreign policy and receptive to efforts, chiefly American, to restrain Japan. In the United States, President Roosevelt had viewed the Japanese challenge to the Russian Goliath with his characteristic sympathy for the underdog; but before leaving office he had come to judge it politic to make a display in the Pacific of American naval might, sending to cruise around the world—and to visit Japan—the "Great White Fleet" of sixteen battleships.

9

It was at this season that Mr. Tōgō (after being graduated from Tokyo Imperial University, where he had specialized in study of German literature) began his diplomatic career—in 1913, as a consular officer in Mukden, then and for long the center of Japanese activities in Manchuria. When world war broke out soon after, the Allies welcomed a companion-in-arms whose Army would subdue Germany's base of Ts'ingtao in the Shantung Peninsula, whose Navy drive Count von Spee's commerce raiders from the central Pacific, occupy the German Carolines, Marianas and Marshalls, and convoy ANZAC troops safely to Europe. They were less happy to see Japan attempt to profit by their preoccupation with the war in Europe to consolidate for herself a position as suzerain of China, by the so-called Twenty-One Demands of 1915, which had they been fully yielded to would have given her substantially an economic and political protectorate. The Allies were willing, too, that Japan should provide the bulk of the troops, and the leadership, for the joint Expeditionary Force to Siberia, in 1918; their complaisance diminished, after their withdrawal in 1920, as they saw their Oriental ally remaining on in occupation of much of the Siberian littoral until 1922 and of northern Sakhalin—seized as reprisal for a Bolshevist massacre of Japanese soldiers and civilians at Nikolaievsk —until 1925.

By the Peace Conference of 1919, however, Japan's claims as one of the victors were recognized by assignment to her of a mandate over the ex-German islands of the Pacific north of the equator, together with Germany's concessions and properties in Shantung. Among the Japanese delegation to the Versailles Conference was Mr. Tōgō, who had had a well-varied experience during the war years. He had been transferred, in the middle of 1916, from Mukden to the newly opened legation in Switzerland, whither he made his way via the Trans-Siberian, Scandinavia, England and France. Typhus contracted en route compelled him to prolong his stay in England, for treatment—but was compensated for, in his view, by the opportunity thereby afforded to receive the impressions of the British national character which remained with him throughout life (he was never thereafter stationed in England). Switzerland was a vantage point from which to survey objectively the nature and effects of war, and to see and appreciate democracy in action. After Versailles he went to the reopened Embassy in Berlin, in which he served from 1919 to 1921. Germany provided firsthand evidence that war does not pay, while enabling Mr. Tōgō to extend his studies in European civilization—including that postwar manifestation of it, communism. Residence in Germany brought him also a bride, a German lady whom he met in Berlin and in 1921 married in Tokyo. His return to Japan at the end of his tour abroad had been made by way of the United States, where—he remembered—he felt "an exhilaration of the spirit at coming to the country which stood for freedom."

A sequel to the First World War which was to influence the course of Far Eastern history down to the Second, and after, was the cluster of treaties entered into at the Washington Conference of 1921–22. The conference had two objectives: one, to rectify the new balance of power which during the war years had advanced Japan to a position of dominance in East Asia; the other, to put an end to the naval-building race by imposing some system of limitation on the world's chief navies. The latter goal was achieved by the Treaty Concerning the Limitation of Naval Armament, setting the capital-ship ratio of the American, British and Japanese navies at 5:5:3, prescribing a limit on the size of vessels to be built and declaring a ten-year "holiday" on new

11

construction, and freezing the status quo of fortifications and naval bases in the Pacific.

The other purpose of the Washington Conference—rectifying the balance of power in Asia—meant the restraining of Japan. To this end, first the Anglo-Japanese Alliance—the bulwark to which Japan owed so much of her success in extirpating the Russian menace from Northeast Asia and establishing herself securely in Manchuria—had to be terminated. When this was done (not without Japanese repinings for the "cornerstone of the foreign policy" of two decades), the alliance had to be replaced by the Four Power Treaty by which the United States, Great Britain, France and Japan pledged mutual respect of rights and territories in the Pacific area. Next, the traditional American policy of the "Open Door" in China was to be legislated into treaty form. For this purpose, there was conceived the Nine Power Treaty guaranteeing the sovereignty, independence and integrity of China, and binding the signatories to refrain from taking advantage of conditions in China to seek special rights or privileges. This treaty was signed by eight foreign Powers with interests in China —the United States, Great Britain, France, Japan, Italy, Holland, Portugal and Belgium—and by China herself. Japan also agreed by separate treaty to restore to China the sovereignty over the Shantung Peninsula which had been assigned to her at Versailles.

One Asiatic Power had been conspicuously absent from the Washington Conference. Russia, since 1917 the land of Bolshevism and terror, was an international outlaw and not bidden as guest to respectable gatherings. To Russian relations, however, a Japan with interests in Asia could never be indifferent, and it was necessary that Japan regularize those relations now. When Mr. Tōgō returned home from Europe, in mid-1921, he was urged to take the First Section of the European-American Bureau of the

Foreign Ministry, in charge of Russian business; he did so, and as a consequence spent a large part of his subsequent career in the field of Soviet affairs.

In 1921 the question of the hour was what to do about the involvement in Siberia, which was obviously going to continue productive only of increasing tax bills and the mounting suspicion of Japan's late allies. One school of thought was that, so far from entering into relations with the Soviet regime, Japan should support and make use of the Cossack Ataman Semenov, or some other of the adventurers struggling for supremacy in Siberia, should continue or extend its occupation of Russian territories, and settle down to permanent exploitation of them. Mr. Tōgō successfully advocated the opposing view—that the Soviet state was a fact, and would prove stable, and recognition should be extended to it; that military occupation of others' territory was unjustifiable, and the Japanese forces should be withdrawn; and that outstanding disputes should be settled by negotiation with the successors to the Russian Empire. As the first step in implementing this policy, the Maritime Province of Siberia was evacuated in October 1922, in conformity with Japan's promise given at the Washington Conference. The resumption of relations was then attempted, but several efforts, in *pourparlers* with representatives of the Moscow government or the ephemeral Far Eastern Republic, proved abortive. Only after the establishment of the U.S.S.R. did protracted negotiations, in which Mr. Tōgō had much of the responsibility, result finally in the two countries' concluding in January 1925 a "Basic Convention," by which relations were resumed on terms of Soviet reaffirmance of the Treaty of Portsmouth, granting of coal- and petroleum-concessions in northern Sakhalin (which was then evacuated), and expression of regret for the Nikolaievsk massacre.

The nineteen-twenties were leisurely, uncrowded days, with little activity of moment on the diplomatic front. Mr. Tōgō, after completion of his work on the Russo-Japanese Basic Treaty, was transferred as First Secretary of Embassy to Washington. He was accompanied, then and always thereafter, by his wife and their only child, a daughter. There was time in Washington, for him, to form impressions, accurate and enduring, of the American character, economy, industrial organization—impressions which were to influence his whole public life thenceforward. In Japan, the twenties were tranquil enough at first. For a few years following the Washington Conference, Japanese foreign policy under the dominating personality of Baron Shidehara [4] expressed faithfully the Washington treaties' spirit of peaceful intercourse, equal opportunity and the Open Door. Domestically, since 1919 party cabinets had held sway, and the nation seemed on the way to establishing for the first time a tradition of responsible parliamentary democracy.

This misnamed "period of normal government" did not long continue. During and for a time after the world war Japan had experienced a great war boom; the war had cost her little, while offering lucrative opportunities of access uncontested to the markets of Asia which the European nations were for the time being too busy to supply, and industrialization of the nation and a metamorphosis of its economy had progressed in pace with the resulting unprecedented prosperity. But with the return of peace

[4] Baron Shidehara Kijūrō (1872–1951), the most prominent spokesman of a conciliatory policy toward China, had been Ambassador to the United States from 1919 to 1922, and meanwhile a member of the delegation to the Washington Conference. He became almost a fixture of official life during the twenties, serving as Foreign Minister in five cabinets, 1924–27 and 1929–31, and as Premier ad interim during the mortal illness of the assassinated Premier Hamaguchi, in 1930–31. After many years in retirement, he emerged after the Pacific War to be Premier briefly in 1945–46, and thereafter Speaker of the House of Representatives from 1949 to his death.

and the re-entry of the Western nations into competition, the bubble burst, and to the predictable *après-guerre* restlessness was added the economic stringency of an industrial plant without outlet for its product, encouraging the recrudescence of the old economic and political urges to expansion, with the fresh motive of maintenance of the new economy. By the mid-twenties the voice of the militarists, which had been unwontedly still since the Siberian fiasco, began again to be heard in the land, raised in animadversion on the "weak-kneed Shidehara diplomacy," the necessity of a "positive policy" toward China, the threat to the national security involved in schemes of disarmament. "Positive" policy or negative, they had the same objective—to promote the China trade, to develop the market of China for Japanese goods; the disagreement was in the means to be employed. By allaying Chinese ill will and cultivating a true friendship and a peaceful coexistence grounded in a sincere respect for Chinese sovereignty and territorial integrity, insisted Shidehara; by the use of force as needed to advance Japan's special interests in China—and especially in Manchuria—cried the "positivists."

The positive policy won out. At this epoch the Nationalist Chinese forces of the Kuomintang, battling their way up from the South under the captaincy of Chiang Kai-shek to "subjugate the North," were recording much progress in their revolutionary venture of unifying China under one government. As this unification threatened to extend to Manchuria—Marshal Chang Tso-lin, war lord of Manchuria, master of Peking and Japanese coadjutor, gave evidence of having under contemplation going over to the Kuomintang—it was apparent that it would not be compatible with the historical goal of a Japanese hegemony there. The cry for resort to a positive policy to counter the threat of exclusion from Manchuria brought about installation in Japan of a Cabinet

15

in which one of its advocates, General Baron Tanaka, was Premier and Foreign Minister, and direct military intervention in China began. Expeditions were dispatched to Shantung, in 1927 and again in 1928, to "protect the lives and property of Japanese nationals"—and to warn off the Nationalists; Chang Tso-lin was murdered, by a bombing of his private train, never satisfactorily explained, in 1928, his son the "Young Marshal" Chang Hsüeh-liang succeeding, under the National Government, to lieutenancy in Manchuria, and Jehol of Mongolia; boycotts of Japanese goods became epidemic throughout China; pro-Kuomintang movements took form in Manchuria itself. Most ominous of all, the Chinese began to build or plan rail lines paralleling Japan's South Manchuria Railway—the road which, running from Port Arthur north to junction at Chang Ch'un with the Russians' Chinese Eastern, had been taken from Russia in 1905 and had become "Japan's lifeline in Manchuria." The Chinese government was scheming, patently, to eradicate Japanese influence from Manchuria. Japanese military ambition was restive in the face of the growing threat of China's resumption of dominion over its territory. "Incidents" multiplied.

While events were building up to a test in Manchuria, international relations were ruffled by developments in other fields. The American Congress saw fit in 1924 to embody in its new Immigration Act a prohibition on Japanese immigration into the United States. It was an action without relevance to the attainment of any American national policy, a "Gentlemen's Agreement" of 1907, scrupulously observed, having halted Japanese emigration to the United States for near two decades; as with the earlier refusal of the Allied Powers at Versailles to incorporate into the Peace Treaty an affirmation of the principle of racial equality, this could but be taken by the Japanese as a gratuitous affront, and it was an unfortunate blow to good feeling. In 1930, naval limitation came up, with the London Conference to revise and expand the scope of the Washington Treaty. Japan demanded a 10:10:7 ratio, was refused it, finally agreed to continuance of the existing ratio to the end of 1936; but eventual breakdown of the system of naval limitations was here adumbrated.

The definitive military adventure was delayed until 1931; when it came, its agent was the Kwantung Army, in Manchuria. Originally a mere garrison for the Kwantung Leased Territory and the South Manchuria Railway Zone, this military establishment had come to regard itself as the chosen instrument of Japan's manifest destiny on the continent, and as such the *corps d'élite* of the Army; and it had developed a certain impatience with civilian governments which failed to evince a sufficient concern for Japan's prestige as a continental Power. It was this institution which on 18 September 1931 precipitated the Manchuria Incident.

The story was that a Chinese bomb was detonated on the tracks of the South Manchuria near Mukden. Whether it ever happened, no one knows; but the Kwantung Army acted swiftly in "self-defense"—it burst out from the Leased Territory and the Railway Zone to seize strategic points, Chinese garrisons were disarmed, the Mukden area was placed under martial law. The government in Tokyo, upon receipt of the news, within twenty-four hours adopted a policy of nonaggravation of the incident, and so instructed the military authorities and the Commander in Chief of the Kwantung Army. But it was too late; the call of destiny which the Army was hearing drowned out the voice of a mundane government. Fighting broke out at points more and more distant from the locale of the original incident; the Kwantung Army was reinforced; within a few months the Chinese garrisons had been driven from the whole of Manchuria, and all its chief cities occupied by Japanese forces.

China appealed the "Manchuria Incident" to the League of Nations, in the first test of that body's ability to enforce pacific settlement of international disputes. The League acted, vigorously enough—though in the end it declined to attempt enforcement— by dispatching to Manchuria for investigation the famous Lytton Commission. The result of the commission's activities was a report unanimously rejecting the Japanese plea of self-defense and finding Japan guilty of aggression. When the League Assembly voted by 42 to 1—the one, Japan's own vote—to adopt the Lytton Commission's report, the chief Japanese representative, Mr. Matsuoka,[5] led Japan's delegation from the floor, in February 1933. While the League had debated, an irresistible "independence movement" had brought about the separation from China of Manchuria and the establishment, on 1 March 1932, of the new state of Manchoukuo, "the country of the Manchus." Manchoukuo attained promotion in 1934 to an Empire, presided over by the "Boy Emperor" whom China had dethroned in 1912, P'u Yi, now the Emperor K'ang Te—an Empire in the interim since 1932 expanded to include Jehol of Inner Mongolia, China's Imperial Province par excellence, commanding Peking.

At this juncture it was that Mr. Tōgō came home from Germany (to which he had been transferred, as Councilor of Embassy, from Washington in 1929) to fill, in February 1933, the important post of Director of the European-American Bureau of

[5] Matsuoka Yōsuke (1880–1946) had gone to the United States at the age of twelve, and there received his education through college. Returned to Japan, he entered the foreign service, but midway of a promising career left it to become vice-president of the South Manchuria Railway for two years, 1927–29, then to enter politics as a member of the House of Representatives. After his appearance at Geneva he was President of the South Manchuria, 1935–39, and in July 1940 became Foreign Minister. He died of illness while on trial by the IMTFE.

the Foreign Ministry. It was a fateful hour for Japan. The Manchurian question was, when Mr. Tōgō assumed his post, still under debate in the League, but its issue was foregone, and the government's decision to withdraw from the League upon an adverse vote had already been made. The United States had laid down, and the League had put its imprimatur on, the doctrine of "non-recognition of the fruits of aggression"—the "Stimson Doctrine" —and Japan, isolated, without an adherent, was faced with ostracism from international society. As his first task as Bureau Director, Mr. Tōgō prepared at the request of the Foreign Minister, Count Uchida, an analysis of Japan's international position with recommendations of a policy for extricating the nation from its plight. Before he completed the assignment, Japan had notified her withdrawal from the League, on 27 March; it was in these circumstances that Mr. Tōgō wrote "A Foreign Policy for Japan following Withdrawal from the League of Nations." [6] In this forceful document—it is very long—the author pointed out that

As a result of the conflict of views between Japan and the League of Nations concerning fundamental principles for the establishment of peace in the Far East, rendering it no longer possible to co-operate with the League, the Japanese government has recently given notification of its withdrawal therefrom. Now that Japan is outside the League and henceforth will have to assume a position in international political affairs quite different from that of the past, it is incumbent upon us to give the most careful and thoughtful consideration and study to Japan's foreign policy, that we may successfully and without miscarriage go through the critical time for our country lying ahead.

Mr. Tōgō then reviewed the relations between Japan and each of the nations with which his bureau was concerned, and postulated certain general principles which should actuate his country

[6] IMTFE Exhibit No. 3,609A, Record of Proceedings, p. 35,362. The document is dated "the middle of April 1933."

19

in its dealings with them. The conclusion of the study is worth quotation at some length, not only because it is of interest for what it reveals of the thinking of a leading maker of policy of the Foreign Ministry in those years, but for the light which it throws on the character and the subsequent activities of its author, particularly as they relate to the events of which his book treats.

Since the Manchuria Incident, the nations of Europe and America have charged Japan with having embarked on aggressive action in disregard of her treaty obligations. It is an incontestable fact that the Powers are apprehensive that Japan will engage in further aggression whenever opportunity is afforded. As a result, Japan has, since the year before last, as much forfeited international confidence as she has enhanced her military prestige. In modern international society resort to force is a matter of the utmost gravity, especially among the Great Powers, and every possible effort should be made to avoid it. Instances are not few in history of unjustifiable resort to force's resulting in disaster. We should not repeat acquisition in defiance of principle, then in reliance on the principle insist upon retention of the gains. Good faith must be alike among nations as among individuals, for it is manifest that when a nation forfeits international confidence it will ultimately be the loser. The urgent task for Japan at this hour is the development of Manchoukuo, which will entail no small expenditure of time, effort and money. If we succeed in this, the position in the Far East will be stabilized, and our assumption of our place as one of the world Powers thereby facilitated; but if we fail, all our efforts will have been for nothing, and we shall be compelled to withdraw wholly from the continent. In the existing circumstances, we must be extremely cautious until we shall have demonstrated substantial achievement in development of Manchuria and Mongolia. To launch recklessly upon adventure, without careful consideration of all factors—whether military, financial, economic, or otherwise—and their interrelation is most inappropriate. It is only last February that forty-odd Powers in concert opposed Japan at Geneva, and the embers from that blaze have not yet died down. It would be extremely difficult for us to win over any one of those Powers, and should the world be threatened with a renewal of such strife, it can be expected that they will in combination deal with Japan. It is essential therefore that for many years to come, while we are striving for the proper development of Manchoukuo, we avoid conflicts with other countries, unless conflict be forced upon us. As regards China, we are now confronted with armed resistance and may be obliged to cope with it, but we should when any opportunity offers immediately lay down our policy for the speedy restoration of good will, and by strictly abiding by it prove to the world our good faith. . . .

. . . the basic policy toward the United States should be to seek American reconsideration of her Far Eastern policy and to prevent war. As the United States does not welcome the exercise by Japan of a hegemony over the entire Far East, Japan on her part should not make this her policy in the foreseeable future. Our concern is the development of Manchuria and Mongolia, whereas the actual desire of the United States is to promote markets and develop enterprises in China and other parts of the Far East. This being the case, the interests of the two countries could be adjusted if the principle of the Open Door and equal opportunity were realized in the Far East.

Japan did not follow the road pointed out by Mr. Tōgō. Where to him the Manchuria Incident had taught anew the necessity of observance of international good faith, to Japan's expansionists its lesson was that they had got away with it. Under the encouragement of this apparent success, they were only too ready to try their luck again, and expansionism and its servitor militarism enjoyed a renascence. Notwithstanding a full measure of drama in domestic events, the true history of Japan was, during the years 1931 to 1937—as in other times—being written on the continent. The story of those years is a monotonous one of an almost unrelieved growth of tension in China building up to an explosion. Manchoukuo was pacified with efficient expedition, but even before the mopping-up of the Chinese forces there had been completed, "incidents" were cropping up south of the Great Wall, in

China proper. In common with the other treaty Powers, Japan had the right under the Boxer Protocol to station troops at certain points between Peking and the sea, a right which unlike the other Powers she had exercised by maintaining a considerable army in the Peking-Tientsin area. To these North China forces now passed the initiative. The presence of such an army of occupation—and in an area traditionally the preserve of native war lords and their armies—could not but result in collisions; frequent incidents, of attacks on Japanese troops or residents, of destruction of Japanese property, of anti-Japanese boycotts, occurred or were alleged, each incident made the occasion for service by the North China forces of demands for reparation, accompanied by ultimatums entailing the withdrawal of Chinese troops and the delegating by the central government of political authority to local regimes under direct intimidation of the Japanese arms. While the sovereignty of the Chinese state was thus diluted by infiltration, its territory was taken in flank by the Kwantung Army, which—developing a marked tendency to act without reference to the government at home—extended its activities from Manchoukuo westward into Mongolia, and even on occasion crossed the Great Wall to menace Peking. "Autonomous regimes" sprouted throughout the North China and Mongolia area; dealing with these puppets, rather than with the central government of China, the Japanese forces extorted, in the name of "economic co-operation," further abdications of sovereignty. The Chinese reaction to these phenomena was a resurgence of nationalism which from around 1935 enabled the National government to make steady progress toward internal unity, while confirming it in a growing determination to clear from its soil Japan and all her works and to resume control of its country. That which was uniting China was, in large measure, the spirit of resistance to Japan. A sense of impending doom was ubiquitous.

At home, in step with these developments in China, a strong tide of chauvinism had set in after the Manchuria Incident. Any who opposed aggrandizement and militarism were stigmatized as "corrupt politicians" or "selfish financial magnates," who must be silenced. Ready to hand as silencer was a tool of ancient tradition in Japanese politics, assassination, now put to use by militarists, joined with a heterogeneous rabble of ultranationalists and other fanatics. Already, in the years between 1918 and 1932—the "period of normal government"—three premiers and assorted other public figures had met death by violence because their views on subjects of interest to the bravos were unsatisfactory: views on disarmament, on rural reform, on what-not (typically, these assassins were vague concerning their motives), but never at a far remove from China problems.

Many were the evidences of the growth of totalitarianism. Premier Inukai had been murdered in 1932—following in the same spring his Finance Minister and the managing director of the great Mitsui *zaibatsu*—murdered by Army and Navy officers in uniform. Nineteen thirty-three and 1934 spawned more conspiracies, which, if they spilled little blood, helped inculcate the discipline of terror. Despite the turmoil which by 1935 had developed in China and at home, the Army's more dedicated authoritarians were yet dissatisfied with progress toward their objectives, and in that year one of them, a lieutenant colonel, murdered with a sword the Director of the Military Affairs Bureau, General Nagata, at his desk in the War Ministry—a moderate, the general had been instrumental in trying to disperse the Army clique demanding a "renovation" of the national life to place it under a military absolutism.

All this was but preludial to the climactic orgy of terrorism

23

which distinguished 1936. On 26 February of that year—"2-26," in Japanese memory—elements of the First Army Division in Tokyo mutinied under the leadership of their junior officers, seized the Premier's Official Residence, the Diet Building, the War Ministry and other public buildings, and for four days imposed a state of paralysis on the national functions. Others of the officers and men were occupied meanwhile in murdering such high officials of state as they could hunt down. The great Finance Minister, Takahashi Korekiyo, the Lord Keeper of the Privy Seal and former Premier, Admiral Viscount Saitō, and the Inspector General of Military Education, one of the Army's "Big Three," were mowed down with submachine guns; Premier Admiral Okada, Count Makino, former Lord Keeper, Grand Chamberlain Admiral Baron Suzuki, by various chances survived the butchery, some with wounds, some without. These mutineers had published a manifesto declaring their motives and arraigning the Elder Statesmen, the financial magnates, government officials and political parties for the state of Japan's international relations, for disarmament, for the failure to take appropriate steps to propagate the national glory throughout the world.

The breakdown of discipline demonstrated on 2-26 was more than even an army riddled with fascism could tolerate, and the ringleaders of the mutiny were court-martialed and shot—a requital not the tradition for predecessor military or civilian assassins of statesmen. Notwithstanding the failure of these attempted coups to achieve any immediate goals—most of them had purposed installing, in one form or another, a military dictatorship —the spirit expressed by them had taken a hold on the popular imagination, and they did much to prepare the nation for the domestic "renovation" and the further freebooting adventure which came in later years. The result was not arrived at without a considerable internal struggle; voices of moderation and decency were, of course, raised against totalitarianism at home and aggression abroad, but they were not audible for the martial music. In the atmosphere of glorification of militarism and force created by the successful Manchuria Incident, the Army's prestige had been so enhanced that it had become able to dictate the composition of Cabinets, and from 1932 onward it permitted the formation of no government not a supraparty one headed by a general, an admiral or a safe civilian reactionary. Even one of its most famous officers, General Ugaki, was unable in 1937 to carry out the Imperial mandate to form a cabinet when no general could be found willing to serve as War Minister under the man who himself as Minister, back in the twenties, had consented to a reduction in the size of the standing army.

In Europe, it was the period of Hitler's ascendancy. Japan began to move toward *rapprochement* with authoritarian Germany, under the impulse first of the sense of friendlessness and isolation of which both were conscious after withdrawal from the League. The Army's traditional hostility to Russia and affinity to Germany, and the growing sympathy for the totalitarian ideology, with admiration for the German dictator's victories, hastened the contracting of an engagement, and fascism became the national policy when Japan entered into the Anti-Comintern Pact with Germany in November 1936 (Italy adhering in the following year), and the Axis came into being. The Anti-Comintern Pact was aimed ostensibly only at halting the spread of the communistic ideology, but it plainly implied military and political alliance against the Soviet state (which in fact was provided for by the secret protocol to the pact).

By the close of 1936, the conjunction of unrest in China and the triumph of authoritarian principles in Japan gave clear warning that a major venture of aggrandizement was gestating. It was born, on 7 July 1937, at Lukouch'iao, the famous "Marco Polo Bridge," outside Peking, to be promptly christened "the China Affair."

The China Affair had had its origin in a brush between Japanese units, conducting night maneuvers at Lukouch'iao, and Chinese troops in garrison in the area. It was only such another rencounter as had become routine, and it was a matter of mere chance that it was not, like its forerunners, settled locally, but was accepted by both sides as the decisive test of political control of North China. Perhaps the opposing commanders' judgment was affected by the pervading sense of uneasiness; this time, at any rate, the incident arrived at no settlement, skirmishing continued, both armies were reinforced and large-scale battles gradually developed, with Japanese forces occupying Peking and Tientsin, driving far into Inner Mongolia to cut communications with the U.S.S.R. and pushing westward into Shansi Province. When in August the hostilities spread to Central China, the incident had become a war. Fighting broke out in Shanghai, which fell to Japanese assault, by land and sea, after a bitter battle of three months; thence the way was clear for a drive up the Yangtze to Nanking, which was taken in December. The Chinese government, routed from its capital, fled farther upriver, taking refuge first at Hankow, then at Chungking in the far west; by the end of 1937 there was no longer any thought on either side but to accept the fact of war. Hostilities came to South China in 1938, when Canton was taken by a seaborne expedition; but, having achieved so much, the Japanese forces found themselves overextended, their armies mired in the vastness of China, and they could only settle down to hold the cities, rail lines and rivers which they had seized, to blockade the coast, and to bomb Chungking and the

Burma Road. Throughout 1939 and 1940 Japanese gains were negligible; it was a stalemate, which remained unbroken when the China Affair became one aspect of a larger war on 8 December 1941.

With the developments in China which were to lead Japan in time to war with America and the British Empire, Mr. Tōgō had, as Director of the European-American Bureau, nothing to do (the American business had been detached, in 1934, and made the charge of a new American Bureau of the Ministry). Rather, the chief activity in his bureau during his five years as director was, again, Soviet affairs. Mr. Tōgō's acute consciousness of the importance to Japan of Soviet relations was emphasized by the fact of his devoting to that subject nearly half of his 1933 "Foreign Policy for Japan." As he had there pointed out, "there are many difficult issues between the two countries, and it is not to be expected that they can be settled at a stroke. If, however, things be left as they are, mutual distrust cannot be dispelled, and the relations of the two countries may come to be dominated by our domestic problem of communism or by the complication of Soviet-Manchoukuoan problems." Accordingly, he rejected the idea, then gaining popularity, of severing diplomatic relations with the U.S.S.R., proposing instead that Japan should establish with her "the relations of a good neighbor." Specifically, he recommended that arrangement be made for purchase of the Soviet Chinese Eastern Railway; that demarcation of the Manchoukuo-Mongolia boundary be carried out, to put an end to border disputes; and that a nonaggression pact and a commercial convention be concluded. He was able to see substantially all his recommendations transmuted into the national policy of the following years vis-à-vis the Soviet Union.

Outstanding among the problems of Russo-Japanese relations

which Mr. Tōgō managed as bureau director was that of purchase of the Chinese Eastern Railway. For the quarter-century since the end of the Russo-Japanese War, Manchuria had tacitly been recognized to be reserved to spheres of influence, south and north, of Japan and Russia. The Chinese Eastern—the Trans-Siberian's shortcut across Manchuria—had been the focus of Soviet interests in northern, as the South Manchurian of Japanese in southern, Manchuria. Until the Manchuria Incident there had been relatively peaceful coexistence there; but the Soviet position thereafter was not a happy one, with Japan and Japanese troops in *de facto* occupation to the Siberian borders, and those borders never quiet. As incidents eddied about the enclave of the Chinese Eastern line the road began to seem a liability; at last the U.S.S.R. decided to cut its losses, and offered, just after Mr. Tōgō's assumption of the bureau directorship in the spring of 1933, to sell out. The offer precipitated a struggle with the Army. All agreed that Russian control of the road should be ended, whether with motive of improvement of Soviet-Japanese relations or of consummating the independence of Manchoukuo, hardly feasible with an alien railway of imperialistic heritage traversing the heart of its territory. But the Russians' first asking price was high; the "incidents" along the line were making its operation very difficult already, and could in time be counted on to render the Soviet position untenable; the Army considered it fancifully extravagant to buy, at any price, what must eventually fall ripe into the waiting hand. Mr. Tōgō had, in his "Foreign Policy," given the conclusive answer to this argument: "since we cannot justifiably obtain Russia's interest in the railway by forcible measures," he had written, "it is only reasonable that we purchase their share in it. It is true that the price is high, but resort to other means such as force would raise it still higher, inasmuch as it would result in

the loss of international confidence by Japan and Manchoukuo."
The argument for honesty prevailed, this time, and it was settled
that Manchoukuo should buy the Chinese Eastern. The actual
conduct of the negotiations devolved upon Mr. Tōgō (Manchou-
kuoan foreign affairs being entrusted to the Japanese government); after almost two years of continuous haggling in Tokyo,
from time to time interrupted by the happening of new "incidents" on the far plains of Manchuria, the sale was brought to
fruition, and a major threat to Japanese-Soviet relations was
eliminated. The sale was widely believed at the time to represent
final liquidation by the Soviet Union of Tsarist imperialism in the
Far East.

Mr. Tōgō wished to capitalize on the Japanese-Soviet cordi-
ality prevailing after settlement of the Chinese Eastern problem
by undertaking removal of other perennial causes of conflict. To
the elimination of two of these, in particular, he devoted much
time and thought, though in the end his efforts were frustrated by
developments in another quarter. First was demarcation of the
frontier between Manchoukuo and the Soviet Outer Mongolia;
where the actual boundary was, no one knew—the area was a
wasteland, and had never been regarded as worth anyone's while
to survey—and clashes over it were occurring with some frequency. Mr. Tōgō wanted to see border demarcation carried out,
to obviate the clashes and as a prelude to a nonaggression pact,
and his negotiations to this end had reached the point of agreement on commissions to perform the demarcation, when announcement of the Anti-Comintern Pact gave the quietus to the
new era of good feeling, and the border-demarcation convention.
Another agreement, to put on a long-term basis the concessions
for the fishing off Sakhalin, which had been requiring year-to-
year renewal, had, before a like end overtook it, progressed even

further, the convention having been signed and being in process of ratification. The wisdom of Mr. Tōgō's insistence on acting to prevent border disputes was evidenced not long afterward, when a 1938 "incident"—involving possession of the hill of Changku-feng, at the point where Manchuria, Korea, and the Maritime Province march together—developed into a respectable battle and for a time threatened to bring on war. But by then Mr. Tōgō had been transferred to Germany, as Ambassador.

With the Anti-Comintern Pact, also, Mr. Tōgō had connection, as the responsible bureau director. This agreement had been negotiated in Berlin by the Japanese military attaché, at the direction of the Army high command, in the intention of creating a defensive military alliance against the U.S.S.R. By the time it reached bureau directors, it represented the national policy; but Mr. Tōgō disliked it. He disliked seeing Japan enter into a liaison with Nazi Germany, in any event; he disliked the pact for its obvious effect on Soviet relations, he disliked it out of apprehension that it would further estrange England from Japan. The most that he could do was to effect some toning down of its language —the original draft, he commented, "read like a Nazi manifesto"—and to obtain insertion into the annexed secret protocol of a significant limiting adjective, so that it should provide for military assistance only in case of the other signatory's becoming "the object of an *unprovoked* attack." Mr. Tōgō insisted also that if policies of state demanded conclusion of such a pact with Germany, efforts must concurrently be made to establish an *entente cordiale* with England; this proposal was approved by the Cabinet, and the negotiations were put in train, just in time to be halted by outbreak of the China Affair.

A last question which was Mr. Tōgō's concern as bureau director was that of naval limitation. The limitations adopted at

Washington in 1922, as extended at London in 1930, would expire with the year 1936 if any signatory exercised its right to denounce the Washington Treaty. It had been apparent since the time of the London Conference that the Navy would consent to no further continuance of the system which allowed Japan only sixty per cent of the capital-ship strength of her chief rivals, and renewal of the naval race seemed to be in the cards. With this deadline of 1936 in view, there had for some time been much military talk of that year as destined to be "the year of crisis," and the talk and attendant accelerated armament had in their turn further enhanced the authority of militarism. Mr. Tōgō's views on naval limitation and the crisis of the 1935 London Conference had already been formulated, and stated in the "Foreign Policy" of 1933:

In the light of present international developments, a conflict of opinion is likely to occur between the two countries [Japan and the United States] at the naval-limitation conference scheduled for 1935. If matters be left as they stand, accord will naturally fail to be reached, and as a result the agreement for maintenance of the *status quo* with respect to fortifications in the Pacific area will be abrogated. The consequences which would ensue—an armaments race, leading to a Japanese-American war—would ultimately bring about a world war. How unfavorable would be the result to Japan has already been pointed out. We on our part should make every effort at this time to induce the United States to reconsider her Far Eastern policy, and, at the same time, should review our course of conduct in regard to disarmament.

Working throughout the years 1934 and 1935 on preparations for the London Conference, Mr. Tōgō endeavored to persuade the government to reconsider its disarmament policy, as here proposed. He was unsuccessful; Japan denounced the Washington Treaty, demanded parity at London, and walked out of the conference when refused it, leaving the world without restraint on naval building; and Mr. Tōgō's prophecy was realized within the decade.

Shortly after the outbreak of the China Affair, Mr. Tōgō had been designated Ambassador to Germany, where he arrived to take up his post on Christmas Eve of 1937. He cannot be said to have been a success, in any usual sense, in Germany. He had known Germany under widely differing regimes—in the chaos of the immediate postwar days, again at the death struggle of democratic government, in the early thirties. Now, in Hitler's heyday, he did not like what he found there. He disliked Naziism and Nazis; he objected to the improvement of Japan's German relations at the expense of those with Britain, the U.S.S.R. and the United States; above all he opposed any move to take Japan into an alliance based on an ideology of force. The agenda at that moment was the formation of a tripartite alliance, German-Italian-Japanese—Hitler's "great *Weltpolitik*-triangle"—euphemized as "strengthening the Anti-Comintern Pact." That Germany was about to embark on a course of aggression could not be doubted; Mr. Tōgō saw that she would be defeated when a test came, and he didn't want Japan to become *particeps criminis* with her and share her fate. (He objected, additionally, to the method by which negotiations for the alliance were being carried on, by the military attaché behind the Ambassador's back.) Mr. Tōgō was very unaccommodating in this, the only major question of Japanese-German relations arising during his time in Berlin; his stubbornness—rendered none the more palatable by the undiplomatic bluntness of speech for which he was noted—made him acutely unpopular with his hosts, and he was abruptly transferred to Moscow after only ten months' service in Germany. He quit Germany in October 1938—the month after Munich—feeling, he said, like one fleeing for his life from a conflagration.

The Moscow post had long been Mr. Tōgō's goal. In 1938 he arrived there at a time when Russo-Japanese relations, which after conclusion of the Anti-Comintern Pact had become difficult altogether, stood at their worst since 1925. Even the establishment of Manchoukuo, bringing Japanese soldiers and Russian face to face across one border, had not stimulated the U.S.S.R. to any great activity; but with full-scale war in China there began to be evidences that Soviet strength in the Far East was rapidly developing and that any offer to make trial of it would be accepted: very substantial aid was given to China, the might of the Far Eastern Army was freely advertised, border clashes were of increasing frequency and gravity. The stiffened Soviet attitude was displayed in the first business which Mr. Tōgō as Ambassador had to manage, that of the fisheries agreement. Since the failure in 1936 to conclude a permanent convention implementing the Treaty of Portsmouth, it had been necessary to negotiate annual agreements governing the terms for Japanese exercise of their fishing rights. In 1938, upon Mr. Tōgō's arrival in Moscow, he found that owing to the deterioration in relations consequent upon the Changkufeng Incident, no progress had been made toward settlement of the annual *modus vivendi.* Only after protracted negotiations with Foreign Commissar Litvinov was he able to reach a solution of this problem, which had threatened to become very troublesome, for the fishing season was about to open, and the fishing fleets were proposing defiantly to sail, convention or no.

When Mr. Tōgō had been in Moscow less than a year, the European war broke out. The Japanese Ambassador, however, had already his own war to manage. In May 1939, some skirmish of patrols occurring on the Manchurian-Mongolian frontier, each side had charged the other with violation of its territory, and

33

brought up troops to defend its "border." The troops involved were the Kwantung Army, on behalf of Manchoukuo, and the Far Eastern Red Army, representing the Mongolian People's Republic. In the Nomonhan area, over the remote and desolate steppes of Outer Mongolia, raged throughout July and August the first large-scale battles of armor in history. There was talk of Russo-Japanese war. It became Mr. Tōgō's duty to prevent this affray from developing into war, and to arrange a solution of it by diplomacy rather than by arms—no easy task, with each of the armies dogmatic that it was defending its indubitable territory against an invader, and both seeming ready and willing to carry matters to a military conclusion. In late August, Mr. Tōgō obtained from his government carte blanche to make a settlement, then after considerable debating persuaded the Russians to agree to a truce. This, announced as a communiqué by the Ambassador and Foreign Commissar Molotov on 16 September, put an end to the fighting on terms of holding of current positions by both sides and designation of a joint commission to fix the boundaries. Not yet, however, was the Nomonhan Incident closed. The commission on the spot—consisting of representatives of Japan and Manchoukuo, the U.S.S.R. and Mongolia—disagreed on fundamental questions of the location of the frontier, and the dispute had to be referred back to Moscow, for further consideration by Ambassador and Foreign Commissar. The two reached a conclusive accord, the "Tōgō-Molotov Agreement" fixing the general lines of the boundary, in June 1940, and the work of actual border demarcation got under way in the field at last (to be finished in 1942). Thus for a second time in Ambassador Tōgō's service in the U.S.S.R. was a rupture averted.

A Russo-Japanese neutrality or nonaggression pact had been under discussion, desultorily, for a dozen years past, but for various reasons nothing had ever come of it. Mr. Tōgō had long viewed the making of such an agreement as a *sine qua non* to lasting Russo-Japanese friendship; in his "Foreign Policy" of 1933 he had devoted many pages to review of the pros and cons of the question, his verdict being that "a nonaggression pact should be concluded as soon as possible." Now he felt strongly that the period of friendly feeling after the pacific settlement of the Nomonhan Incident should be taken advantage of to open negotiations for such a treaty; but he had first to convince his government of the desirability of the move. In 1939, still, this was not easy, but after repeated urging he received approval to go ahead, and the negotiations got under way around the year end. A neutrality pact had been reduced to draft form, its signature delayed only by the failure of efforts to consummate concurrently a trade agreement, when Mr. Tōgō was ordered home, at the end of August 1940.

In two years in Moscow, he had been able to see the substantial realization of his policy of 1933 for making a friend of the Soviet Union—the cardinal points of which had been rationalization of the northern-fisheries rights, agreement on a method of establishing Manchoukuo-Mongolia boundaries and conclusion of a neutrality pact. The reorientation of relations which he had achieved was signalized when Foreign Commissar Molotov, at the farewell banquet which he tendered to the Ambassador on the eve of his return to Japan, toasted him in the words: "In my public life of many years I have never known any man who insists so earnestly and so frankly as Mr. Tōgō on what he believes to be right. I respect Mr. Tōgō not only as a distinguished diplomat and statesman, but as a man."

If relations with the Soviet Union had become friendlier, those with the Western democracies were sinking to a nadir. The cause was the old one: China. The establishment of Manchoukuo, and subsequent development there of a Japanese economic monopoly in violation of the principle of the Open Door, had brought Japan into collision with the Powers whose commercial interests were being expelled, and especially with the United States, the leading champion of the principle. The China Affair seriously intensified this collision.

The China Affair had commenced not long after the installation of a Cabinet led by Prince Konoe,[7] who by virtue of aristocratic lineage and absence of military connections gave the appearance of being a liberal, or at any rate a moderate, but who had collected together into his government a remarkable group of reactionaries. This government had, again as in 1931, professed the policy of localization of the fighting and nonaggravation of the incident; again, nonaggravation had not been consistent with the Army's desires—or its capabilities. As Japanese occupation of China spread—from North China to Shanghai and the Yangtze Valley, to Canton and the southern provinces, to Hainan and lesser islands of the China Sea—it was accompanied by the swinging shut of the Open Door, the vanishing of equality of commercial opportunity, and China was rapidly being made a Japanese economic satellite. Foreign commercial and other interests were progressively curtailed until they faced extinction, while incessant diplomatic *démarches* protesting violation of the Nine Power Treaty and promotion of Japanese monopoly of access to China met only with the response that those conditions

[7] Prince Konoe Fumimaro (1891–1945) was the head of one of the highest ranking of the old Court-noble families, and as such titular chief of the great Fujiwara clan which for centuries had played a leading role in Japanese national affairs and Court life. His hereditary position led naturally to his filling such offices in modern Japan as President of the House of Peers (1933–37) and of the Privy Council (1939–40). The Prince was thrice Premier, 1937–39, 1940–41, and July–October 1941. He committed suicide upon being designated a "war-crimes" suspect after the surrender of Japan.

were the inevitable incidents of war, that the way to end them was to discontinue the aid to China which was prolonging the war. For America, followed at some distance by Britain, had promptly moved to the assistance of China. Already, in October 1937, President Franklin D. Roosevelt had sounded his call for "quarantining the aggressors," and during the years 1938 to 1940 Anglo-American aid to China mounted in a steady crescendo: American "moral embargoes" on shipment of munitions to Japan were followed by credits of millions to China, then by mandatory embargo on export of aviation gasoline, of machine tools, of scrap iron. The Burma Road was opened, to send in through the jungle a thin trickle of the munitions which could not pass the blockade by sea; the American Flying Tigers brought moral support, more valuable than their squadrons of P-40s. Clearing the way for full economic sanctions against Japan, the United States in 1939 abrogated the commercial treaty in effect with her since 1911. Events were demonstrating that, as Mr. Tōgō had written in 1933, "as a matter of course the United States will not countenance the establishment by Japan of a hegemony over all the Far East."

As for Japan, she had early accepted the fact that she had on her hands an all-out war. By January 1938 the Konoe Cabinet, satisfied that the Chinese government meant to resist to the end, declared that it would thenceforward refuse to deal with it, but would "look forward to the establishment and growth of a new Chinese regime, harmonious co-operation with which can really be counted upon." Shortly afterward, the nation went officially on a war footing, with passage by the Diet of the National General Mobilization Law, empowering the government to control and employ the entire national human and material resources without recourse to legislation. Japan had a million men in her armies in China. Her war aims were disclosed with the announcement, in November 1938, of the "New Order," based on Japanese-Manchoukuoan-Chinese mutual aid and collaboration "to insure the permanent stability of East Asia." For such collaboration, however, a new Chinese government was requisite; accordingly, after several years of fumbling attempts to create satisfactory local regimes, there emerged at Nanking in March 1940 the "Reformed National Government of the Republic of China." To serve as President of this government, the Japanese were fortunate in being able to secure as big a figure as Wang Ching-wei,[8] who had crowned his long and loyal service to the Kuomintang by a spectacular defection and flight from Chungking in December 1938. In November 1940 Japan entered into a "Treaty of Basic Relations" with Wang's regime, which by a simultaneous "Joint Declaration of Japan, Manchoukuo and China" extended recognition to Manchoukuo, and the "Greater East Asia Co-Prosperity Sphere"—the later incarnation of the New Order in East Asia—seemed well launched.

Pari passu with these developments in the China war, totalitarianism was tightened up at home. The natural wartime predominance of the military oligarchy and subordination of the civilian government was increasingly accentuated after the National General Mobilization Law. With state-regulated strategic industries being expanded and nonessential ones severely restricted, with wages, hours and profits being controlled and rationing instituted, the capitalistic system of free enterprise was superseded by an economic dictatorship. Censorship of word and

---

[8] Wang Ching-wei (1885–1944) had been a trusted lieutenant and a political heir of Sun Yat-sen in China's revolutionary days, and was for a generation one of the foremost of the Kuomintang leaders of the new nation. During the years from the Manchuria Incident to his desertion he had been, as Foreign Minister and Premier of China, an outstanding opponent of Japanese aggression. He remained President of his "National Government" until his death, in Japan, during the war.

thought was extended, "the new national structure" began to be a familiar term.

As the growing antagonism to the Western Powers drew Japan closer to her Axis partners, a succession of Cabinets flitted by, short-lived and ephemeral—the military alliance with Germany (the same against which Mr. Tōgō in Berlin had contended unsuccessfully) provided the major preoccupation of five of them. Negotiations for the alliance had been nearing conclusion when announcement of the Russo-German nonaggression pact, in August 1939, put a temporary end to them (and, as it then appeared, to the Berlin-Rome-Tokyo Axis) and brought the reactionary Hiranuma Cabinet tumbling down in consternation after a life of seven months. The successor government of General Abe, which adopted a policy of "keeping out of the European war and concentrating on settlement of the China Affair," lasted five months, overthrown in part by inability to reach an understanding with the United States which would leave Japan free to defeat China. Admiral Yonai, a relative moderate, followed, to be forced out of office after six months when the Army revived the idea of the German alliance and demanded that the reluctant government go forward with it.

At this stage—July 1940—Prince Konoe was again called upon to form a government. The new national structure, of fascistic orientation, domestically and internationally, was expeditiously completed by the Second Konoe Cabinet. The existing political parties—the last surviving organized opposition to absolutism—were dissolved, to be replaced by the "Imperial-Rule Assistance Association," a sort of corporate party ("in Japan it is the privilege of all His Majesty's subjects to assist the Throne") with the Premier as president. The last objections to the German alliance were overborne by the brilliant sweep of the Wehrmacht

39

through Western Europe, and on 27 September 1940 Japan climbed on the band wagon with the signature at Berlin of the pact which brought into being the Tripartite Alliance of Germany, Italy and Japan. At the same period, German pressure on Vichy was availed of to extort the consent of prostrate France to the grant of "military facilities" in French Indochina, by virtue of which the northern part of that colony was occupied for the purpose of "settling the China Affair" by severing China's major land route of supply from without. A treaty of friendship with Thailand had already been made; agreements for economic collaboration in Indochina followed in the spring of the next year.

The Tripartite Pact—by whatever considerations its timing may have been dictated—was not simply a reflection of a spirit of opportunism. It had been realized in Japan since early in the China Affair that Japan would have to settle with the United States, at least, or the China Affair itself would be insoluble. Some halfhearted moves toward a Japanese-American understanding had even been made, but it was obvious that no expectations could be entertained of them while the war with China was to be pressed on with. As the world began to cleave into an alignment of democracy against totalitarianism, Japan had to choose sides, and, given "the immutable national policy" toward China, it was Hobson's choice. The Tripartite Pact, by which she irrevocably threw her lot in with the Axis, frankly created a military alliance: reciting mutual recognition of the leadership of Germany and Italy and of Japan in "the establishment of a new order" in Europe and Greater East Asia respectively, and pledging co-operation to attainment of that end, it provided for assistance "by all political, economic and military means if one of the three Contracting Powers is attacked by a Power not at present involved in the European War or the Sino-Japanese conflict."

Assurance was carefully added that the pact "in no way affects the political status at present existing between each of the three Contracting Powers and Soviet Russia"; there was even talk of inducing the U.S.S.R. to adhere to the alliance. If the Anti-Comintern Pact was ostensibly directed against international communism, the Tripartite Alliance was unmistakably enough antidemocratic in intention—specifically, anti-America.

Japan's professed purpose in entering into the alliance was "to facilitate the settlement of the China Affair." The United States —the argument ran—was more and more coming to the support of China; she must be prevented from undertaking any decisive intervention, if the China Affair was to be won—or even was not to continue perpetually. By the threat of the Tripartite Pact —the threat of having to deal with Japan's allies as well as with Japan—the United States would be deterred from further involvement, and Japan left free to defeat China without interference; the same considerations were applicable, from the German point of view, to the European War. Thus, as Japan's Foreign Minister explained it, the pact was not directed against, but in truth was for the benefit of, the United States, since it was designed to keep her neutral, for her own good.

The Foreign Minister responsible for these sentiments, and for Japanese diplomacy under the Second Konoe Cabinet, was Matsuoka Yōsuke. Under the auspices of this brilliant but erratic politician, that diplomacy had been full of surprises, the culmination of which was reached in the spring of 1941. In March, Matsuoka had visited the Axis capitals to improve relations with the new partners of the Tripartite Alliance. In returning he stopped over in Moscow, where, following in Germany's footsteps, to the general astonishment he suddenly executed with Molotov a neutrality pact, providing—in terms substantially identical with

41

the draft developed in the preceding year by Mr. Tōgō—for maintenance of peaceful and friendly relations, for mutual respect of territorial integrity, and for observance of neutrality if the other signatory should be attacked by a third Power.

Simultaneously with his move toward the Axis alliance, Matsuoka had conducted a wholesale purge of the diplomatic service, recalling all but a handful of Japan's ambassadors and ministers "because of their unsuitability to the trend of the new era." Of those blown out of office by the "Matsuoka Hurricane," Mr. Tōgō inevitably was one.

The rest of the chronicle is his.

THE AUTHOR
WHEN FOREIGN MINISTER IN THE TŌGŌ CABINET
1942

Part One

THE ROAD TO WAR

CHRONICLE OF EVENTS LEADING TO THE OUTBREAK OF THE PACIFIC WAR

[Far Eastern events expressed in East Longitude dates]

1936

November 25   Anti-Comintern Pact signed by Japan and Germany

1937

July 7   China Affair begins at Lukouch'iao

1939

July 26   Japanese-American Commercial Treaty of 1911 abrogated by the United States

September 1   European war begins with German invasion of Poland

1940

March 30   "Reformed" National Government of China under Wang Ching-wei established at Nanking

June 17   France asks an armistice

July 22   Second Konoe Cabinet formed

September 22   Northern French Indochina occupied under agreement with Vichy

September 27   Japanese-German-Italian Tripartite Pact signed

1941

April 13   Russo-Japanese Neutrality Pact signed

April 14   Japanese-American negotiations begin

June 22   Russo-German war begins

July 2   Imperial Conference approves the "Outline of National Policy"

July 18   Third Konoe Cabinet formed

July 21   Southern French Indochina occupied under agreement with Vichy

July 26   Japanese assets in the United States frozen

August 14   Atlantic Charter published

September 6   Imperial Conference approves the "Outline of Execution of National Policy"

October 18   Tōjō Cabinet formed

December 1   Imperial Conference approves decision for war

December 8   Pacific War begins

44

I Become Foreign Minister

IN 1940 I had been Ambassador in Moscow for about two years, years which had been fruitful in the settlement of a number of irritating disputes between the two countries. I was recalled as one of the incidents of the "Matsuoka Hurricane" which raged throughout the Japanese diplomatic service during the autumn of the conclusion of the Tripartite Alliance of Germany, Italy and Japan, and after my recall and return to Japan in November I was given no assignment, remaining an ambassador without post. Foreign Minister Matsuoka a time or two requested me to submit my resignation from the diplomatic service; I refused, saying to him that to do so would be tantamount to approval by me of his policies, and that if he wanted to rid the service of me he could always discharge me. Nothing further happened.

In reports which I had made upon my return—to Premier Prince Konoe and Matsuoka, and to the Emperor—summarizing the condition of Europe as I saw it, I pointed out especially that relations between Germany and the U.S.S.R., since the conclusion of the Tripartite Pact, were not friendly, whereas our pending negotiations for a Russo-Japanese neutrality pact were approaching consummation. Particularly, I stressed to Matsuoka that the Tripartite Pact would not contribute to solution of the

China Affair, but that that solution must depend mainly on self-restraint by Japan. To the Emperor I reported on the domestic situation of the U.S.S.R., emphasizing chiefly that her productive capacity was increasing under the Five-Year Plans, and that the communist ideology amounted to a religious faith, grounded in the idea of world revolution.

During this period I occasionally met high officials of the Foreign Ministry and of various other offices; but, as I have said, I retained only nominally the position of ambassador, and had nothing to do with the business of the Ministry. Having no duties, I had plenty of time at my disposal, and I utilized my leisure in traveling extensively within Japan, and refreshing my knowledge of my own land.

Conditions in the country had changed a great deal in the three years since my departure for Europe. There was in some quarters a feeling of frustration that the China Affair, now three years old, showed no sign of coming to an end. Nevertheless, it was noticeable that popular enthusiasm for the Tripartite Alliance persisted, and respect and unbounded admiration for Germany were everywhere evident; those not familiar with international politics were even saying that the Axis Alliance would be "eternal." Hard as it is now, after the war, to conceive of such a state of affairs, its existence in those days would be simple enough to demonstrate. I was astonished not only at the number but at the ascendency of those who put their trust and reliance in the Tripartite Pact; they prevailed in political, in journalistic, even in intellectual, circles. That phenomenon of the times resulted in part perhaps from German propaganda, but mainly, I think, from the fear of "missing the bus" at a time when Germany was achieving dazzling war gains in Europe.

What caused me most concern at that period was that the

government seemed to be basing its policies on the notion that Japan could easily solve her international difficulties by force of the Tripartite Pact alone. I expressed my views on this fallacy as occasion offered itself—to Premier Konoe and Foreign Minister Matsuoka, in particular—but I soon realized that it was rather widely established. I felt also that many in Army and Navy circles, the younger officers especially, were fascinated by the increasingly formidable military strength of Japan. The Army, having devoted the major part of its appropriations since the beginning of the China Affair to mechanization, felt that its fighting power had been vastly enhanced; the Navy, confident of its fleet (which, since the abrogation of the Naval Limitation Treaty, had come to include types of vessels peculiar to Japan), believed itself invincible.

Thus, while Japan was irritated at the prolongation of the China Affair, there was little evidence of any intention to try to reach a reasonable settlement with the National government through self-abnegation of Japan. On the other hand, it was apparent that the scheme, pursued since the time of the First Konoe Cabinet, of unification of China through the Wang regime of Nanking was unrealistic, that regime being entirely incapable of achieving such unification.

It was in those circumstances that the idea of restraining the United States by force of the Tripartite Pact, while concurrently by negotiation with her solving the China Affair, could be observed to be gaining support. But the concept underlying the Tripartite Pact was, as is clear from its text, that of dividing the world into three, each party dominating one part; and as the pact was in that sense hostile to the United States, negotiating with her for solution of the China Affair was incompatible with its spirit, and it was only to be expected that in any such negotia-

47

tions she would raise objection to the pact. When I learned that since around the time of the appointment of Ambassador Nomura [1] high government, Army and Navy and other officials who advocated or favored the pact had been considering the opening of Japanese-American talks, I was therefore amazed at the lack in Japan generally of understanding of international politics. My apprehension was that if such negotiations should be commenced without prospect of successful conclusion, and should ultimately fail, relations would be worse than at the beginning, and the end result would be a clash between the United States and Japan. As Ambassador to Moscow, in 1939, with instances of such occurrences in mind, I had entered into negotiations over the Nomonhan Incident only after having obtained from Tokyo the commitment that the incident would not be allowed to develop into war even if the efforts for a truce should fail. So as to negotiations with the United States, it was quite possible to anticipate that, if they failed, the disagreement would go out of control, when a war between the two countries would be by no means improbable. I therefore seized every opportunity to insist that we should not start negotiations without the determination to make, if necessary, great concessions in connection with the two chief points of contention, the Tripartite Pact and the China Affair. In any event, I could not comprehend why moving through the United States should be expected to produce better results for solution of the China Affair than would a direct approach to the Chiang Kai-shek regime; nor was it to be wondered at that

---

[1] Admiral Nomura Kichisaburō (1877–   ) had had the experience of being Foreign Minister in the short-lived (1939–40) Abe Cabinet. His selection as Ambassador, to which position he was designated in December 1940, was influenced by the fact that, as attaché in Washington and member of the delegation to the Washington Conference, he had formed a personal acquaintance with Assistant Secretary of the Navy Franklin D. Roosevelt. After the outbreak of the war and his repatriation to Japan, he held no public office.

Chiang would not treat with us so long as the Nanking "government" continued to exist.

At this point—in April 1941—before I heard any more about Japanese-American negotiations, Foreign Minister Matsuoka returned to Japan from his visit to the Axis capitals and Moscow, to be received with popular plaudits for the conclusion of the Russo-Japanese Neutrality Pact. Matsuoka himself was in an ebullient mood, as was apparent from—among other evidences —his public speech at the Hibiya Hall, in which he glowingly belauded the Axis and Axis statesmen. Negotiations with the United States were again rumored. In truth, the negotiations did get under way at about this time, though I was not aware of the fact then—as the whole subject was classified as "State Secret," and anyone responsible for a violation of security in connection with it was subject to heavy penalties, I had no accurate knowledge of developments, nor was I in a position to inquire of those who had. Being thus possessed of no information concerning the policy of the government, I knew only what came to me piecemeal from persons in political, business and press circles, all of which were keenly interested. When toward the end of May I heard that the policy of the government was fidelity to the obligations of the Tripartite Pact, together with the safeguarding of what had been achieved on the continent since the Manchuria Incident, I was much disturbed over the prospect for the negotiations, and could only hope that somehow they might succceed. Spring drew on into summer, and after a long absence I resumed life in the mountains, at Karuizawa,[2] whence throughout the season I came down to Tokyo from time to time. In Karuizawa

[2] A mountain town in Nagano Prefecture, a hundred miles northwest of Tokyo, long a favorite summer resort of diplomats, resident foreigners and well-to-do Japanese. During the war many among these classes rusticated in Karuizawa to escape the difficulties of wartime urban life, and later the air raids.

I sometimes had visitors who, interested in the Japanese-American negotiations—which had become the pivotal national problem—asked my opinion on the subject; to them I could only repeat that I was uninformed, but earnestly prayed for a solution.

During one of my visits to Tokyo, I was caught by reporters and asked about the possibility of a Russo-German war, then being rumored—a possibility which they understood that the governmental authorities did not credit. It requiring no clairvoyance to see whither events were trending, I gave the reasons for the likelihood of such a war. When it commenced, soon afterward, more reporters visited me to ask my views on the military prospects, pointing out that the Germans were boasting that within a few weeks they would capture Moscow and overthrow the Soviet government. I replied that, however effective the invasion might be, I doubted that the Germans could capture Moscow within a matter of weeks, or that the Soviet government would so easily be brought to the point of collapse even if Moscow did fall, as the Russians were prepared to move their capital into the industrial area east of the Urals and continue resistance from there.

The Russo-German war broke out on 22 June. During its early days there were various rumors going about, such as that Matsuoka was insisting on our attacking the U.S.S.R., despite the Neutrality Pact, that the government and the military high command were jointly studying the idea of a move northward or southward, or that our forces in Manchuria were being hastily reinforced—of all which there was no confirmation. The thing which caused me the greatest misgivings was, however, the course of the Japanese-American negotiations. In the beginning they had been said to be promising, but by the end of June—after the outbreak of the Russo-German war—it was understood that they were making little progress. As we entered July, it was even rumored that negotiations could not continue unless Matsuoka were eliminated as Foreign Minister; and his ouster in fact came about, when on 18 July the Third Konoe Cabinet was established with substantially the same personnel as its predecessor, but without Matsuoka. Just before the reconstitution of the cabinet I heard that Japanese military forces would be moved into southern Indochina. I was much astonished at this story, and had supposed that any such plan would have been dropped with the change of cabinet; toward the end of July, however, the movement was carried out. The immediate sequel was President Roosevelt's order freezing all Japanese assets in the United States, and thereby imposing an embargo on petroleum exports to Japan, on 26 July.

1941

Shortly after these events, a high official of the government confided to me that consequences of such gravity had not been anticipated. I was appalled at this naïveté; but even one of the directors of the Yokohama Specie Bank, a man who should have been familiar with foreign affairs, told me that he too had not expected the United States to resort to such extreme retaliatory measures. After imposition of the embargo, the Navy seemingly became gravely perturbed—not without reason—at the thought that the two-year supply of petroleum which it had accumulated would have to be drawn upon, and would gradually be exhausted. The Japanese-American negotiations now no longer revolved about the China problem alone, but brought the United States and Japan into direct confrontation.

I occasionally met the new Foreign Minister, Admiral Toyoda,[3]

[3] Admiral Toyoda Teijirō (1885–   ), upon retirement in 1941 after a long naval career which had included several years as an attaché in London in the midtwenties, had become Minister of Commerce and Industry and of Overseas Affairs in the Second, and of Foreign Affairs in the Third, Konoe Cabinet. He subse-

who had replaced Matsuoka, but I learned nothing concrete of
the negotiations, he saying merely that they were not progressing
satisfactorily. I gathered that in fact they were at an impasse, and
that a proposal by Prince Konoe for a personal meeting with
President Roosevelt had been rejected. A pessimistic outlook on
the diplomatic scene had thus come to prevail. At the same time,
the tone of the press toward Britain and America had turned
increasingly intransigent. The propaganda of the armed forces
seemed to be succeeding in beguiling the people to trust all to the
power of their country; the growth of a spirit of bravado, of seizing this "opportunity of a thousand years" for the glorification
of Japan, without shrinking from a war against Britain and
America, could be observed throughout the country. I continued
to preach the necessity of doing everything possible for success in
the negotiations, with the result that it soon became routine for
the representatives of the Kempei [4] to visit me two or three times
a month to inquire into my views, they seemingly feeling it necessary to keep me under surveillance.

About the end of September, I heard from a high official of the
Foreign Ministry of the existence of a "deadline," agreed upon
between the government and the high command, for conclusion
of the negotiations. This news, which I heard for the first time,
made it easy to conceive that conditions had become serious. By
early October, it was rumored that on the ground of the "deadline" the military officials were insisting on abandonment of the
negotiations, which were making no progress. After 12 October,

---

quently filled the position of Minister of Munitions in the Suzuki Cabinet of 1945,
since which time he has been engaged in business. His reputation was as one of
the ablest of the naval officers of his time, and as one of the most cosmopolitan
in outlook.

[4] The Kempei, nominally an approximate equivalent to the American Military Police,
possessed also an extensive power of "thought control" and censorship, and a considerable degree of autonomy.

I began to hear that the government's tenure on office had become very precarious; and on the 16th the Konoe Cabinet resigned en bloc, "on account of internal disunity."

After a conference with the Senior Statesmen,[5] Lord Keeper of the Privy Seal Kido [6] recommended to the Throne appointment of General Tōjō,[7] Minister of War in the Konoe Cabinet, as new Premier, and, on the 17th, Tōjō received the Imperial mandate to form a cabinet. At half-past eleven on the night of the 17th, I was called on the telephone at my home by Tōjō, who requested me to visit him immediately at the War Minister's Official Residence. Upon my arrival, after telling me that he had been designated Premier, he asked me to enter the Cabinet as Foreign Minister and concurrently Minister for Overseas Affairs.

I told Tōjō that although I had no accurate knowledge of recent political conditions or of the development of the Japanese-American negotiations, I had heard that the previous Cabinet had ended in disunity brought about by the recalcitrance of the

[5] "Senior Statesmen" was the term applied to the unofficial body composed of all former Premiers, which in some measure succeeded to such functions of the Genrō—the "Elder Statesmen" of earlier days—as advising the Throne on selection of a Premier.

[6] The Lord Keeper of the Privy Seal was the Emperor's political adviser and the channel of liaison between Court and government, as such having a wide but vaguely defined area of influence and authority.

Marquis Kido Kōichi (1889–   ), grandson of a leading statesman of Restoration days, after a bureaucratic career leading to the posts of Minister of Education, Minister of Welfare and Home Minister, became Lord Keeper in 1940, occupying the position until it was abolished in 1945, after the surrender. He was charged before the IMTFE with responsibility for "aggressive war," and was convicted and sentenced to life imprisonment. He was paroled in 1955.

[7] General Tōjō Hideki (1884–1948) had been employed as Chief of Staff of the Kwantung Army, Vice-Minister of War and Inspector of Aviation, but had first become known outside Army circles when, as lieutenant general, he became Minister of War in the Second Konoe Cabinet. Upon designation as Premier, he was promoted general and kept on the active list, the first active military officer in a quarter of a century to be Premier. At his resignation as Premier, War Minister, Minister of Munitions, President of the Imperial-Rule Assistance Association and Chief of the General Staff, in July 1944, he was retired and held no office subsequently. Pursuant to conviction by the IMTFE, he was hanged with others of the defendants, on 23 December 1948.

Army over the negotiations; therefore, I told him, I must first be
informed of those circumstances before deciding whether to
accept his offer. Half an hour's discussion followed. Tōjō at first
said that it was quite true that the collapse of the Konoe Cabinet
had resulted from the uncompromising attitude of the Army
toward the stationing of Japanese troops in China, which was
one of the main issues between Japan and the United States. He
said that he felt moreover that since the Imperial command had
fallen upon him, despite his having been the spokesman of the
Army's views in the preceding Cabinet, he could continue to
maintain a resolute stand in the negotiations. At that, I told him
that I would have to decline his offer of the Foreign portfolio, for
if the Premier and the Army were going to continue obdurate,
even if only on the one question of the stationing of troops in
China, the negotiations would certainly break down. Both further striving for a diplomatic solution and my assumption of the
Foreign Ministership being meaningless if the new Cabinet was
to be born under such auspices, I could not accept the offer of
the portfolio.

Tōjō then explained that what he had said represented merely
his "feeling"; but I answered him that even such a "feeling" of
the Premier was obstacle enough to the negotiations. I added that
if I were to become Foreign Minister I should do it with the
determination to succeed in the negotiations; and therefore I
could not accept the position unless the Army would agree to
make genuine concessions in reconsidering the troop-stationing
question, and also would consent to reviewing the other problems involved and to making the necessary abatement of its
demands to enable us to reach a settlement on a reasonable basis.
Tōjō said that if there was a possibility of the negotiations' succeeding, he would be in agreement with the desire to see them

concluded; nor, he assured me, had he any objection to reviewing the problem of troop stationing, as well as the other issues—which others however were, according to the reports from Washington, virtually solved. He required that I give an immediate answer whether I would enter the Cabinet, because he wanted to submit the list of Ministers to the Throne early the next morning.

I knew that the Japanese-American negotiations had already reached a point at which the Navy must be peculiarly concerned with their outcome. I was therefore interested in the choice of Navy Minister, and I asked Tōjō if it was true that, as rumored, the Navy portfolio would go to Admiral Toyoda Soemu.[8] Tōjō said that it would not; Admiral Shimada [9] would be Navy Minister. Although not acquainted with Shimada, I knew that at least he also did not belong to the "stronger" faction of the Navy; I therefore thought that I could count on the Navy's not obstructing diplomatic exertions.

Having thus come to the conclusion that I would have scope for activities offering some vista of success in the negotiations, I told Tōjō that I would accept the offer of the Foreign and Overseas portfolios. The investiture ceremony was held on the following day, 18 October, and the Tōjō Cabinet was established.

Some, outsiders, seem to have had the idea that the Tōjō Cabi-

---

[8] Admiral Toyoda Soemu (1885–   ), modern Japan's most distinguished naval officer, was at that time Commander in Chief of the Kure Naval District. As the war progressed, he was called to the most responsible positions in the Navy—Commander in Chief of the Combined Fleet, 1944–45, and Chief of the Naval General Staff from May 1945 to the end of the war. Admiral Toyoda was tried by an Allied military tribunal in Tokyo, in 1948–49, for responsibility, as chief of the Naval high command, for atrocities, and was acquitted, since which time he has lived in retirement.

[9] Admiral Shimada Shigetarō (1883–   ), before becoming Navy Minister, had held among other posts those of Vice-Chief of the Naval General Staff and Commander in Chief of the China Fleet. In February 1944, while Navy Minister, he became concurrently Chief of the Naval General Staff for a few months, but quit office on the fall of the Tōjō Cabinet and thereafter played no part in affairs. He is at present on parole from a sentence of life imprisonment imposed by the IMTFE upon conviction of "planning aggressive war."

net was determined from the moment of its formation on waging a war; this, of course, is not true, as will be apparent from the following pages. So far as I myself am concerned, my conversation with General Tōjō just related—even disregarding my later efforts—is proof that my purpose in entering the Cabinet was not to start a war, but to avert one. My mistake lay in believing that I could achieve a solution merely within the terms of my understanding with Tōjō, when neither of us was aware that relations had so far deteriorated that the other party to the controversy had already determined on war—there was at that moment, indeed, no one on the Japanese side who had yet recognized the full gravity of conditions. It is certainly no longer necessary to deny that the Tōjō Cabinet was the alter ego of a "Tōjō Clique" —a term frequently heard in earlier days—ample evidence having been produced at the IMTFE trial to dispose of the suggestion that any such "clique" had existence. I was often asked, immediately after my entry into the Tōjō Cabinet, how I had come to accept the ministership; I answered frankly to all questioners that my purpose was to bring the negotiations with the United States to a successful ending, and I explained to them my bargain with Tōjō.

When I took office I was, naturally, conversant with the general course of the development which our foreign policy had taken. Military intrusion into the field of diplomacy had first become marked in matters pertaining to China, and with its extension to German and Italian relations the Tripartite Pact was born. In the decade of warlike atmosphere following the Manchuria Incident, the soldiers' prestige had become enhanced, and it had become increasingly difficult for a foreign minister to realize the expression of his views in the national policy. This was why at my entry into the Cabinet I had requested from Tōjō

(who continued as War Minister) the assurance of his co-operation in my diplomatic efforts, and had specially questioned him
about the choice of a Navy Minister. As to the Japanese-American negotiations in particular, I had, as I have said, only frag-
mentary information, but no accurate knowledge of the terms or
other details. From what I had gathered, the United States
seemed to have been quite uncompromising, but not to have
manifested a purpose to oppose our desires in their entirety; I
was therefore—perhaps overoptimistically—of the opinion that
there was still some ground for hope of the negotiations if Japan
would make substantial concessions. Furthermore, since the military services seemed to wish this success and to be amenable to
reconsidering their previous stand, as promised by General Tōjō,
it was not a case of the Cabinet's being bent from the moment
of its formation on war; and I was resolved to devote myself to
the utmost of my abilities to succeeding in the negotiations, however dark the prospect and however great the possibility of failure. One can, no doubt, insure one's personal safety by evading
the undertaking of the task in such circumstances, but in so
doing one must certainly betray the cause of one's country and
of the peace of the world. War did engulf us, disappointing my
aspirations; and, now I am within prison walls, I regret certain
errors of judgment, but there is still no doubt in my mind that
my decision to assume the Foreign Ministership was beyond all
question right.

Upon entering on the duties of the office, I immediately undertook a comprehensive review of the Japanese-American negotiations. I shall discuss in detail in the next chapter the results of
this study; but here I wish to mention a few subsidiary matters.

The transfer of the office and its business from my predecessor
was very simple. In his remarks upon turning the office over,

Admiral Toyoda discussed the activities of the Foreign Ministry, and incidentally suggested a special embarrassment which he as a naval officer in the Ministry had felt when he said, "You, not being an adopted son, can be quite *sans gêne*." In connection with the Japanese-American negotiations, he informed me that the Konoe Cabinet had resigned on account of the opposition of the Army to the setting of a time limit on the stationing of troops in China, though the setting of such a limit could have resulted in the consummation of an agreement; for the details of this, he referred me to the documents. Toyoda said further that this troop-stationing question was the only stumbling block remaining in the way of the negotiations. This being consistent with the fact that the intracabinet strife resulting in the downfall of the Third Konoe Cabinet had arisen from that question alone (and with Tōjō's recent statement that Ambassador Nomura was reporting from Washington that the issues other than that one had in general been settled), I was encouraged at the possibility that a solution might be found if that was the only current problem in the negotiations. (Later, however, it was gradually discovered that this information was incorrect, and that the other two major issues as well still remained at large.)

I gave much thought to the choice of the subordinates who would support me in my mission. For Vice-Minister I selected Nishi Haruhiko,[10] who had been Chief of the Russian Section of the European-American Bureau when I was bureau director, and had since worked closely with me. As Director of the American Bureau—hence the official who would be in charge of the Japanese-American negotiations—I assigned the Director of the East

[10] Nishi Haruhiko (1893–   ) is a career diplomat who prior to 1941 had accomplished the routine advancement through varied posts at home and abroad. Resigning the Vice-Ministership in 1942 when Mr. Tōgō left office, he became wartime Minister to Manchoukuo. From 1952 to 1955 he was Ambassador to Australia, and since 1955 has been Ambassador to England.

Asiatic Bureau, Yamamoto Kumaichi, to act concurrently (Yamamoto had, in the East Asiatic Bureau, worked from the early stages on the negotiations, then involving mainly the China problem). Under him, Kase Toshikazu, whom I had known since he was an attaché, was continued as Chief of the First American Section, directly responsible for the negotiations. Kase was concurrently designated Secretary to the Minister. Shortly afterward I asked former Foreign Minister Satō,[11] a senior of the Ministry with long experience in Europe, and former Ambassador Kawagoe, an expert on Chinese affairs, to put their experience at our disposal as Advisers to the Ministry.

In connection with personnel, I might mention also that I carried out a small-scale "purge" within the Ministry. At once after assuming office, I requested and received the resignation of an ambassador who was known to have been working for promotion of the policy of southward expansion. I planned also the suspension from office of two section chiefs and another official, whom I regarded as radicals and violators of the discipline of the service; they, however, resigned in preference to accepting the order of suspension. These measures served as an effectual warning to certain Ministry officials who were advocating a "strong" foreign policy, especially vis-à-vis Britain and America, and who had occasionally gone even further and plotted or conspired with military officers or other radical elements.

Recognizing the paramount necessity of familiarizing myself, by study of the documents and otherwise, with what had already passed in the Japanese-American negotiations, I declined all

---

[11] Satō Naotake (1882–   ), a professional diplomat, after some years as Ambassador to Belgium and to France had become briefly Foreign Minister in 1937. He was Ambassador to the U.S.S.R. during the war years (1942–45). Quitting the diplomatic service after the end of the war, he was elected to the House of Councilors, the upper house of the National Diet, of which he was President from 1949 to 1953.

invitations and evaded all affairs and callers not absolutely inescapable, and for the first week in office devoted literally all my time—save for attendance at meetings of the Cabinet and the Liaison Conference—to analysis of the negotiations. Performance of this chore was not facilitated by the disorder in which I found the documents of the Foreign Ministry. As for the business of the Ministry of Overseas Affairs, I was interested in it but would evidently be able to spare no attention whatever for it, during the time of travail lying before me; soon after taking office, therefore, I asked to be relieved of the position of Minister of Overseas Affairs. My request being granted without demur, I was freed to dedicate all my energies to the Japanese-American negotiations.

The extent of military interposition into and predominance in our diplomacy was emphatically borne in upon me when I learned that at that time copies of purely diplomatic correspondence went habitually to the military authorities, a procedure which seemingly had been followed since the Manchuria Incident. The Foreign Ministry, needless to say, received none of the telegrams of the Army or the Navy, not even those dispatched by their attachés in the diplomatic missions abroad; on the other hand, I was informed immediately upon assuming office that every incoming and outgoing telegram relating to the Japanese-American negotiations was provided to the War and Navy Ministries and the two General Staffs, without instruction from the higher officials of the Foreign Ministry (important messages were in the same manner sent to the Lord Keeper of the Privy Seal as well). The Director of the Military Affairs Bureau, General Mutō,[12] once described to me how every morning there was a

[12] The Military Affairs Bureau of the War Ministry was the center of the Army's political activities, and occupancy of its directorship was the usual prelude to succession to the highest places of the Army.

pile of telegrams from the Foreign Ministry waiting on the desk of War Minister Tōjō, who carefully read them all, and if any number was missing demanded that it be supplied.

Lastly, I should mention the theft of the Foreign Ministry's cipher. This came to light in the course of the hearings of the Pearl Harbor Investigation Committee of the United States Congress, when it was revealed that since the time of the Second Konoe Cabinet, in 1940, the Ministry's telegrams had been intercepted and deciphered. Immediately after becoming Foreign Minister, recalling that our ciphers had been known to the American government during the Washington Conference of 1921–22, I had inquired of the Chief of the Cable Section whether our communications were secure. He assured me, "This time it's all right!"—technical experts are generally confident of their specialties. After the war, when I learned of the disclosure by the Congressional investigation, I called upon Mr. Kameyama, who had been Chief of the Cable Section at the time of the Japanese-American negotiations, to investigate. He told me that such deciphering could have been possible only by acquisition of the secret of the sending-and-receiving machines; but whatever the means by which the United States became possessed of our ciphers, the occurrence was a humiliation for the Foreign Ministry. I do not believe, however, that this leakage of private communications did substantial damage to the negotiations in my time; for there was, I think, already no room for bargaining at that last stage.

Lieutenant General Mutō Akira (1892–1948) reached the position in 1939, remaining to April 1942; he was thereafter a division commander in the East Indies, then Chief of Staff of the 14th Area Army, in the Philippines, from October 1944 to the end of the war. He was hanged pursuant to conviction by the IMTFE on charges of vicarious responsibility for atrocities.

CHAPTER 2

The Japanese-American Negotiations under the Konoe Cabinets

THE REVIEW of the development of the Japanese-American negotiations to which I devoted my first weeks in office left me with the distinct feeling that, conceding Japan's demands to have been excessive, the attitude of the United States had undergone a marked change in the course of the negotiations from the time of the original Draft-Understanding with which they had commenced in April. The United States had shown no sign of making concessions, merely reiterating after the latter part of June her position as taken at that time; and especially, after the freezing of Japanese assets at the end of July, she had become extremely uncompromising, and seemed only to be trying to prolong the discussions rather than to reach an agreement. I got the impression that the American attitude could indicate nothing but a resolution to risk a failure of diplomacy, and consequently war. I thus came to comprehend Matsuoka's calling for termination of the negotiations in anticipation of a possible breakdown, and I could not understand the preceding Cabinet's optimism for succeeding by diplomacy in the absence of relaxation of the demands on our side.

A determination on war on the part of the United States, underwritten by joint military conferences of the "ABCD Powers"—America, Britain, China and the Netherlands—was in any event our estimate in those days. I had confirmation from American sources of the correctness of this estimate in 1942 when I read *How War Came* by Forrest Davis and Ernest Lindley; by revealing that the United States had been resolved on war at the time of the Atlantic Conference in August, the book verified my suspicion. Further corroboration came when in the winter of 1945–46 I read the record published by the Pearl Harbor Investigation Committee.

My study of the history of the negotiations suggested to my mind many ambiguities and doubts. To explain these, and to relate chronologically how the facts became known to me, would be the method most faithful to the truth and the most interesting to me personally, but it would be tedious for the reader. In the following pages I shall, therefore, describe in outline the evolution of the negotiations, prior to my becoming Foreign Minister, on the basis of what I discovered in the course of my review of them, of what came to be known to me later from the record of the Congressional investigation of Pearl Harbor,[1] of the evidence brought out at the IMTFE, and of other sources. The documents relating to the Japanese-American negotiations will for the most part be merely summarized, they having already appeared in such State Department publications as *Peace and War* and *Foreign Relations of the United States—Japan: 1931–1941*, and in *Gaikō Shiryō: Nichibei Kōshō Kiroku [Diplomatic Reference Materials: Record of the Japanese-American Negotiations]*, compiled by the Foreign Ministry. I may add that there

---

[1] *Pearl Harbor Attack (Hearings before the Joint Committee on the Investigation of the Pearl Harbor Attack, 79th Congress, 1st and 2nd Sessions)*, 1946 [cited hereinafter as *"Pearl Harbor Attack"*]. T.S.

are many works of reference to which now, being in prison, I have no access for quotation; such are the record of the Pearl Harbor investigation, mentioned above, and the published memoirs of various high American officials.

The Japanese-American negotiations had their inception when Secretary of State Hull requested Ambassador Nomura, on 14 April 1941, to obtain from his government instruction whether he might commence negotiations on the basis of the so-called Japanese-American Draft-Understanding. The origin of this "Draft-Understanding" has been much mooted; but whatever its nature, it was in fact the genesis of the ensuing Japanese-American negotiations, and I must summarize it here to render intelligible my further discussion of them.[2]

The document declared in its preamble that, motivated by the desire to establish a just peace in the Pacific, the two governments felt it necessary to arrive at mutual understanding concerning seven points:

1. "The concepts of the United States and of Japan respecting international relations and the character of nations."
2. The attitude of the two nations toward the European War.
3. The China Affair.
4. Naval, aerial and merchant-marine relations in the Pacific.
5. Commerce and financial co-operation between the two nations.
6. Economic activities in the Southwest Pacific area.
7. Political stabilization in the Pacific.

In relation to these, the draft proposed the making of agreement, the main points of which were as follows.

[2] The "Draft-Understanding" is given in full as Appendix "B."

1. The two nations were to "acknowledge each other as equally sovereign states and contiguous Pacific Powers," and to "assert the unanimity of their national policies as directed toward the foundation of a lasting peace and the inauguration of a new era of respectful confidence and co-operation among our peoples." They were further to declare it to be their conviction that "nations and races compose, as members of a family, one household; each equally enjoying rights and admitting responsibilities with a mutuality of interests regulated by peaceful processes and directed to the pursuit of their moral and physical welfare, which they are bound to defend for themselves as they are bound not to destroy for others."

2. Japan was to declare that "the purpose of its Axis Alliance was, and is, defensive and designed to prevent the extension of military grouping among nations not directly affected by the European War"; but, "with no intention of evading its existing treaty obligations," it was to declare further that its military commitments under the alliance were to come into force "only when one of the parties of the alliance is aggressively attacked by a power not at present involved in the European War." The United States, in return, was to declare that "its attitude toward the European War is . . . determined by no aggressive alliance aimed to assist any one nation against another," but solely by considerations of its self-defense.

3. As to the China Affair, the United States was to request Chiang Kai-shek to negotiate peace directly with Japan, on the basis of the terms following:

(*a*) The independence of China.

(*b*) Withdrawal of Japanese troops from China, in accordance with agreement to be reached between Japan and China.

(*c*) No acquisition of Chinese territory.

(*d*) No imposition of indemnities.

(*e*) Re-establishment of the "Open Door," as that term should thereafter be interpreted by agreement between the United States and Japan.

(*f*) Coalescence of the governments of Chiang Kai-shek and Wang Ching-wei.

(*g*) No large-scale emigration of Japanese to Chinese territory.

(*h*) Recognition of Manchoukuo.

If the Chiang regime should refuse to negotiate peace, the United States would discontinue aid to it.

4. Each nation was to refrain from such dispositions of naval or air forces as would menace the other. Japan would, if desired, use its good offices to procure release for charterage to the United States of a percentage of its merchant tonnage.

5. The two nations were to supply to each other commodities respectively required and available, and to resume normal commercial relations by a new Treaty of Navigation and Commerce. The United States was to extend to Japan a gold credit sufficient to establish sound economic conditions in the Far East and to permit of sustained economic co-operation between the countries.

6. In consideration of Japan's pledge that its activities in the Southwest Pacific would be carried on by peaceful means, American co-operation should be given for the procurement of natural resources required by Japan.

7. For political stabilization in the Pacific, the two nations should not acquiesce in future transfers of territories to or conquests thereof by European Powers, and should jointly guarantee the independence and the defense of the Philippines. Japan "requests the friendly and diplomatic assistance" of the United

States "for the removal of Hongkong and Singapore as doorways to further political encroachment by the British in the Far East." Japanese immigration to the United States and the Southwest Pacific "should receive amicable consideration" on a non-discriminatory basis.

Finally, it was provided that upon conclusion of the understanding a conference to implement it should be held at Honolulu, between President Roosevelt and Premier Konoe with necessary staffs.

In transmitting this document to the Foreign Ministry, Ambassador Nomura had explained that "Informal preparations have been made to sound out the concurrence of the United States in this Draft-Understanding. Having got confirmation that Secretary Hull agreed with it in general, I have privately participated in its preparation and have had my subordinates work on it. As the result, this Draft-Understanding was drawn"; and in another communication he said, "I have studied the document very carefully with the Embassy staff, the Army and Navy attachés, Colonel Iwakuro and others." As I then understood it, the original idea of this agreement had been the outcome of the visit to Japan of Bishop James Edward Walsh and Father James M. Drought of the Maryknoll Mission, toward the end of 1940, and the draft itself had resulted from the activities in the United States of Colonel Iwakuro, an officer detached from the Military Affairs Bureau of the War Ministry "to assist Ambassador Nomura," and Mr. Ikawa Tadao, an official of the Finance Ministry serving on Nomura's staff and a man close to Prince Konoe. I understood also that, as Ambassador Nomura said, Secretary Hull not only concurred in the draft but had participated in its preparation; when it was received in Tokyo, at any rate, the Japanese authorities took it as an overture by the United States,

67

and even expected that it would be possible to have its terms modified to our advantage in the course of subsequent negotiations.

On the other hand, Bishop Walsh, in an affidavit [3] submitted to the IMTFE, testified that Matsuoka had requested him to communicate to the United States government the intention of the Japanese government to initiate negotiations aimed at the adjustment of relations. Matsuoka, he said, did not express himself clearly concerning any concrete terms, but other government officials informed him that Japan's basic terms were (1) nullification of the Tripartite Pact, not explicitly, but in some definite way which should be at once effectual and complete, and (2) withdrawal of all troops from China and restoration of China's territorial and political integrity. Where the bishop could have acquired such erroneous ideas, I do not know. If these reported terms had been the policy of the Japanese government, an understanding with the United States could readily have been reached without recourse to any negotiations or to employing anyone as go-between. In any event, it is sure that this misunderstanding was conveyed to the American authorities, and possibly led them to entertain the belief that Japan would if pressed recede to these terms; and the later negotiations were certainly complicated thereby.

The contents and phraseology of the text of the Draft-Understanding indicated that specialists of the United States had worked on it. Nevertheless, it could have been expected that differences of opinion would result from the many ambiguous and vague terms used in it, and this did in fact happen. It will be noted that this draft was in many ways more advantageous for Japan than subsequent proposals of the United States. Among

[3] IMTFE Exhibit No. 3,441, Record of Proceedings, p. 32,978. T. S.

such points are, for example, the provisions of Article 1, that nations and races compose, as members of a family, one household, each equally enjoying rights; those of Article 3, calling for fusion of the governments of Chiang Kai-shek and Wang Ching-wei and recognition of Manchoukuo; and those of Article 7, providing for Japanese immigration to the United States and the Southwestern Pacific area on a basis of equality with other nationals and freedom from discrimination. However, Secretary Hull had made it plain that this draft should be the point of departure, by asking Ambassador Nomura when it was submitted to obtain authority to proceed with discussions on the basis of it; but, even more, the very thought of initiating negotiations had been repeatedly advanced by the President and the Secretary of State, as is shown in the American record [4] of the conversations between Hull and Nomura. It will not be overlooked, in evaluating this fact, that at that time the German offensive against Britain, though somewhat blunted, still constituted a very grave menace.

As soon as the Draft-Understanding was received in Tokyo, the government authorities immediately commenced examination of it. On 18 April it was discussed at a Liaison Conference of the government and the high command, and some favored immediate acceptance. It was decided, however, to make inquiries of Ambassador Nomura concerning some ambiguities in the provision relating to the Tripartite Pact, and to delay a final reply until after the return of Foreign Minister Matsuoka, then en route home from his trip to Europe.

Pursuant to this decision, Prince Konoe—who was acting as his own Foreign Minister in Matsuoka's absence—inquired of

[4] *Foreign Relations of the United States—Japan: 1931–1941*, 1943 [cited hereinafter as *"Foreign Relations"*], Vol. 2, pp. 387–8, 393–4, 397–8. T. S.

Ambassador Nomura if the proposed understanding was not contradictory to the spirit of the Tripartite Pact, in that by means of it the United States might be disembarrassed of concern over Pacific affairs and freed to concentrate on aid to Britain. The Ambassador replied that since Japan's obligation under Article 3 of the Tripartite Pact—the military-assistance clause—would remain in full vigor even after conclusion of a Japanese-American understanding, any threat of war between the United States and Japan inherent in the pact likewise would continue unimpaired, and the understanding would therefore not dispense the United States from attention to the Pacific. Nor, the Ambassador insisted, would the Japanese-American settlement conflict with the spirit of the Axis Pact, because although American aid to Britain might be increased after conclusion of the understanding, Japan could by force of the agreement itself restrain the United States from actual entry into the European War. As to relations between the United States and Japan in case of failure to reach understanding, he said, economic pressure on Japan would be intensified and the danger of war increased. Prince Konoe returned the question whether Britain and American might not suppress Japan, despite the understanding, if they won the war, just as they had done after the First World War. The Ambassador's response was that the best way to cope with postwar developments would be, by means of the understanding, to improve Japanese-American relations, to settle the China Affair and to open the way to securing raw materials, thereby leaving us with hands free to cultivate our strength.

In fine, the concept of the understanding as it was presented by the Ambassador was to preserve the Tripartite Pact effective and intact, while at the same time restraining the United States from entering the European War. Not only did this directly contradict the impression received by Bishop Walsh, but it would put Japan in the position of flatly rejecting the United States' desires. Obviously, in these circumstances success of the negotiations could from the beginning hardly have been hoped for. Admiral Nomura, I felt, had made these explanations out of a sincere desire to see negotiations got under way; but the result was to confuse subsequent proceedings unnecessarily.

When Foreign Minister Matsuoka received the telegram, on his way back to Tokyo, informing him of receipt of the Draft-Understanding and requesting him to hasten his return, his impression of what had occurred seems to have been at variance with the actualities. He had been hoping—as I learned from one of his suite—to persuade President Roosevelt to mediate between Japan and China, and when in Moscow en route to Europe had prevailed upon American Ambassador Steinhardt there to cable to the President his suggestion to that effect. When he heard of the American proposal he was thus at first much pleased with the news, thinking that this was in response to his approach through Ambassador Steinhardt. As it gradually became clear, however, that such was not the case, Matsuoka developed a coolness to the Draft-Understanding; evidence accumulated, after he learned of its contents, that he was displeased by the commencement of negotiations on the basis of it—though, as I have mentioned, Bishop Walsh testified that Matsuoka had previously asked him to convey to Washington the intention of the Japanese government to open discussions. It was of course not necessary for Matsuoka to ask the bishop to act as go-between, and if he really made such a request it must have been because of some quirk of his character. Matsuoka was a shrewd politician, but he acted often enough in devious ways, of which this was a good example.

71

Matsuoka, in his instructions to Nomura prior to the Ambassador's departure for his post, and after his arrival there, had emphasized Japan's obligations under the Tripartite Pact, and had pointed out that the establishment of the Greater East Asia Co-Prosperity Sphere implied only the finding of ways and means for self-supply and self-support in the area. He had merely instructed Nomura to work to make this understood in the United States, but had not directed him to commence any negotiations. What Matsuoka intended was by means of the "grandeur"—so he conceived it—of the Tripartite Pact to force the United States to reconsider its course and to exercise self-restraint; his Oral Statement cabled to Nomura on 3 May makes it clear that he adhered to the policy of not prejudicing the position of Germany and Italy, in accordance with the pact.

It is, I think, unnecessary here to offer any appraisal of the Tripartite Pact, my unequivocal and long-continued opposition to which is a matter of record. It should, however, be noted that Matsuoka being, as the one who concluded the pact, a believer in it, it was only logical that he should have felt little enthusiasm for the Japanese-American negotiations. Matsuoka's views were important to their future because it was chiefly on the basis of them that the Japanese counterproposal to the United States was prepared. The most significant provisions of this document, which was handed to Secretary Hull on 12 May, were three. With regard to the attitudes of the two governments toward the European War, it declared that "Japan maintains that its obligations of military assistance under the Tripartite Pact . . . will be applied in accordance with the stipulation of Article 3 of the said Pact"; but it required the United States in its attitude toward the European War not to resort to "such aggressive measures as to assist any one nation against another." As to the China problem, it referred to the Konoe Statement,[5] the Treaty with the Nanking government and the Joint Declaration of Japan, Manchoukuo and China, and provided that the United States, accepting the principles enunciated in those documents and in reliance upon Japan's policy of friendship and good-neighborliness, should "forthwith request the Chiang Kai-shek regime to negotiate peace with Japan." Finally, the counterproposal dropped—as more appropriately to be dealt with after relaxation of the tension—the provisions of the Draft-Understanding relating to disposition of naval and aerial forces (Paragraph IV*a*), release of Japanese shipping for charterage (Paragraph IV*c*), the gold credit (Paragraph V), and nonacquiescence in transfer of Far Eastern territories (Paragraph VII*a*). The guarantee for the Philippines also was to some extent weakened.

In Tokyo, the estimate of conditions in America around this time was based to a large extent on a long report sent by Ambassador Nomura on 8 May. According to the Ambassador, President Roosevelt more and more had tended, since the passage of the National Defense Act, to be dictatorial, and was actually creating so-called public opinion; most Americans were determined on standing by England to the end, and the British-German war was likely to develop into an American-German one. It was, he reported, possible that the United States would, even at the risk of war, start convoying to assist Britain, and opinion could

[5] On 22 December 1938 the First Konoe Cabinet had issued a statement which set the tone for the later Treaty of Basic Relations between Japan and (Nanking) China and Japan-Manchoukuo-China Joint Declaration (see the Translators' Introduction, p. 38). This statement asserted that Japan, Manchoukuo and China would be "united by the common aim of establishing the new order in East Asia and of realizing a relationship of neighbourly amity, common defence against Communism, and economic co-operation," that Japan respected the sovereignty of China, and that Japan "does not intend to exercise economic monopoly in China, nor does she intend to demand of China to limit the interests of those third Powers, who grasp the meaning of the new East Asia and are willing to act accordingly" (*Foreign Relations*, Vol. 1, pp. 482–3).

be heard that the United States should immediately go to war to help recoup British losses in the Balkans and the Near East. It was conceivable, he concluded, that in the delicate international situation the United States would endeavor to utilize the Draft-Understanding to adjust relations with Japan—less dangerous than Germany—in order to avert a two-front war.

In response to Ambassador Nomura's presentation of the Japanese counterproposal of 12 May, Mr. Hull stated that there was no longer any guarantee against Japanese advance to the south, and made inquiries concerning our concrete terms for peace with China. On 16 May, in an informal Oral Statement, he declared that the United States considered her aid to Britain a part of her self-defense, and he attached excerpts from his speech of 24 April, in which it was asserted that the right of self-defense might be exercised by resistance wherever such resistance would be most effective for the United States. With regard to the China question, he asked for a spelling out of Japan's peace terms. In Tokyo, meanwhile, Foreign Minister Matsuoka had disclosed to the German and Italian Ambassadors the fact that Japanese-American negotiations were in progress, and the developments therein. German Foreign Minister Ribbentrop expressed regret that Japan had entered into discussion with the United States, and protested against its continuing unless Germany was first consulted.

On 21 May, Secretary Hull told Nomura that he had no objection to quoting the Konoe Statement, as proposed by the 12 May draft, but could not agree to the treaty with the Nanking government and the Japan-Manchoukuo-China Joint Declaration. He was agreeable also to the principle of joint defense against communism (although he disapproved of use of the term "communism"), and seemed, according to the Ambassador, to take no exception to the idea of Japanese troops' being stationed at specified points in China for that purpose. On 27 May, President Roosevelt, stressing in a "fireside chat" the need to thwart the designs of Hitler, declared that as a matter of self-defense the decision whether, where and when the rights and interests of the United States were threatened rested with the United States itself. He did not mention Japan specifically.

On 31 May the Embassy received from the State Department an interim proposal, to which on 4 June it countered with its own modification, but the positions of the two parties remained divergent. Ambassador Nomura endeavored earnestly to bring Secretary Hull around to his view; but before the Ambassador's efforts had borne any fruit, the American proposal of 21 June was presented.

The United States' draft of 21 June embodied the position to which it clung throughout the subsequent negotiations down to Secretary Hull's note of 26 November. Its main points of difference from earlier drafts were the following.

1. With regard to the attitudes of the two governments toward the hostilities in Europe, it was to be clarified that the aim of the Tripartite Pact was defensive and "designed to contribute to the prevention of an unprovoked extension of the European War." In an exchange of notes which was proposed, the United States— after making reference to Secretary Hull's 24 April speech—was to request that Japan confirm that "with regard to the measures which [the United States] may be forced to adopt in defense of its own security," the government of Japan "is not under any commitment which would require Japan to take any action contrary to or destructive of the fundamental objective of the present agreement, to establish and to preserve peace in the Pacific area."

2. As to means for solution of the China Affair, the Japanese government was first to communicate to the United States "the

general terms within the framework of which the Japanese Government will propose the negotiation of a peaceful settlement with the Chinese Government, which terms are declared by the Japanese Government to be in harmony with the Konoe Principles . . . and with the practical application of those principles," after which the United States would "suggest to the Government of China" that it enter into negotiation of the peace. There was a proposed annex and supplement on the part of the Japanese government, embodying the basic terms of the Sino-Japanese peace. Concerning Manchoukuo, however, the annex and supplement provided only for "amicable negotiation in regard to Manchoukuo."

3. Problems of commerce in China were raised by a separate sheet posing three questions: (1) "Does the term 'economic cooperation' between Japan and China contemplate the granting by the Government of China to the Japanese Government or its nationals of any preferential or monopolistic rights which would discriminate in favor of the Japanese Government and Japanese nationals as compared with the Government and nationals of the United States and of other third countries?" (2) Could the Japanese government indicate the approximate time within which would be effected removal of "existing restrictions upon freedom of trade and travel by nationals of third countries in Chinese territory under Japanese military occupation"? (3) "Is it the intention of the Japanese Government that the Chinese Government shall exercise full and complete control of matters relating to trade, currency and exchange?"

4. The annex and supplement on the part of the United States declared that "It is understood that during the present international emergency Japan and the United States each shall permit export to the other of commodities in amounts up to the figures

of usual or pre-war trade, except, in the case of each, commodities which it needs for its own purposes of security and self-defense."

On 22 June, Ambassador Nomura, having requested an interview with Secretary Hull, told him that he could not transmit to his government the notes, which the Secretary proposed be exchanged, concerning the Tripartite Pact and the peace terms between Japan and China, they being wholly unacceptable to Japan. The 21 June proposal itself in effect demanded of Japan an assurance in blank that she would stand out, regardless of the provisions of the Tripartite Pact, if on the plea of self-defense the United States joined in the war in Europe; it required submission of peace terms with China which should be acceptable to the United States (though slightly moderating the American stand on Manchoukuo); and it made plain that the United States would recognize no preferential status for Japan in trade and enterprise in China. Moreover, it would have enabled the United States even after conclusion of the agreement to embargo such commodities as petroleum and steel, which Japan required, whenever it deemed it necessary for its self-defense.

With the proposal, Secretary Hull had handed to Ambassador Nomura on the 21st an Oral Statement in which he said that there was accumulated evidence that some Japanese leaders in influential official positions were definitely committed to a course calling for support of Nazi Germany and envisaging Japan's fighting on the side of Hitler should the United States become involved in the European hostilities. Hence, he said, he had come to the conclusion that he must await some clearer indication than had yet been given that the Japanese government as a whole desired to pursue peaceful courses such as constituted the objectives of the proposed understanding. Upon seeing this Oral Statement

77

Foreign Minister Matsuoka instructed Nomura to return it immediately to the Secretary, on the ground that "it constitutes criticism of officials of a sovereign state and urges changes in the organization and policy of another government in a manner almost unprecedented." (This incident must have lain behind Matsuoka's animus toward Admiral Nomura. When, after many years, I met Matsuoka in Sugamo Prison in May 1946, he startled me by exclaiming immediately, without even delaying for greetings, "Nomura must have been a nuisance to you, too! He's impossible!"; and he continued with many harsh remarks. Upon my answering, "It was you who selected him, wasn't it?" "I didn't know he was like that," he said; and I still recall vividly the extreme antipathy with which he spoke of Nomura.)

Even before receipt of the United States' 21 June proposal—because despite Japanese urging we had received no favorable response to our suggestions—many in the government and the military services had begun to complain of the way Ambassador Nomura was conducting the negotiations in Washington. Some were even going so far as to say that it would be better to discontinue diplomatic endeavors; according to the memoirs of Prince Konoe,[6] the government had already been considering cessation of the negotiations and going to war against the United States. The lower ranks, particularly of the Army, had become very restive. The occupation of French Indochina having been decided upon, Prince Konoe goes on to say, preparations for a war against Britain and America were put under way in earnest; as these preparations progressed, they in turn resulted in further stimu-

---

[6] The Konoe memoirs were published in part in Japan as *Heiwa e no Doryoku* [*Endeavors for Peace*], 1946; the original Japanese manuscript was, before it could be published in full, "lost" in the General Headquarters, Supreme Commander for the Allied Powers. A translation, under the title *The Progress of Japanese-American Negotiations during the Time of the Second and Third Konoye Cabinets*, appears in *Pearl Harbor Attack*, Part 20, Exhibit No. 173, Exhibits page 3,985.

lating the opposition to the Japanese-American negotiations. What Konoe says explains how the progress of the war preparations encouraged the military faction to grow in the confidence that they would not be defeated, and consequently to demand with increasing peremptoriness that diplomacy yield place and war be launched. In any event, the 21 June proposal being as a whole irreconcilable with Japan's position—so flatly so that our Ambassador had even demurred at transmitting one part of it to his government—it is evident why Tokyo was much discouraged and dissatisfied, and why argument for cessation of the negotiations should have resulted.

Meanwhile, unexpectedly—so far as the Japanese government was concerned—war broke out between Germany and the U.S.S.R. Some in the Army urged that Japan should seize this opportunity to attack Russia from the east simultaneously with the German offensive from the west; the Navy, however, was reluctant from considerations of defense in the Pacific to concur in the idea. It was reported that Foreign Minister Matsuoka, upon learning of the outbreak of the Russo-German war, submitted to the Throne his opinion to the effect that Japan should attack the U.S.S.R. in co-operation with Germany, and that we would eventually fight Russia, America and Britain. Prince Konoe, dumfounded at Matsuoka's representations to the Emperor, tried to restrain the movement for a Russian war.

The movement would not so easily be stopped. The Army dispatched to Manchuria a large draft of troops, under the operational code name "Kwantung Army Special Maneuver." Discussions at the Liaison Conference of government and high command even resulted in agreement on an "Outline of National Policy Attendant upon the Changing Situation" as a program to be followed in consequence of the Russo-German war. This outline, which was adopted at an Imperial Conference on 2 July, consisted of three "policies," with elaboration of provisions for implementing them.[7] The policies were:

1. Regardless of changes in world conditions, Japan shall firmly adhere to the policy of establishment of the Greater East Asia Co-Prosperity Sphere, thereby contributing to maintenance of the peace of the world.

2. Japan shall continue to press forward with efforts for solution of the China Affair, and shall proceed with the southward movement to secure the basis for self-sufficiency and self-defense. The Northern problem will be dealt with in accordance with changes in the situation.

3. Japan shall overcome all obstacles to attainment of the foregoing objectives.

The gist of the provisions for implementing these policies was that Japan should not for the time being go to war against the U.S.S.R., but should strive to gain victory over the Chiang Kai-shek regime by arms; that moves in the South should be carried out even at the risk of war with Britain and America; and that America's entry into the European War should be prevented by all possible means, diplomatic or otherwise, but that if America did involve herself Japan should act in accordance with the Tripartite Pact. It was expressly provided that Japan should continue "necessary diplomatic negotiations with nations concerned in the southern regions," and "for this purpose we shall make preparations for a war with Britain and the United States." The general tone of the Outline of National Policy is one of virtual abandonment of the Japanese-American negotiations.

After having arrived at this decision regarding Japan's over-all policy, the Liaison Conference proceeded on 10 and 12 July to deliberation on the Japanese-American negotiations. The Konoe memoirs relate the developments thus:

[7] The "Outline of National Policy" is printed in full as Appendix "C."

The attitude of Foreign Minister Matsuoka became more and more uncompromising, and it became evident that he tended to be openly opposed to going on with the negotiations. . . . According to him, the American proposal [of 21 June] had been made with malicious intent either to force Japan's capitulation or to throw her into confusion. . . . Above all, he demanded that the "Oral Statement" attached to the American proposal be returned to the United States forthwith. He contended that the Japanese-American negotiations must be ended, the only question being how and when they should cease.

If the "Outline of National Policy" actually represented the national policy, Matsuoka was to a large extent correct, as negotiations with the United States in the face of such a policy had no expectancy of success. The case of those advocating continued diplomatic efforts could be maintained only if the "Outline" was, despite its formal importance as having been adopted by an Imperial Conference, mere verbiage, an exercise in composition. That it was not mere verbiage quickly became evident when the measures vis-à-vis the South were effectuated by the movement of Japanese forces into southern Indochina. This advance cut the ground from under diplomacy, and rendered an eventual war between Japan and the United States inevitable.

There was thus an antinomy between the Imperial Conference decision and the continuance of the negotiations, and it was utterly paradoxical that the Army and Navy leaders who so strongly advocated an advance southward and had brought about adoption of the decision should simultaneously have insisted upon persevering with the negotiations. The only possible explanation is that the Premier and Army and Navy miscalculated the attitude of the United States.

Despite Matsuoka's deprecating of the prolongation of the negotiations, many favored it, and he acquiesced in it. A Japanese proposal modifying the American draft of 21 June was prepared and sent to Admiral Nomura on 15 July. Conformably with the opinion of the Army and the Navy, this proposal embodied the following three points: (1) that the attitude of Japan toward the European War would be decided in accordance with the requirements of treaty obligations and self-defense; (2) with regard to the China problem, that the United States should recommend peace on the basis of the Konoe Principles, but should not interfere in the peace terms; and (3) that Japan reserved her right to the use of force in the Pacific when necessary.

While Matsuoka was preoccupied with the "Oral Statement" received from the United States, Prince Konoe had come to entertain the belief that the negotiations would not prosper so long as Matsuoka remained as Foreign Minister. For that reason, and partly motivated also by personal feeling, the Prince planned the reconstruction of the Cabinet with the aim of eliminating Matsuoka; this was carried out when on 18 July the Third Konoe Cabinet was formed, with Admiral Toyoda Teijirō taking the Foreign portfolio. The Cabinet having been established with the announced aim of continuation of the negotiations, it was the general expectation that it would at least try to expedite them; there was therefore profound astonishment when the first act of the new government was the occupation of southern French Indochina, on 21 July. This, however, was merely a revelation of the discongruity between the 2 July decision and continued negotiation. I heard it said in defense of the new Cabinet that, the move having been decided upon by its predecessor, it was precluded from doing other than carrying it out—both the Premier and the Foreign Minister having been members (the latter as Minister of Commerce and Industry and of Overseas Affairs) of the Second Konoe Cabinet, they could only have felt that they were in no position to recant their allegiance to the national policy adopted by it.

It was disclosed at the IMTFE trial that meanwhile, on the other side of the Pacific, an official in the State Department had divulged confidentially before 2 July that the Japanese-American negotiations would be terminated by the United States, and Japanese assets frozen.[8] The plan for freezing of assets thus antedated the occupation of southern Indochina, having originated roughly at the time of the demands in Japan for cessation of the talks upon receipt of the American 21 June proposal. In any event, American designs for economic sanctions against Japan were no recent thing. At the time of the Manchuria Incident, in 1931, Secretary of State Stimson had purposed application of sanctions jointly with the League of Nations. The plan was abandoned because of President Hoover's apprehension that such action would conduce to war; but when Roosevelt, as President-Elect, had his meeting with Secretary Stimson on 9 January 1933 he fully concurred in Stimson's ideas. And, as it turned out, Roosevelt as President gave notice of abrogation of the Japanese-American Treaty of Commerce, in July 1939, and imposed an embargo after September 1940 on export to Japan of scrap iron and other strategic materials, thereby seriously deranging Japan's international trade.

Resort to expedients such as these was only natural, there being many in the United States who were confident that Japan could ultimately be driven to submission by economic pressure, as well as many favoring a strong policy toward Japan in general. Some in the American government were already by this time calling for the imposition of an embargo on petroleum, but President Roosevelt had been unwilling to go this far, lest it should lead

[8] *Foreign Relations*, Vol. 2, p. 496; see also *Id.*, Vol. 2, p. 501. T. S.

to war. This was explained by him in a speech on 24 July; if he had cut off the supply of petroleum to Japan, he said, "they probably would have gone down to the Dutch East Indies a year ago, and you would have had war." Therefore, he had let the petroleum supply flow to Japan "with the hope—and it has worked for two years—of keeping war out of the South Pacific for our own good, for the good of the defense of Great Britain and the freedom of the seas."

Prior to the movement of the Japanese forces into southern French Indochina, Japan had entered into negotiations with the Vichy government concerning joint defense of the colony, a protocol embodying the agreement therefor finally being signed on 29 July. The United States had earlier obtained from various sources advance information of the movement southward of the troops, and Mr. Hamilton, Chief of the State Department's Division of Far Eastern Affairs, brought up the subject with Ambassador Nomura on 5 July, referring to the press reports. The Ambassador explained that as the United States was aiding the Chiang regime not only financially but by supply of planes and other munitions and the sending of pilots to China, Japan was compelled to take necessary counteraction. He called attention to the fact that Japan was being militarily encircled, with the American fleet visiting Australia, staff conferences being held (and their subject matter becoming known) among American, Dutch and British Far Eastern representatives, and American-Soviet mutual assistance being rumored; now that he was hearing of the probability of a petroleum embargo, he said, he wanted to ask reflection on the part of the American authorities. To further inquiries by the same official, on the 15th, concerning a move into southern Indochina, the Ambassador gave a similar reply.

The Japanese counterproposal (sent to Ambassador Nomura

on 15 July) to the American proposal of 21 June was not delivered. There being in it no relaxation of Japan's attitude, and the atmosphere in the United States having become worse, Nomura withheld it in the hope that the change of cabinet in Tokyo might bring a favorable turn. Nomura later even said that "the advance into southern French Indochina was the greatest crisis in the Japanese-American negotiations." On 23 July he made a report to Foreign Minister Toyoda on the reaction of the United States to the operation, and on the same day explained in detail to Under Secretary Welles the necessity of carrying it out for promoting a settlement of the China Affair, as well as for assuring to Japan an uninterrupted supply of foodstuffs and other raw materials. To the Under Secretary the Ambassador expressed his fear that a petroleum embargo would exacerbate the national feeling of Japan, and on the 24th he reiterated this opinion to the President, and reviewed the pending issues in the negotiations. In connection with Indochina, the President said to the Ambassador that it had been for the sake of peace in the Pacific that he had resisted popular pressure for an embargo, but that if Japan should invade the Netherlands Indies, Britain immediately, and then the United States, would go to their aid. The President here made a suggestion of neutralization of French Indochina; if Japan would withdraw her troops, he said, he would spare no effort to obtain from the interested countries solemn guarantees of the neutrality of the area and of the right of acquisition by Japan of supplies and raw materials therefrom on a basis of equality.

On 26 July the President issued the executive order freezing Japanese assets in the United States and embargoing exports of petroleum. The Japanese press expressed astonishment and indignation at the action, but most dismayed by it was the Navy. The Navy's alarm was by no means unreasonable, for once the supply

85

of petroleum from the United States and the Indies was cut off, the stockpile which it had accumulated would gradually be used up, and the fleet which it had constructed at the cost of abrogation of the Naval Limitation Treaty would soon become worthless to it. Subsequent developments made it clear that this action was —as had been foreseen by the United States—the decisive factor in the coming about of war.

To the President's suggestion of 24 July of neutralization of Indochina, Siam was later added. The idea was studied by the Japanese authorities; but our forces could not be withdrawn from southern Indochina unless the whole southward drive was to be abandoned, the Indochina move having been based on the 2 July Imperial Conference decision, and the first implementation of the policy of southward advance therein prescribed. A counterproposal was therefore drawn in Tokyo, and sent to Ambassador Nomura on 5 August. Its chief points were that Japan should not station troops in areas in the Southwest Pacific, except for French Indochina, while the United States, Great Britain and the Netherlands should cease their military preparations; that the issues, including that of supply of raw materials, pending between Japan and the Netherlands should be resolved; and that normal trade relations between the United States and Japan should be restored. The United States was also to render good offices for the negotiation of peace between Japan and the Chiang Kai-shek regime, and in future to recognize Japan's special position in French Indochina.

It is true that this American proposal of 24 July was a selfish one, which Japan could scarcely accept in its entirety. It aimed merely at forestalling Japan's southward advance by the suggested neutralization of Indochina, without offering any palliative for the freezing of Japanese assets and the embargo on petroleum

—both intimately connected with the movement into southern Indochina. No more, however, was it to have been expected that the Japanese counterproposal, which dwelt only upon such issues among those pending in the Japanese-American negotiations as might be developed advantageously to Japan, would be acceptable to the United States. It is no wonder, therefore, that when Nomura presented the Japanese plan to Secretary Hull on 6 August the Secretary showed little interest in it, and that the Ambassador should have concluded that the United States was prepared "for any eventuality"—that is to say, that she was prepared to go to war.

In this state of affairs, the Japanese government as an emergency measure fixed upon a scheme to which great importance was attached in Tokyo, and to which in coming weeks the government pinned its highest hopes for a settlement with the United States. This was the project of Prince Konoe's meeting in person with President Roosevelt—Honolulu was the locale thought of—to study possibilities for averting a crisis. The idea of such a conference had been included in the Draft-Understanding at the outset, but it had never been pursued in the negotiations, and now reappeared with an air of novelty. The meeting was duly proposed by Ambassador Nomura to Secretary Hull on 8 August, but the Secretary vouchsafed no expression of opinion concerning it.

The United States considering the Japanese move into southern Indochina to represent a decisive turning point in Japan's policy, it was natural enough that she felt compelled to settle her own course of action. It chanced that President Roosevelt was just at that time to meet with Prime Minister Churchill, and for a week, beginning on 9 August, they held at sea the Atlantic Conference. Although the details of this meeting afloat have not yet been fully disclosed, the memorandum [9] submitted to the Congressional Pearl Harbor Committee by former Under Secretary Welles, who attended the meeting, makes known that one of the points agreed upon between the President and the Prime Minister concerned an arrangement for parallel ultimative action toward Japan. According to Welles' memorandum, the President exhibited to Churchill the Japanese draft agreement presented by Ambassador Nomura to Secretary Hull on the 6th, and various alternative strategies vis-à-vis Japan were considered. It was in the end agreed that Japan's proposal should not be rejected outright, but that a strict warning would be administered to her, while talks were kept going; Roosevelt, as reported by Welles, stated on that occasion that he believed that the starting of a war by Japan could thereby be staved off for thirty days. Davis and Lindley are more specific on this latter point; [10] according to them, when Churchill expressed fear that no further respite could be hoped for, the President said, "I think I can baby them [the Japanese] along for three months" (the word "baby," according to these authors, was a favorite of the President's).

In view of this evidence, it is interesting that when President Roosevelt received Ambassador Nomura on 3 September, the Ambassador reported him as saying categorically (and even giving the reasons therefor) that the contents of the Japanese-American negotiations had not been referred to at his meeting with Prime Minister Churchill.[11] The making of this statement by the President can only be supposed to be true, as Ambassador Nomura could have had no reason so to report if it was untrue; the import

---

[9] *Pearl Harbor Attack,* Part 14, Exhibit No. 22C, Exhibits page 1,275. See also Under Secretary Welles' *viva voce* testimony, *Id.,* Part 2, pp. 458 ff.; and compare Churchill, *The Second World War,* Vol. 3, *The Grand Alliance,* 1950, pp. 438 ff.

[10] Davis and Lindley, *How War Came,* 1942, pp. 9–12. T. S.

[11] Telegram, Nomura to Toyoda, IMTFE Exhibit No. 2,894, Record of Proceedings, p. 25,798. T. S.

of Mr. Roosevelt's having made such a false statement will not be overlooked. At any rate, the warning mentioned by Welles was read to Nomura by the President on 17 August. It was in very stiff terms, to the effect that the United States would resort immediately to any and all action which it might deem necessary if Japan should take any further steps in pursuance of a policy or program of military domination, by force or threat of force, of neighboring countries. According to Ambassador Nomura, the President remarked to him upon pronouncing the warning that he did not like to say those things, but said them because he thought it best for the two countries.

A second document handed to Nomura by the President on 17 August dealt with the suggestions by the Ambassador of a meeting of chiefs of state and of resumption of negotiations. After detailing developments since the Japanese advance into southern Indochina, it went on that if the Japanese government desired and was in a position to suspend its expansionist activities and to embark upon a peaceful program for the Pacific, the American government "would be prepared to consider resumption of the informal exploratory discussions which were interrupted in July." However, it continued, the government of the United States would feel it helpful if, before such resumption of conversations was undertaken, the Japanese government would furnish a clearer statement than had yet been given of its attitude and plans, "just as this Government has repeatedly outlined to the Japanese Government its attitude and plans." Ambassador Nomura reported that the President observed, as he handed over this document, that he could not go to Honolulu, as proposed by Prince Konoe, for the tête-à-tête, but might be able to go to Juneau.

In response to these documents, the Japanese government sent to Ambassador Nomura on 26 August a message from Premier

Konoe addressed to President Roosevelt, as well as a long exposition of the peaceful intent of Japan. When the Ambassador saw the President on the 28th to present these communications, the latter, according to the Ambassador, even dwelt on possible times and places for the meeting with the Premier—thus palpably "babying" Japan. (The way the President "babied" us was very affable, according to Nomura's report—just like a great actor's playing of Molière. The people in the Kremlin later in a similar manner cozened us, through our ambassador, in connection with the Teheran and Yalta Conferences; but the President remains to me the better actor.) Konoe's Cabinet, heartened by this good augury for the meeting, proceeded even to select the suite to accompany the Premier to American territory.

The meeting of the chiefs of state soon, however, began to appear doubtful of realization. On 3 September the President handed to Ambassador Nomura a reply to Prince Konoe, in which he pointed out that he could not avoid "taking cognizance of indications of the existence in some quarters in Japan of concepts which, if widely entertained, would seem capable of raising obstacles to successful collaboration between you and me." In these circumstances, he said, he felt constrained to suggest the desirability of taking precautions toward the success of the proposed meeting, "by endeavoring to enter immediately upon preliminary discussion of the fundamental and essential questions on which we seek agreement."

The President at the same time handed over an Oral Statement criticizing the attitude of the Japanese government as conveyed on the 28th. This document, referring to Secretary Hull's statement at the inception of the negotiations, said that the four principles maintained by the United States as fundamental to international affairs were:

1. Respect for the territorial integrity and the sovereignty of each and all nations.
2. Support of the principle of noninterference in the internal affairs of other countries.
3. Support of the principle of equality, including equality of commercial opportunity.
4. Nondisturbance of the *status quo* in the Pacific except as the *status quo* may be altered by peaceful means.

The Oral Statement emphasized that stability in the Pacific area could be attained only through adherence to these principles, and requested that Japan give an indication of its concurrence in the attitude of the United States.

On the following day, the 4th, Secretary Hull told Ambassador Nomura that affirmation of the Four Principles should be given prior to a meeting of the chiefs of state. According to Nomura's reports, the United States had in the beginning clung to the Four Principles, but the negotiations had proceeded—at the insistence of Japan upon not becoming engrossed in debates on abstractions —without going into them. Now Secretary Hull not only reinstated them in the forefront, and demanded of Japan to accept them unconditionally, but further requested Japan's full concurrence in the American position concerning such concrete problems as attitudes toward the European War, nondiscriminatory treatment in trade, and withdrawal of Japanese troops from the continent.

Before Secretary Hull's statement reached Tokyo, however, Ambassador Nomura had received new instructions, which crossed his report of it. He was directed thereby to propose agreement on three points. First, that Japan would make no military advance without justification, whether northward from Japan or against areas adjoining French Indochina. Second, that if the United States should enter the European War, Japan's interpretation and application of the Tripartite Pact would be independently defined by her. Third, that Japan was ready upon the realization of a general peace and restoration of normal relations between Japan and China to withdraw her armed forces from China as soon as possible, in accordance with agreement to be reached between the two countries. The United States, in return, was to rescind immediately the order freezing Japanese assets, to cease the rendering of aid to China, to suspend military preparations in the Far East and the Southwestern Pacific area, and to remove the prohibition on the passage of Japanese vessels through the Panama Canal. Ambassador Nomura presented this proposal as directed, on the 6th, pointing out when he did so that the first and second points in particular would meet with the desires of the United States. He again urged that the conference of the two chiefs of state be promptly held.

It is significant that about this time the British Ambassador in Tokyo, Sir Robert Craigie, reported to his government that it was the best opportunity in years for bringing about a just solution of Far Eastern issues, and that the policy of procrastination on the part of the United States ("the Americans seem to be playing for time") was the obstacle blocking the Japanese-American negotiations.[12] The 6 September proposal of Japan could not, however, have aroused any interest in President Roosevelt, who, resigned to the inevitability of a war against Japan unless she would agree to the United States' proposals in their entirety, had been trying to gain a few months' time. His only interest was to prolong the diplomatic phase by managing Japan adroitly; in those circum-

[12] Telegram, Craigie to Eden, 30 September 1941, IMTFE Exhibit No. 2,908, Record of Proceedings, p. 25,847. T. S.

stances the plan for the meeting of the chiefs of state was moribund from birth.

The military services in Tokyo now began to consider that there was no future for the Japanese-American negotiations. The Navy, especially, perturbed since the placing of the embargo on petroleum, felt that if the negotiations were destined to prove futile Japan should take her stand before her opportunity was lost. The growth of this feeling led to the calling, on 6 September, of another Imperial Conference, at which was adopted a resolution by which war became an imminent possibility. As will be seen, the new policy for the Japanese-American negotiations established as one item of this Imperial Conference decision was in fundamental conflict with the Four Principles of the United States. It therefore did not accord with the realities when Prince Konoe declared at the Imperial Conference that he was still working to realize promptly the meeting of the chiefs of state; and it was in square contradiction of the decision that on the very day of the conference he told the American Ambassador that he fully subscribed to the Four Principles (and that he later, in order to forward the meeting with the President, sent his secretary Ushiba to Councilor Dooman of the American Embassy to say that influential elements in Japan had consented to the Premier's giving to the President assurances which would satisfy him). Prince Konoe's sincerity in trying every expedient for a peaceful solution is commendable, but the many self-contradictions in his course are to be deplored. In particular, if his purpose was to agree to a strong decision in Tokyo, then after going abroad to swallow the other party's demands *in toto*, his attitude can only be regarded as unmanly, in that he would have put the entire burden on the shoulders of those remaining behind. It is easy enough to send recommendations from abroad; ambassadors often cable recommendations without care for whether they fit the case. This is a reprehensible habit. The problem is the feasibility of the plans. As I studied the history of the Japanese-American negotiations, I was impressed with the feeling that in this case the Premier should have set out for the rendezvous only after the settling in Tokyo of Japan's basic terms for an understanding with the United States.

The gist of the decision at the Imperial Conference of 6 September was as follows.[13] "In view of the current grave state of affairs, and especially of the offensive against Japan precipitated by the United States, Great Britain, the Netherlands and other countries, the situation of the U.S.S.R., and the resilience of our national strength, Japan will carry out the action vis-à-vis the South" determined upon by the Imperial Conference of 2 July. "With the determination not to decline war" with the United States, Britain and the Netherlands, Japan should have completed her preparations by the end of October; meanwhile, *pari passu* therewith, she should "endeavor to exhaust diplomatic measures to attain her demands vis-à-vis the United States and Britain," the minimum points of demand and the limits of Japan's concessions to be as stated in an appendix. If by the beginning of October there should appear no hope of fulfillment of Japan's demands through negotiation, war "shall be forthwith determined upon." Particular efforts would be made to prevent formation of a Russo-American front against Japan.

In the appendix were defined in detail Japan's minimum demands and maximum concessions, including noninterference by the United States and Britain in the disposition of the China Affair and the making of peace on the basis of the Sino-Japanese Treaty of Basic Relations and the Japan-Manchoukuo-China

[13] The decision is printed in full as Appendix "D."

Joint Declaration, and the cessation of aid to the Chiang regime; abstention by the United States and Britain from further strengthening of their armaments in the Far East, and recognition of the "special relations" existing between Japan and France; and restoration of commercial relations with Japan and facilitating of her obtaining materials indispensable for her existence. Japan in return would go to the extent of agreeing to make no military movement, based on Indochina, into any area save China, and to withdraw from Indochina upon establishment of an equitable peace in the Far East, and would guarantee the neutrality of the Philippines. The Tripartite Pact was not to be brought up spontaneously in the negotiations, but any inquiries were to be answered with the statement that there was no change in Japan's obligations under the pact; similarly, inquiry concerning the Japanese attitude toward the U.S.S.R. was to be answered that no initiative in military action would be taken by Japan so long as the U.S.S.R. respected the Neutrality Pact and did not threaten Japan or Manchoukuo.

It was understood that after adoption of this decision the Army and Navy high commands accelerated their war preparations in no small degree. At the same time—according to the reports from the Washington Embassy—the Gallup Poll showed the American public opinion favoring the stopping of Japan at the risk of war to have risen from 51 per cent in July to 70 per cent in September, and the prospect of a war with Japan to be more popular than that of one against Germany.

The Japanese proposal of 4 September produced, even as late as the 19th, and despite Ambassador Nomura's inquiries, no substantial reply from Secretary Hull, who merely posed questions. Foreign Minister Toyoda, thinking thereby to get the negotiations moving again, therefore on the 22d presented to Ambassador

Grew, in Tokyo, the basic terms of peace between Japan and China which he wished communicated to the Secretary of State. These terms were:

1. Neighborly friendship.
2. Respect for sovereignty and territorial integrity.
3. Cooperative defense between Japan and China.

Cooperation between Japan and China for the purposes of preventing communistic and other subversive activities which may constitute a menace to the security of both countries and of maintaining the public order in China.

Stationing of Japanese troops and naval forces in certain areas in the Chinese territory for a necessary period for the purposes referred to above and in accordance with the existing agreements and usages.

4. Withdrawal of Japanese armed forces.

The Japanese armed forces which have been dispatched to China for carrying out the China Affairs [*sic*] will be withdrawn from China upon the settlement of the said Affairs, excepting those troops which come under point 3.

5. Economic cooperation.
    (*a*) There shall be economic cooperation between Japan and China, having the development and utilization of essential materials for national defense in China as its principal objective.
    (*b*) The preceding paragraph does not mean to restrict any economic activities by third Powers in China so long as they are pursued on an equitable basis.

6. Fusion of the Chiang Kai-shek regime and the Wang Ching-wei government.
7. No annexation.
8. No indemnities.
9. Recognition of Manchoukuo.

A general proposal embodying these basic terms of peace was prepared on the 25th, and presented to the United States government in Washington on the 28th. It was, however, little changed from previous drafts; the United States sent a memorandum to Japan on 2 October, reiterating her viewpoint as theretofore expressed. The Japanese government offered various explanations, in Tokyo and in Washington as well, of its position. It was around this time that both American and British Ambassadors in Tokyo were urging upon their respective governments that it was the opportune time to restore to normal Japanese-American relations or to cause Japan to come over to the British and American side.[14] The attitude of the United States, however, manifested no change.

The Imperial Conference decision of 6 September had provided (Paragraph 3) that "Should there be no prospect, by early October, of attainment of our demands through . . . negotiations, war against the United States (and Britain and the Netherlands) shall be forthwith determined upon." The 2 July Imperial Conference decision had made a Pacific war inescapable; that of 6 September made it definite. Those who did not acquiesce in prolongation of the Japanese-American negotiations, therefore, after the latter part of September grew in their antagonism to it, urging that Japan should decide upon war at once, as it was necessary to commence hostilities by the end of October at latest. The government, however, contended that diplomacy was not entirely hopeless; and a series of "Ogikubo Conferences"—so called from their locale, Prince Konoe's villa in the Tokyo suburb of

[14] Telegram, Grew to Hull, 29 September 1941, *Foreign Relations*, Vol. 2, p. 645; Telegram, Craigie to Eden, 30 September 1941, IMTFE Exhibit No. 2,908, Record of Proceedings, p. 25,847. See also Grew's telegram to Hull of 18 August 1941, *Foreign Relations*, Vol. 2, p. 565; and compare Grew, *Turbulent Era*, 1952, Vol. 2, Chapter XXXIV.

Ogikubo—was held, after 5 October, for exploration of the subject by Premier, Foreign Minister and War and Navy Ministers. A telegram sent by Ambassador Nomura on the 3d is worthy of note in connection with these conferences. Nomura said that although the Japanese-American negotiations had come to a "deadlock," it was not necessarily an insoluble one. Japan's outlook would become favorable relative to the United States, he considered, in the event of a separate peace between Germany and the U.S.S.R., or if the United States came to feel it safe to undertake serious commitments in the Atlantic; but in the existing circumstances the United States would achieve the objectives of war against Japan by mere economic warfare. Finally, he observed that two of the three pending issues between the countries had been virtually settled, with that of the stationing of troops in China the only one remaining unsolved—but as to that one, he added, considering the actual conditions in China, a complete withdrawal could not be thought of for some years to come.

The Ogikubo Conference of 12 October was practically the last debate on the question of war or peace. On the authority of the Konoe memoirs, on that occasion Navy Minister Oikawa first stated that, now Japan was faced with the alternative of war or no war, he would leave decision to the Premier. Prince Konoe at once responded that if it was to be decided there and then, he would vote for continuing the negotiations. Here War Minister Tōjō interposed, saying that the Premier was too hasty, that it must first be settled whether there was any possibility of success through diplomacy, as it was vital that Japan should not let slip her opportunity for a war by devotion to palavering which arrived nowhere. Foreign Minister Toyoda pointed out that, the major obstacle to agreement being the recognition of the right to maintain troops in China, the negotiations were not beyond hope if the Army would consent to some concessions, however slight, on that head. To this, according to Konoe's memoirs, Tōjō rejoined that the Army could make no concession in regard to the stationing of troops, a matter of life or death to it.

The discussions at the Ogikubo Conferences thus dealt almost exclusively with the troop-stationing question—because, apparently, of Admiral Nomura's telegram, above mentioned, reporting the other two of the three pending issues substantially solved. As I shall later explain, this report of Nomura's was incorrect, the other two issues not having been settled, and it was therefore a grave blunder that the Ogikubo Conferences should have been limited in their scope to consideration of this one. At any rate, these conferences having arrived at no conclusion on that problem, on the 14th the Premier asked the War Minister's reconsideration. Tōjō not only refused to comply with this request, but at the Cabinet meeting on that day exhorted upon the ministers the necessity of breaking off the Japanese-American negotiations. It was this which drove Prince Konoe to submit the resignation of the Cabinet on the 16th. At a meeting of the Senior Statesmen the following morning it was decided to recommend Tōjō as the new Premier, nominations of Prince Higashi-Kuni and General Ugaki having been opposed by Lord Keeper Kido.

Such was, as disclosed by my later study of the documents and by other sources of information, the tide of events from the inception of the Japanese-American negotiations to the establishment of the Tōjō Cabinet and my assumption of the Foreign Ministership.

Prince Konoe's course as Premier during this period, and his

99

traits of character which dictated that course, are a fruitful field for speculation. He was indubitably very sincere in his desire for the improvement of relations between Japan and the United States; but his actions subsequent to commencement of the negotiations betray many incongruities. While undertaking diplomatic activity aimed at improvement of Japanese-American relations, he quite readily consented to terms of negotiation widely discrepant with the United States' position; he rendered a war inevitable by the Imperial Conference of 2 July; and while soliciting a personal meeting with President Roosevelt as an issue from the impasse brought about by execution of the July policy, by concurring in the 6 September Imperial Conference decision he made the coming of the war quite definite. Basically there was, whether in the United States or in Japan, hardly anyone, aside from extreme militarists, who wanted war; but it is meaningless to protest one's attachment to peace and abhorrence of war if one merely stands on one's demands and makes no concession. And, needless to say, whether one's demands conform to justice and international good faith should first be pondered; to look merely to one's own advantage, without consideration for the other party's position, cannot be said to be the way to work for peace.

Prince Konoe's self-contradictions are not made comprehensible even by his memoirs. I recall many conversations with him, during the war when we were both out of office and I was passing much time, as was he, in Karuizawa. In one such conversation he referred to the irresponsible attitude of the Navy, and his surprise at it. He said to me indignantly that while the advance southward, which was ultimately the Navy's concern, had had such irredeemably evil results, yet at the cabinet crisis in October 1941 the Navy had abdicated to the Premier the decision concerning the war which was actually its affair. I told the Prince, "I agree with your view that the Navy was irresponsible, but you yourself were no less so. You left behind you when you resigned a time bomb—you created all the obstacles to Japanese-American agreement, you let Japan in for it by the advance into southern French Indochina, and you had a hand in the war decision on 6 September which resulted in war preparations' proceeding. This lighted the fuse of an explosive. Although it was understood after the Third Konoe Cabinet resigned that the war decision was to be re-examined, I was greatly troubled by being unable to lay hand on the bomb, the fuse of which continued to sputter throughout the subsequent re-examination of the position."

The Prince, sober and for him unusually chastened, answered, "For that, I make apology to the nation and the Emperor."

CHAPTER 3

The Historical Background
for the Negotiations

WHEN THE THIRD KONOE CABINET made its exit, leaving behind it the ominous legacy of which I have made mention in foregoing pages, relations between Japan and the United States were on the brink of such a denouement as would admit of no further diplomatic parleyings. The development of the Japanese-American negotiations of 1941, and the crisis in relations to which they had led by October, when I took office, I have considered in detail in the preceding chapter. But had this crisis been engendered only after the commencement of the negotiations?

Japan purposed, in the Japanese-American negotiations, obtaining the mediation of the United States for settlement of the China Affair, and inducing her to discontinue her aid to Chiang Kai-shek, in order to hasten a Japanese-Chinese settlement. But the United States was not to be content merely to see China and Japan extricated from the warfare then in progress: she had taken her stand solidly behind China. The problem, that is to say, was not only Japan's violations of the Nine Power Treaty or infractions of the principle of the Open Door in China; application to history teaches that the Nine Power Treaty itself had originally been contrived to curb Japan, after the First World War. The deterioration in Japanese-American relations thus did not come about at a stroke, in a few months of 1941, but had originated long since in Japan's conflict with the outer world attendant upon her expansion into the Asiatic continent. To discover the origins of the Greater East Asia war is impossible without a full and correct understanding of events on the international stage from about the time of the Russo-Japanese War of 1904–05, with reference to Japan's relations not only with China but as well with Britain, Russia and other countries.

Now that the Pacific War is ended, it may seem futile, or even a disservice to the cause of friendship between Japan and the United States, to indulge in critical analysis of their relations of the past. If no constructive purpose would be served by such an analysis, I should indeed be reluctant to undertake it; but our hopes that such tragic events as the recent Pacific War may not recur must look for their realization to a recognition of the true facts of history. The United States Department of State having sent its expert on Japan, Mr. Ballantine, to testify at the IMTFE trial [1] that Japan since her emergence as a modern state had undeviatingly pursued a policy of double-dealing and military aggrandizement, I feel it a duty to state, as a text for the future, the facts as they were.

Intercourse between Japan and the United States dates from Commodore Perry's expedition to the Far East in 1853–54. It is evident from American sources [2] that Perry's purpose was to establish American bases in such places as the Ryūkyū (Okinawa) and Ogasawara (Bonin) archipelagoes; his foresight certainly

---

[1] Affidavit of Joseph W. Ballantine, IMTFE Exhibit No. 1,245, Record of Proceedings, p. 10,711. T. S.

[2] *Official Correspondence of Commodore Perry*, U.S. Senate Ex. Doct., Serial No. 751, Doct. No. 34, 33d Congress, 2d Session, 1855. T. S.

seems imbued with the prophetic, in view of the strategic importance assumed by those islands in the recent war. Perry's "opening" of Japan was followed by a period in which good relations were cultivated by the efforts of such gentlemanly men as Townsend Harris,[3] America's first consul general, who worked devotedly for Japanese-American friendship, and his successors. With the opening of the country to foreign intercourse, however, Japan had been compelled to accept treaties with the world Powers granting to their nationals extraterritoriality in Japan and in other ways limiting her own sovereignty; and the early years of the Meiji period—say from the "Restoration" of 1867 to the end of the century—were devoted to securing revision of the "unequal treaties" and achieving national independence and emancipation. Until even after the Sino-Japanese War of 1894–95, therefore, Japan's industrial structure had not yet assumed capitalistic form, and her external policy had not yet come to represent an implementation of imperialism.

United States Secretary of State John Hay in 1899 produced his doctrine of the Open Door in China.[4] Rather than at restraint of Japan, this action was aimed at forestalling any such political or economic partition of China as that which Britain, France, Russia and Germany designed on the occasion of the Boxer Rebellion. The United States had at that time, through its war with Spain, acquired possession of the Philippine Islands in the Pacific, and was expanding its imperialistic activities in the Far East. The

---

[3] Townsend Harris (1804–1878), after a life as a merchant in New York City, obtained appointment as first American envoy to (and first foreign diplomatic representative in) Japan—Consul General in 1855, under Perry's Treaty of Kanagawa, Minister Resident in 1859, following ratification of the first Japanese-American commercial treaty, which he negotiated. By his fairness, plain speaking and pertinacity, Harris attained a tremendous influence over Japanese officialdom, and left a reputation which still lives, and has even transmuted him into a legend, in Japan today.

[4] See *Foreign Relations of the United States, 1899*, 1901, pp. 128 ff.

European Powers having pre-empted the available bases in China, the policy—the Open Door—championed by the United States with a view to securing for herself necessary markets in China was quite different from that which she was pursuing in the Philippines, and it was thus not necessary that the United States in those days aim directly at Japan. The China problem nevertheless turned out to be the major issue in the Japanese-American negotiations. For Russia had meanwhile advanced southward into Manchuria, and the Russo-Japanese War came about when Japan determined to eliminate the pressure thus brought to bear upon her, and Britain to assist Japan in order to safeguard her rights and interests in China proper. The sudden rise of Japan, by this war, as a new Power in the Pacific posed a threat rather to the United States than to Tsarist Russia; and the sequel was an increasing coincidence of the foreign policies of the United States and Russia—not a theory conceived by me, but the conclusion of such American authorities as Beard [5] and Dulles.[6] During the Russo-Japanese War, President Theodore Roosevelt had at first patently rejoiced in Japanese successes; but as they continued uninterruptedly he gradually came to doubt whether a too complete victory of Japan might not prejudice the interests of the United States, and out of this apprehension he maneuvered at the Portsmouth Peace Conference for a peace which should balance the influence of Russia and Japan in China.

It must therefore be said that the Russo-Japanese War marked a turning-point in Japanese-American relations, an epoch from which the policy of the United States developed in the direction of restraint of Japan's expansion on the continent. This new positive policy found expression in American railway politics in Man-

[5] Charles A. and Mary Beard, *The Rise of American Civilization*, 1927, Vol. II, pp. 459–98. T. S.

[6] Foster Rhea Dulles, *The Road to Teheran*, 1944, p. 6. T. S.

churia: first the scheme of the rail magnate Harriman, with tacit State Department approval, for gaining control of the South Manchuria Railway, which Japan had won by her war with Russia; then the obtaining by American and British interests of a concession to build a Chinchow-Aigun railway (a scheme abandoned in consequence of Japanese protests that the line would parallel the South Manchuria); and finally Secretary of State Knox's proposal, in 1909, of internationalization and neutralization of all lines in Manchuria, the South Manchuria included. This American policy encouraged a *rapprochement* between Russia and Japan, and when the two countries came to an understanding by which northern and southern Manchuria were recognized as their respective spheres of influence, a temporary lull in the competition of the Powers fell upon this part of the world. I had been struck by this increasing closeness of Russo-Japanese relations when serving, in my first diplomatic post, in the consulate in Mukden, in 1913–16.

During the First World War there arose two disputes affecting Japanese-American relations, that of the so-called Twenty-One Demands on China, and that of the activities of the Japanese troops, dispatched as an element of the Allied Expeditionary Force, in Siberia. These incidents were eventually disposed of; but at the postwar Washington Conference the United States, working to perpetuate the policy of the Open Door in China, succeeded in bringing about the abrogation of the Anglo-Japanese Alliance and its supersession by the Nine Power Treaty, while restricting Japan's power in the Pacific through the Naval Limitation Treaty.

Japanese-American relations continually deteriorated thenceforward. It can safely be said that Japan's guiding purpose in the years between the wars was that of freeing herself from the obligations of the treaties concluded at the Washington Conference. The Nine Power Treaty in particular exerted a great influence on subsequent Japanese-American relations. The Naval Limitation Treaty had a fixed period of validity, and was permitted by Japan (over my strenuous protests as responsible bureau director of the Foreign Ministry) to lapse with the expiration of the term—its demise promptly making still worse the relations between the United States and Japan. The influence of the Nine Power Treaty was, however, even more far-reaching, for it had no fixed term, and continued in effect all through the subsequent period and the Japanese-American negotiations, in which it was the source of much controversy. Japan, and especially the Foreign Ministry, never comprehended how resolute was the United States' commitment to the Nine Power Treaty, and to the principle of the Open Door on which it was based, how obstinate the American intention to stand on it to the end, even at the risk of going to war for it; that state of affairs had of course existed from before the outbreak of the Manchuria Incident, as well as in the days of Matsuoka and thereafter.

As Japan had come to act and to be regarded as the stabilizing force in the Far East, frictions developed, and she had come also to be in frequent conflict with the United States and other countries. After the Russo-Japanese War, Japan, though a late comer on the scene, hastily reared a capitalistic industrial structure. Her territory being small and meager of resources, however, the only way for her to secure raw materials, as well as markets, was by external expansion; ineluctable geographical considerations dictated that this expansion should be on the continent of Asia. Such a pattern of growth is historically a necessary concomitant of capitalistic and imperialistic maturation; Japan's mistake—or misfortune—was that her progress was too rapid, and brought her into conflict with the vested interests of other Powers. Any nation, in any time, must change and develop continuously, and stagnation will lead but to decay; but no more is too hasty transformation or too precipitate rise of a nation salutary—history affords a plethora of instances (especially those of many revolutions of the past) of an imposing national structure soon crumbling for want of a sound foundation on which to rest. So, in this case, it was Japan's compulsion to expand, and the United States' and Britain's attempting to prevent her, which was the ultimate cause of the hostility which developed into war.

In particular, the tariff policy of the British Empire as settled at the Ottawa Conference of 1932, restricting the import of Japanese commodities, gave an added impetus to the continental orientation. But at the same time, with the rise of the Kuomintang a nationalistic trend had come to prevail in China, and the Chinese had begun to demand restoration of their sovereignty. As an anti-Japanese movement had gained momentum in China and spread over into Manchuria, threatening Japan's sphere of influence gained by the Russo-Japanese War, the Manchuria Incident of 1931 had resulted.

At the time of the Manchuria Incident, as I have mentioned, Secretary of State Stimson took an active interest in its development, urging the League of Nations to impose economic sanctions on Japan and offering on behalf of the United States to co-operate in them, thus to prevent further Japanese continental expansion. Owing to the veto of President Hoover, who feared that such measures would be "roads to war," this plan did not materialize; but the United States maintained its position of non-recognition of the "fruits of aggression," and the American-Japanese antagonism grew serious as time went on.

After Roosevelt's assumption of the Presidency in 1933, he

supported the Stimson Doctrine without reservation, and endeavored to restrain the growth of Japan's political influence on the continent, which he regarded as threatening infringement on the cherished American Open Door policy. It has even been suggested that the main purpose of the American recognition of the Soviet government in November 1933, after many years of non-recognition, was the disruption of Russo-Japanese amity; [7] it was, at any rate, the first step on the long road to Yalta.

These conditions had their natural reflection within Japan. As Japan, in the normal course of her capitalistic development expanding into the continent, found herself opposed at every stage by Britain and America, the militarists and others riding the mounting wave of expansionism began to accept the idea that the nation must prepare for a war as the inevitable end of the confrontation with the Western Powers. Often, indeed, even those who wished to avert a conflict with them were enthusiastic in support of a positive policy toward China. The trend to a strong policy toward America and Britain was evidenced in the talk of Japan's being the stabilizing force in the Far East, or of the "East Asia Monroe Doctrine"; but it was no less evident in connection with the problem of the Naval Limitation Treaty. The treaty, born of the Washington Conference, in 1922, had established the 5:5:3 ratio for American, British and Japanese capital ships and aircraft carriers. The treaty was to continue in effect through 1936, and thereafter unless denounced by a signatory prior to its expiration. Japan did denounce the Washington Treaty, and accordingly it and the London Treaty of 1930 (confirming and enlarging it), which had been ratified by Japan despite widespread demonstrations of militant nationalism, expired at the end of 1936. Meanwhile, the Japanese Navy, with a view to prepar-

[7] Dulles, *The Road to Teheran*, p. 190.

ing Japan for a possible clash with the United States growing out of the China problem, insisted at the London Conference of 1935–36 on the new formula of a "common upper limit" to supplant the 5:5:3 ratio, and when the United States and Great Britain would not accept this formula, Japan quit the conference.

The United States, observing from the mid-1930s Japan's strengthening of her ties with the Axis Powers, began to conceive of her as a nation which must be "quarantined," and gave little evidence of attempt to understand Japan's expositions of the aspirations and needs which she deemed natural and reasonable. Especially, after the outbreak of the China Affair the United States undertook to stiffen the resistance of the Chiang Kai-shek regime to Japan by providing to it not only economic and financial but military assistance. Finally, the conclusion of the Tripartite Pact administered the *coup de grâce* to Japanese-American relations; this treaty not only disturbed the United States in her policy of aiding Britain but, seemingly, gave rise to the fear in America that Germany might, should she by any chance subdue Britain, exert pressure upon the United States itself, in co-operation with Japan. After the conclusion of the Tripartite Pact, therefore, the United States was making the propaganda that Germany and Japan were conspiring for world domination, and denouncing them as the two aggressor states of the world, thus passing condemnation on all of Japan's actions since the Manchuria Incident. This attitude of the United States was a challenge to the military and other obstreperous elements in Japan. It was perhaps inevitable that, each side reacting with increasing antagonism toward the other, the struggle should have been intensified as time went on; but it must be remembered that this state of affairs it was which caused the breakdown of the Japanese-American negotiations and thus brought about the Pacific War.

War and the causes of war offer a fertile field for debate and meditation. Should the occurence of wars be attributed solely to social conditions? If personal elements play a part, what is the relation between them and the individual's freedom of will? (It is, of course, a moot point of philosophy whether the concept of free will, just as that of justice, is not one which the human race has developed—or, more properly speaking, is yet developing.) Again, the relation between the principle of nonintervention in domestic affairs—a fundamental tenet of international law—and ideological war deserves examination. Especially, wars between totalitarianism and democracy and between communism and capitalism call for adequate study; this interesting inquiry, however, lies outside my subject, and I wish here only to advert to one or two points suggested by it.

While the causes of wars vary with the era, wars in modern times have very rarely resulted from desires of individuals, but have almost always been accompaniments of the establishment of national sovereignties and the development of capitalistic economies. Many of them have been incident to the acquisition of colonies, aimed at obtaining raw materials and securing markets. The causes have been mainly economic, and the wars necessary concomitants of recent capitalistic development and economic competition among the Powers. As such wars recurred and as, with the development of scientific techniques, their scale grew larger, efforts to prevent war emerged. The averting of war by means of arbitration of causes of conflict was advocated; but the effort bore little fruit, few nations being willing to accept the unconditional obligation of arbitration. Nor was the renunciation of war by multilateral treaty—such as the Kellogg-Briand Pact— more successful, the nations' insistence on excepting the case of self-defense creating a vitiating loophole. Such efforts at prevention of war as the League of Nations and other collective-security mechanisms, through which sanctions might be imposed upon an offending party, or alliances obligating one party to assist another in case of attack, either proved inefficacious or even aggravated wars. No more did prevention of war by systems of balances of power succeed.

On the other hand, there are many factors working to frustrate efforts to prevent war, as Powers tend more and more to suspicion of one another and to reliance on military might alone to defend themselves. As national boundaries became settled, over the globe, countries with securely established possessions came to be preoccupied with maintenance of their vested interests, and gave little consideration to the needs of those less fortunately circumstanced. Treaties which were discriminatory, or had become unsuitable or unreasonable, were not amended to conform to changing conditions, and thus became causes of wars. National sovereignty having been stressed since the establishment of modern states, it became a principle of international law to confide to the decision of each nation the question of its rights of self-defense; but when in recent days it is asserted by such strong Powers as the United States that the right of self-defense may be exercised at such times and places as defense will be most effective, almost any action of a state can be justified as within the limits of that right, thereby nullifying the efforts at prevention of war. Modern wars having become total wars, the concept of strategic materials has been illimitably expanded; this, together with the practice of Hitler's *Blitzkrieg*, makes the observance of international law a matter of much difficulty.

Hence, although the First World War was fought as a "war to end war," it was promptly succeeded by the Second. While the nations are endeavoring to create a better world after the Second

World War, mankind is thrown into a "cold war" and the Third World War is being prophesied even before the conclusion of peace after the Second. To maintain peace must be recognized as impossible unless the causes of war be earnestly and conscientiously studied, and unless the nations submerge their egoism to follow the path of independence in harmony. Perhaps it is inevitable that more time should yet be required for the attainment of harmony among human beings and co-operation among nations, it having been only some two thousand years since such sages as Buddha, Christ and Confucius awakened to the idea of peace—a very brief period if we consider the history of the race. Nevertheless, men not only should concern themselves with the formal aspect of prevention of war—with alleviation of the symptoms—but should at once set about the contriving of provisions directed to eradication of the ultimate causes. This is urgently needed, in a world the mores of which sanction the use, for the mere purpose of expediting the end of a war, of a weapon of the inhumanity of the atomic bomb, and promise employment of the still more dreadful hydrogen bomb.

Finally, he who really desires peace must put his whole being into fighting for it. It is self-stultifying to act the bystander while events march by, then to speak up after all is over, saying that one has desired peace; it is otiose to assume a safe position, and express peaceful intentions merely in speeches or dispatches. Who truly yearns for peace must endeavor at every opportunity to arouse public opinion, must devote himself—at the risk of his life, if need be—to fighting against the enemies of peace. He must not be guilty of indecision or tergiversation, when the tide of the times runs turbulent—but too many so-called statesmen, all the world over, often have been, often are.

The same considerations are applicable to international intercourse. If in a negotiation a country professes its peaceful intent, but from beginning to end harps on its contentions only and—making no concessions in the concrete issues involved, whatever their nature—demands the complete capitulation of the other party, its attitude cannot be said to be that of one really desirous of peace. Negotiation implies give and take.

CHAPTER 4

The Tōjō Cabinet Sets Its Policy

I HAVE POINTED OUT in earlier pages that the Third Konoe Cabinet had retired leaving behind it the bomb of the Japanese-American negotiations with fuse alight. The United States' attitude after the Japanese move into southern French Indochina having become so adamant as to evidence a determination to accept the risk of war, relations were at such a crisis that there remained scarcely any room for diplomatic negotiation. The efforts which the Tōjō Cabinet, from the day of its formation, devoted to the search for a solution centered about the discussions in the Liaison Conference, an organ to which I have already referred a time or two. It is necessary that before narrating these efforts I explain the nature of the "Liaison Conference," and the relation between the government and the military high command which was the reason for its existence.

The Liaison Conference, a wholly extraconstitutional body, had come into being in July 1940 under the Second Konoe Cabinet, to provide a medium for co-ordination between the government and the high command. Under the Japanese Constitution the high command of the military forces and the direction of affairs of state were in theory separate from and independent of each other: military operations and related concerns were the exclusive province of the high command, the government having no voice therein; while the government had, nominally, full control over nonmilitary affairs, and over the administrative aspects even of military matters certain authority was vested in the service ministers in the Cabinet (who, though military men, in their capacity as ministers represented not the high command but the government). The only headship of a supremacy common to high command and government alike was that of the Emperor, and down to a time after the First World War the Genrō—"Elder Statesmen" of much influence if vaguely defined powers—exercising in his name this authority, performed the function of controlling and co-ordinating the two. But the Genrō were not replaced as they died, and with their passing from the scene the problem of military-civil relations became increasingly an awkward one.

The independence of government and high command was in actuality, however, unilateral. While the government had no power of interference in military operational affairs, in practice it could not manage even its proper nonmilitary business without concurrence of the high command; and a considerable degree of military intervention into affairs of state gradually developed. After the Manchuria Incident of 1931, when the operations of the national government had come to be very complex, the custom was inaugurated of deliberating the general outlines of national policy at a Five Ministers' Conference, consisting of the Premier and the Army, Navy, Foreign and Finance Ministers. With the outbreak of the China Affair, and as the warfare in China grew increasingly serious while at the same time the intrusion of the high command into political affairs became more and more pronounced, the Five Ministers' Conference proved inadequate to the task of achieving unification of the national policy.

In 1940 Prince Konoe, then Premier, accordingly organized the Liaison Conference with a view to achievement of such unification through round-table discussions between the highest authorities of the government and those of the high command. It was a concession on the part of the government that it openly recognized, by establishing this institution, the direct interference of the armed services in the creation of national policy, and the extent of the interference actually increased after the Liaison Conference came into being. The national predicament having by that time become so grave that all important policies had to be considered in relation to the war, the increasing weight of the views of the military men was natural, and some such institution as this was indispensable.

This predominance of military opinion had, with the passing of time, come to have a seriously crippling effect on the operations of the government. The trend to military intrusion into political concerns had been intensified with the growth of the concept of total war—figures relating to military strength were clothed in secrecy, and no explanations of them were vouchsafed to the governmental financial authorities or to the national Diet; pressure was exerted in the name of total war not only upon industry but in cultural fields as well. After restoration in the mid-1930s of the earlier requirement (abandoned in the period of party government following the First World War) that the service ministers in the Cabinet be officers on the active list, the Army and Navy could, by declining to nominate or by ordering withdrawal of a minister, dictate the formation and change of cabinets; they began to boast of being "the driving force of the nation," and to extend their interference to diplomatic affairs. This condition was evidenced in the Manchuria Incident, the China Affair, the conclusion of the Tripartite Alliance and many

117

other instances in which no effective restraint could be imposed upon military ambition. Moreover, as the Manchuria Incident seemed at the time to have been a profitable venture, some officers began to feel that they would succeed whenever they moved decisively in pursuit of their goals—and there were those in civilian circles, too, who catered to them. That point of view worked no small harm to the future of the country.

Events during the period of the Japanese-American negotiations well exemplify the military meddling in diplomatic affairs. The move into southern French Indochina, which led to the negotiations' breaking down, had been planned by the military men. As war preparations were expedited and efforts were intensified to complete them, consequent upon the Imperial Conference decisions of July and September, the soldiers began to nurture an overweening confidence in victory, and—as has been seen in the quotations from the Konoe memoirs—to press for abandonment of the negotiations and early decision for war. The Navy particularly, after the American embargo on petroleum, became much exercised over the necessity of promptly deciding on war if there was no hope from diplomacy. At all times, the military services opposed the moderation of the terms in the negotiations, thereby to all intents and purposes precluding their consummation.

It is not difficult to conceive the extent of the tyranny of the military power from the fact that on the eve of the Pacific War such a fundamental datum as the total tonnage of Japanese naval vessels—not to speak of the displacement of the gigantic battleships *Yamato* and *Musashi*, or the plan to attack Pearl Harbor— was vigilantly withheld from the knowledge of the civilian cabinet ministers. General Tōjō even told me in Sugamo Prison that it was only at the IMTFE that he had first learned that the Japanese task force which carried out the attack on Pearl Harbor had assembled at Hitokappu Bay on 10 November, and weighed anchor for Hawaii in the morning of the 26th! The high command did not divulge its secrets even to the full general who was Premier and Minister of War; it is easy to conceive how other ministers were treated.

My point being to make clear how authoritative the military voice after the Manchuria Incident, and how it dominated the Liaison Conference, the architect of the national policy, we may consider the composition of the conference. The government was represented by Premier, War Minister, Navy Minister, Foreign Minister, Finance Minister and President of the Planning Board, with other ministers participating whenever necessary (in the time of the Tōjō Cabinet, for example, the Agriculture and Forestry Minister and the Communications Minister attended once or twice). The Chiefs and Vice-Chiefs of Army and Navy General Staffs spoke for the high command. The Chief Secretary of the Cabinet and the Directors of the Military Affairs Bureau of the Army and the Naval Affairs Bureau of the Navy served as secretaries of the conference. As the deliberations of the Liaison Conference during my first Foreign Ministership involved external affairs, I arranged for the Director of the American and East Asiatic Bureaus, Yamamoto, always, and Vice-Minister Nishi, occasionally, to be present at the meetings; these two, however, not being officially secretaries of the conference, could not attend the formal meetings in the presence of the Emperor. Since the government and the two high commands were co-ordinate constituents of the Liaison Conference, reports to the Emperor were made separately by the three components. There was no chairman of the conference, nor any order for presentation of views; agenda for meetings were made up by the secretaries on the basis of drafts previously prepared by the staffs of the agencies concerned, but discussions were often at random—although, the number of participants being small, everyone's attention was readily concentrated on any important topics raised.

Such was the nature of the body by which, starting on 23 October, immediately after the formation of the Tōjō Cabinet, and continuing for ten days, our national policy was deliberated. For those ten days the Liaison Conference met almost every day; when the subject was especially important, the discussions often continued from morning to the early hours of the following day, and not rarely became heated. Most of the decisions of the Liaison Conference were subsequently submitted to the Cabinet, and some of the more important ones were presented for approval at Imperial Conferences—an "Imperial Conference" being in substance a meeting of the same officials, in the presence of the Emperor. I recall no Liaison Conference decision from which Cabinet approval was withheld. It is to be noted that in the time of the Tōjō Cabinet the reports to the Emperor on the deliberations and decisions at the Liaison Conference concerning all important national policies—including the question of peace or war —were, following the custom which had prevailed from the days of the Konoe Cabinet, made for the Cabinet by the Premier exclusively. Reports by the Foreign Minister to the Throne were confined to the diplomatic negotiations themselves.

With the meeting on 23 October the Liaison Conference embarked upon an over-all examination of our policy concerning the Japanese-American negotiations. I had found upon reviewing the documents of the Foreign Ministry, from the day after I took office on 18 October, that diplomacy had reached a state of deadlock, and it was touch-and-go whether peace could be preserved between the two countries. It was therefore evident from the beginning that the negotiations were extremely unpromising; my own problem was a dual one—bargaining with the United States to obtain moderation of its stand was but half the battle, for I had also to persuade our own military authorities that they must make concessions. If these objectives could be gained there was, I believed, still some room, however small, for saving the peace.

Here I may recapitulate briefly the position as I then saw it. In forming my judgment I relied especially on Ambassador Nomura's telegram of 3 October, in which he reported that the problems of the Tripartite Pact and nondiscriminatory treatment in trade had in general been solved, with only the issue of the stationing of troops in China remaining. So far as concerned the Tripartite Pact, Japan could not present the United States with an authorization in blank, but she had made concessions to the extent that in case of America's entry into the European War she would act in accordance with her own interpretation of the pact, independently of Germany and Italy; I therefore believed that, as Ambassador Nomura reported, a tacit understanding had been reached. As to nondiscriminatory treatment in trade, also, I accepted his report that no serious difference remained, Japan having promised fair treatment to American interests. I did not apprehend, in any event, that this problem alone would disrupt the negotiations and bring about a war, however obstinately Mr. Hull might invoke the principle of free trade, if understanding was arrived at on the other issues.

It was therefore credible to me that the only serious obstacle remaining in the path to agreement was the question of the stationing of troops in China. In regard to this, I took into account also the written opinion of my predecessor, Admiral Toyoda, setting forth the terms upon which he deemed it possible to consummate the negotiations. In Admiral Toyoda's opinion we should agree to three terms. (1) Japan should cease reinforcement of

French Indochina. (2) The provision for stationing troops in China should be stricken from the peace terms, and Japanese troops should, in accordance with a secret Japanese-Chinese agreement, be withdrawn from China within two years after the establishment of peace between Japan and China. This to be subject to the proviso, however, that Japanese troops might be stationed in certain areas of North China, Mengch'iang (Inner Mongolia) and Hainan for a period of five years after the restoration of peace—a period subject to extension, at its expiration, through consultation between the parties. (3) The Japanese troops stationed in Indochina should be withdrawn when the purpose of joint defense no longer warranted their presence, and not later than the termination of the China Affair.

On the basis of such reports and opinions of the highest Japanese authorities concerned with the Japanese-American negotiations, I naturally harbored the hope that there was some possibility of arriving at an agreement; but at the same time I took for granted that it would be necessary that Japan make substantial concessions, my study of the documents having convinced me that the United States was ready to go to war if necessary. In these circumstances, before the Liaison Conference discussions began I worked out my own terms for a solution, in general, as follows. First, that Japanese troops stationed in China, including those in the special areas of North China and elsewhere, should be withdrawn within five years. Second, that Japan should affirm that she had no intention of disturbing economic activities of third Powers in China conducted on a fair basis, and had no objection to application of the principle of free trade throughout the world—nor, in applying it, to including China, thereby solving the basic issue over China between the United States and Japan. Further, in connection with the Southern problem created by the movement of Japanese forces into southern French Indochina I intended by withdrawing our troops therefrom to demonstrate that Japan had no aggressive designs against those areas, thus manifesting our sincerity and promoting the success of the negotiations. With regard to the Tripartite Pact, I believed that a meeting of minds had already been reached, and that if the other issues were settled this one would amount only to finding a form of expression, as Japan had conceded it in substance.

Provisionally, I instructed Ambassador Nomura on 21 October that the new Cabinet was no less earnest than its predecessor for the adjustment of Japanese-American relations on a fair basis, and that pending more detailed instructions he should try to obtain from the United States a response to our proposal of 25 September.

It was in this frame of mind that I attended my first meeting of the Liaison Conference, on 23 October. The session commenced with Premier Tōjō's stating that, he having been made acquainted at the formation of his Cabinet with the Imperial wish that the Imperial Conference decision of 6 September be re-examined, now, with "the slate wiped clean," the Liaison Conference was to re-examine that decision in its entirety. The Chief of the Army General Staff, General Sugiyama,[1] however, quickly reminded us of the fact that according to the 6 September de-

---

[1] Field Marshal Sugiyama Gen (1880–1945) was the dominating figure of the last decade or so of the Japanese Army. During that time he served as Commander of Aviation Headquarters, Vice-Minister of War and Vice-Chief of the General Staff, as well as filling successively all of the "Big Three" offices of the Army—Inspector General of Military Education, Minister of War and Chief of the General Staff. In the latter position from 1940 to 1944 he had responsibility for preparation of the Greater East Asia War and for its conduct in the early, successful, years, as reward for which he was made a field marshal in 1943. In early 1944 he was ejected from his position—Tōjō took it over—but after Tōjō's fall in July he reappeared as Minister of War in Koiso's Cabinet, and at the end of the war commander in chief of one of the two General Armies into which, for the final defense, Japan was divided. He committed suicide at the surrender.

cision diplomacy was to have primary emphasis and war preparations secondary during the month of September, with war
preparations foremost and diplomacy subordinated after early
October—with all which, he suggested, former Foreign Minister
Toyoda had been familiar. Accordingly, he said, a prompt determination was essential if we were not to lose our opportunity, in
view of the approach of the monsoon season and other circumstances. Army Vice-Chief of Staff Tsukada, even more pessimistic
and more intransigent, then asserted that the Japanese-American
negotiations had demonstrated the bankruptcy of diplomacy, that
America and Britain had already severed their economic relations with Japan and were tightening their encirclement of us,
and that Japan should therefore immediately resort to measures
of self-defense. The Vice-Chief of the Naval General Staff, Admiral Itō, also urged that Japan should quickly make her decision
as to the outlook for the negotiations, as she could afford no loss
of time.

I thus discovered at once that although the 6 September decision was to be re-examined, the war preparations which the high
command had undertaken following the 2 July Imperial Conference remained, undisturbed, like a mine in the path of diplomatic
activity, encouraging the military services to a bellicose attitude
and constituting a formidable obstacle to any progress. Furthermore, as the only newcomers in the Liaison Conference were
Navy Minister Shimada, Finance Minister Kaya and myself—all
the rest had been participants in the 6 September Conference—
the "limits" set by the September decision tended to be taken as
a point of departure for any renewed examination of the subject,
and a resulting sort of psychological inertia made it very difficult
to obtain relaxation of those limits. Nevertheless, I questioned
sharply the premises asserted by the high command, saying that

all avenues offering any chance whatever should be explored, and that for Japan, contending that compromise was impossible, to plunge precipitately into military action was unwarrantable. The Premier, too, insisting that the position should be re-examined upon the launching of the new cabinet, it was in the end decided to have the secretaries prepare a concrete scheme of the items and the method of the re-examination. As I recall, the main items thus submitted by the secretaries were:

1. Is there a prospect of having the United States accept promptly the demands agreed upon on 6 September?

2. What would be the consequences to Japan of acceptance of the United States' Memorandum of 2 October?

3. To what extent can Japan recede from her 6 September decision?

4. What is the prospect of the European War?

5. Is it possible for Japan to fight either Britain or America only?

6. What are the United States' potential and ability for war?

7. How to build up Japan's war potential: increasing production of steel, petroleum, ships and other munitions, and financial strength.

Hours were spent in deliberation of these questions. As to Item 1, accord was readily reached that there could be no expectation of inducing the United States to agree to the demands contained in the 6 September decision. Consideration of Item 2 led to the consensus that if Japan accepted the American 2 October Memorandum, all that had been achieved since the Manchuria Incident would have evaporated, and the established position of Japan in Manchuria and Korea would be prejudiced and Japan would be compelled ultimately to withdraw entirely from the continent. Discussion of Item 3 I postpone to subsequent pages, inasmuch as that inquiry is central to the decision on Proposals "A" and "B," newly worked out for presentation to the United States, which I treat in detail hereafter. The prospect of the European War, called for by Item 4, being based on the Foreign Ministry's observations, was one of pessimism: a German invasion of England was considered very difficult, and it was going to be a long war, in which Germany might suffer setbacks. In connection with Item 5, the Foreign Ministry's view, that it was beyond doubt that if Japan went to war with either Britain or America, the other would come in, was accepted without dissent.

For diagnosis of Item 6, the military and other representatives introduced a detailed and concrete study of the war potential of the United States. There was no questioning of the size of her forces, that having been publicized; and as the conference took at face value the numerous published figures on American productive capacity, it was fully recognized that her potential was beyond comparison greater than that of Japan. Some doubted whether the United States could secure a sufficient supply of rubber, but the general opinion was that she could manage it by use of reclaimed and synthetic material and by imports from South America. Although it required a huge industrial plant to maintain the function of arsenal for the European War, most of the plant had been completed by the autumn of 1941; as this industrial capacity could at any moment be mobilized forthwith for the war against Japan, there was no means, it was unanimously agreed, of directly vanquishing the United States in case of war against her.

It was for this reason that Japan's grand strategy, as I understood it then, rather than consisting of unlimited offensive operations, was to be the occupation of the Southwestern Pacific area and preparation for a long war by maintenance and building up of our fighting strength through the supply of materials from the South. I was therefore amazed when Japan at the outset of the war attacked Hawaii, and subsequently struck at Midway and at areas as distant as Rabaul, contrary to the initial basic principles of our strategy. Looking back from today, when the war is over, I still do not think that our defeat was attributable so much to underestimation of the war potential of the United States as to violation of strategic principles. On the other hand, there is no doubt that lack of foresight in mobilization of science for development of weapons greatly hampered us in many directions; with respect to the talk of atomic bombs, for instance, one of our authorities in that field asseverated a few months preceding the obliteration of Hiroshima that an atomic bomb could not be completed in time for use in this war. This condition I consider to have been a consequence of the general level of scientific knowledge in Japan, which could not be corrected overnight.

The last point for consideration by the Liaison Conference was the building up of Japan's potential for war—of what items, and by what means, production must be increased. I was astonished at our want of the statistical data required for a study of this sort, but even more I felt keenly the absurdity of our having to base our deliberations on assumptions, as the high command refused to divulge figures on the numbers of our forces, or any facts relating to operations. In connection, for example, with shipping—one of the subjects more discussed—I argued that the loss of bottoms at sea would, contrary to the estimate in the plan presented to the conference, be greater in the second year of war than in the first, on account of the expedited construction and extended operations of American submarines. The Navy, however, simply asserted that it had plans for coping with the menace of submarines, and I—being without any way of pursuing the argument further—had perforce to leave it at that. Steel production promised to be insufficient, but it was argued that it would be expanded with the improvement, as the years went by, in the shipping position. The transportation of petroleum from the South also would, it was said, be increased. The problem of shipping, obviously, was one of the most vital; but the ministries concerned asserted that it could be solved.

Opinions were also given us, by those responsible for such things as wartime finance, securing of the food supply, and national morale, that there need be no anxiety in those quarters. Many of the subjects before the conference required technical study, but all participants examined and discussed the whole position very earnestly. Tōjō and the military—especially the Army —representatives took a firm stand from the beginning, but their attitude in these deliberations was very sincere, and I cannot subscribe to the opinion that Tōjō and the others had premeditated war from the moment of formation of the Cabinet.

It was in these circumstances that I submitted to the Liaison Conference my alternative Proposals "A" and "B" for the Japanese-American negotiations. In the negotiations we were at swords' points, and such an impasse had been reached that failure in them would in the circumstances almost inevitably bring about a war. I was determined to prevent this result, so calamitous for the two countries and for mankind at large, but it was my conviction that it could be prevented and the negotiations brought to success only through the making of mutual concessions. My task, therefore, was to work out a fresh proposal embodying our maximum possible concessions. My basic position has been explained a few pages earlier in connection with my preparation for attendance at the Liaison Conference; this position I embodied in Proposal "A," relaxing the 25 September proposal of Japan—that is to say, modifying the 6 September Imperial Conference decision —to the extent shown by the following recapitulation (my ideas in connection with the several subjects of the negotiations are added in parenthesis).

1. Nondiscriminatory Treatment in Trade

Our position on this subject will be modified to provide that the Japanese government agrees to application to the entire Pacific area, including China, of the principle of nondiscrimination, if that principle be applied throughout the world. (This modification was responsive to Secretary Hull's insistence that the principle should be applied universally, and constituted an abandonment of Japan's claim to preferential treatment in China by reason of geographical propinquity. The repeatedly explained intention of Japan not to restrict economic activities of third Powers conducted in China on a fair basis was not changed.)

2. Interpretation and Implementation of the Tripartite Pact

(This subject was left untouched, in view of the report from the Embassy in Washington that general understanding had been reached. It was intended to give further consideration to the form of expression when all other issues should have been settled.)

3. Withdrawal of Troops

a. Withdrawal from China

Troops will be stationed in designated areas of North China and in Mengch'iang and Hainan Island for a necessary period after the establishment of peace between Japan and China, and all other troops will be withdrawn within two years. ("A necessary period" to be five years. Concerning Hainan—to which reference had been made in the written opinion of former Foreign Minister Toyoda—the United States should have been aware of our desire in regard to it, as it was mentioned in the Japan-China Treaty of Basic Relations. Proposal "A" dropped the provision for stationing of troops in the Shanghai Triangular Zone and at Amoy, contained in the Treaty. The United States had repeatedly recognized that the withdrawal would take some time.)

129

b. Withdrawal from French Indochina

(As by the proposal of 25 September Japan had undertaken to make no military movement from Indochina into areas adjacent, the United States should have felt no apprehension of Japanese military action if she understood the sincere intention of Japan. The September proposal, however, had made the withdrawal conditional upon "the establishment of an equitable peace in the Pacific area"; this was nebulous, and it was therefore stipulated in Proposal "A" that the time for withdrawal should be the solution of the China Affair. My intention concerning the withdrawal from French Indochina was expressed in Paragraph 5 of Proposal "B," given below; [2] and I thought that if the United States showed receptivity to negotiation I could work out a final plan by combining those provisions in the two proposals which were advantageous to the United States.)

I encountered bitter opposition in the Liaison Conference to this proposal, as making too great concessions—even within the Foreign Ministry, indeed, there was objection to the provision for nondiscriminatory treatment in trade and abandonment of Japan's long-standing claim to a special position in China based on geographical propinquity. The Liaison Conference was persuaded without too much difficulty to agree to withdrawal of our forces from French Indochina upon the conclusion of peace between Japan and China. But the provision for the withdrawal from China proved, as was to have been anticipated, the most controversial, and drew heavy fire from the military services.

The Army high command declared flatly that it could not agree to placing a time limit on the stationing of troops in China, on the ground that to do so would result in depriving Japan of her gains from the China Affair and would lead to deterioration in the morale of the armed forces. Tōjō tacitly supported the high command by saying that, the question deserving much careful study, he could not lightly approve my plan; the president of the

[2] See p. 134.

Planning Board, Minister without Portfolio Suzuki (also a general), maintained a similar position. Navy Minister Shimada argued for a retention of troops in China on the ground that, according to his observation during his recent tour of duty as commander in chief of the fleet in China waters, Japanese enterprises there could not carry on their operations, or even be secure, in the absence of our troops. Shimada was especially emphatic in stating that he could in no circumstances consent to the withdrawal from Hainan. Even Finance Minister Kaya, who had been of a moderate opinion, joined them, saying that the continued presence of troops was necessary for the sake of our enterprises in China, as he had found in his experience as president of the North China Development Corporation. None in the Liaison Conference came to my support.

The problem of stationing of troops in China having been the cause of the fall of the Third Konoe Cabinet, I had expected that the military representatives would not prove tractable regarding it. I on my part had, however, been resolved from my entry into the Cabinet that I would not remain in office if my plan of setting a time limit should be defeated. I therefore contended tenaciously against the demand for keeping our troops in China with no fixed date for withdrawal, pointing out that it was not reasonable to station troops in territories of other countries indefinitely, and that accordingly the argument that placing a time limit on their retention there would impair the morale of the armed forces was fallacious. The military occupation, I argued, would ultimately do more harm than good even from the point of view of protection of our residents; for Japan to impose military pressure upon her neighbor for a protracted period would not contribute to the permanent peace of the Far East, and such enterprises as could not operate without military support had better be given up.

131

The discussion of this question generated much warmth, and seemed endless. Finally, however, one of the secretaries proposed that we should agree on stationing our troops in China for a period of ninety-nine years. The term of ninety-nine years, of course, I rejected, for it meant no limit; but the making of the proposal was evidence that the military representatives, who had been annoyed at my pressing the point so strongly, felt that they could not escape consenting to the setting of some time limit. After my refusing to accept a period of ninety-nine years, many argued that it must be one of not less than fifty years, but this, too, I rejected, saying that to set a term of as long as fifty years was meaningless, as nobody could tell what might happen in the course of half a century. I continued to contend for the five years which I had first suggested. The general opinion of the conference conceded to twenty-five years, but there seemed no possibility of further shortening it; I proposed eight years, then ten, but all the others became obstinate at twenty-five years, and demanded that I in turn make a concession. I was not satisfied with such a long period, on the basis of which it was doubtful whether negotiations would succeed, but in the atmosphere of the conference nothing better could be gained. I considered, moreover, that once a time limit had been set, it might be possible to re-examine the length of time if the United States should raise the objection that it was too great. A reservation on this point was one of the understandings which, as I shall relate presently, I obtained from Premier Tōjō on the morning of 2 November. I therefore acquiesced in the sense of the Liaison Conference.

It was by this process that for the first time in the course of the Japanese-American negotiations a term came to be set to the stationing of Japanese troops in China. Dissatisfied as I was with the period stated, of twenty-five years, it was my intention first to impress upon the United States that the military occupation was not to be indefinite, and then to find a compromise on the time provided, rather than antagonizing the United States by demanding from the beginning its agreement to the twenty-five years.

My intention was in the end frustrated by the United States' reception of Proposal "A." It may perhaps be that my instruction to Ambassador Nomura transmitting the proposal was not worded with sufficient care; but it remains regrettable that this telegram was intercepted by the United States authorities and translated by them in an extremely malicious way, which did much to complicate the subsequent development of things. I shall recur to this point. The United States would in any event have been cool to Proposal "A" because—as we learned when we heard Mr. Ballantine's testimony at the IMTFE—she had felt no confidence in Japan's professions, especially since the movement into southern French Indochina. Leaving aside the question of the nature of that Japanese move—whether aggressive or otherwise—so long as the United States did not trust the other party the negotiations could never arrive at a fruition unless Japan should accept unconditionally the demands of the United States, and no concession short of that would have sufficed. Some points in America's proposals, however, were not reasonable, and Japan at that time could not accept the American position *in toto* and unconditionally.

It had been far from easy even to get the Liaison Conference to agree to Proposal "A." I had, however, to be prepared for the possibility that Proposal "A" would not bring about a solution, it being evident that the United States was maintaining its stand at the risk of going to war. Against the eventuality of such a failure, I worked out a second plan, Proposal "B," as a *modus vivendi*, to be used as a last resort in arriving at agreement on a few items essential for averting the outbreak of a war. Proposal "B" was as follows.

1. The Governments of Japan and the United States undertake to make no military advance into any of the regions, excepting French Indochina, of Southeastern Asia and the Southern Pacific area.

2. The Governments of Japan and the United States shall co-operate with a view to acquisition of those goods and commodities which the two countries require from the Netherlands East Indies.

3. The Governments of Japan and the United States mutually undertake to restore their commercial relations to those prevailing prior to the freezing of assets.

The Government of the United States shall supply to Japan a required quantity of oil.

4. The Government of the United States undertakes to refrain from measures and actions prejudicial to the endeavor for restoration of general peace between Japan and China.

5. The Government of Japan undertakes to withdraw troops now stationed in French Indochina upon either the restoration of peace between Japan and China or the establishment of an equitable peace in the Pacific area.

The Government of Japan declares that it is prepared upon conclusion of the present agreement to remove its troops now stationed in the southern part of French Indochina to the northern part thereof.

Notes:

1. It may if necessary be promised at conclusion of this agreement to withdraw the Japanese troops upon either the restoration of peace between Japan and China or the establishment of an equitable peace in the Pacific area.

2. The provisions of Proposal "A" concerning nondiscriminatory treatment in trade and the interpretation and implementation of the Tripartite Pact may if necessary be added to this agreement.

The aim was, by Paragraph 1 to allay American suspicion concerning any further Japanese advance into the south. Paragraph 2, in no way a new proposal, envisioned co-operation for the acquisition of such necessary materials as petroleum, tin and the like. It was intended by Paragraph 3 to reinstate the commercial relations in effect prior to the freezing of assets in July; special provision for the petroleum supply was made in view of the attitude of the United States and conditions within Japan at the time. As to Paragraph 4, requesting the United States to suspend her aid to Chiang Kai-shek, which was inimical to Japan, the thought was that it was not reasonable for the United States to continue to assist the Chiang regime while Japan was bending her efforts to bringing about peace with China. It was intended to solve the China Affair through direct negotiations, but Japan was ready to accept American mediation, as was later evidenced by her embracing President Roosevelt's suggestion to that effect of 17 November; I had my own plan formulated for adjustment of relations between Japan and China on an equitable basis of moderate terms, in case of direct negotiations. Paragraph 5, in declaring that Japan would withdraw from southern into northern Indochina immediately upon conclusion of the agreement, represented an entirely new proposal, which could but be recognized as proof of Japan's abandonment of the policy of southward advance, and as revelatory of the sincere intention of the Japanese government for peace.

The whole concept of Proposal "B" thus was—as I made clear in my telegram of 20 November instructing Ambassador Nomura to present it—to restore relations, then critical, to their condition prior to July, and to eliminate the United States' suspicions by demonstrating in deed that Japan had no design of southward advance, thus calming the atmosphere and averting war. Mr. Ballantine of the State Department testified at the IMTFE that the reason for the United States' lack of interest in Proposal "B" was that she put no trust in our promises; the withdrawal from southern French Indochina, he said, was meaningless, because the troops even if withdrawn could again be dispatched thither within a matter of a day or two. Evidently, the negotiations themselves were meaningless if one party took a position of mistrust of the other. That the United States was suspicious without reason is proved by the fact that Proposal "B" was furiously opposed by the military services at the Liaison Conference, altercation over it raging until the conference almost broke up, because the soldiers considered it to yield too much to the United States.

In the discussion of Proposal "B" I argued that war must at all costs be avoided, and that it was imperative for that purpose to re-establish the status as it had been prior to the movement into southern Indochina and the subsequent freezing of assets, thereby relaxing the tension. The high command fought me vehemently, Chief of Staff Sugiyama especially saying that the Army high command could not accept such an extreme concession to the United States as withdrawal from southern Indochina while many important problems remained pending between the two countries. This time, too, I clung to my position and took issue with General Sugiyama on various grounds, being prepared to resign if Proposal "B" failed of obtaining approval by the conference. It was finally approved, after much acrimonious and exhausting contention. General Mutō, who as director of the Military Affairs Bureau attended the conference as one of the secretaries, later told me that he and some of the other participants had been very much worried, seeing that the Foreign Minister was evidently chancing his resignation. When the acceptance of Proposal "B" was in the balance, he related, he had persuaded the Chief of Staff to yield, asking him, "If the negotiations fail on account of the Army's opposition to the Foreign Minister's proposal, can the Army take the responsibility?" Also, he said, they were at great pains to arrange how to cope with any dissatisfaction of the forces at the front in case the negotiations should be consummated on the basis of Proposal "B." It is lamentable that Proposal "B," thus worked out at such effort, finally proved unavailing.

Proposals "A" and "B" being agreed to, the basis upon which the Tōjō Cabinet was to go forward with the Japanese-American negotiations was thus settled. While, however, it would be most fortunate for the cause of peace if our proposals should result in conclusion of the negotiations, there was a clear possibility, considering the inflexible attitude of the United States, that they would not. In view of this possibility, the Liaison Conference had proceeded with other calculations, concurrently with discussion of Proposals "A" and "B," and the question finally presented itself inescapably for decision, what steps Japan should take in the event of the negotiations' breaking down. The military representatives urged that we should make our plans against such an eventuality, and submitted three alternative courses of action. These were, (1) to decide immediately to commence war; (2) to exercise patience, awaiting a change in circumstances; and (3) to continue negotiations, with the determination to go to war in case of their failure. Over this question, again, a controversy marked by much asperity went on in the Liaison Conference, from 1 November into the small hours of the following day. I had considered the problem one which must be expected to arise, especially in view of the 6 September decision; and I had anticipated (as I have explained in connection with my entry into the Cabinet) that the Army would continue obstinate, but had based my plans on the assumption that the Navy would be moderate. My astonishment had been considerable to find the Navy's attitude as I have mentioned in connection with the troop stationing and other problems. Now, in order to do all that I could to obtain tempering of the Navy's views on this question, I requested the intercession of former Premier Admiral Okada, who was influential in the Navy; I was later informed that he had caused his opinion to be expressed to the naval authorities, who however intimated that intervention from outside was not welcome.

On 1 November the Liaison Conference met in the morning. The Army high command—taking its usual strong tone—demanded that the negotiations be broken off now in accordance with alternative (1), above, as the United States was extending its encirclement of Japan and had imposed economic sanctions, and moreover had no sincere intention to conclude the negotiations. In such circumstances, they said, Japan would be foolish to defer decision and lose the opportune time for war. I countered that we were not faithful to our trust to the nation if, while there remained even the smallest room for negotiation, we threw the country into war without having exhausted all possible efforts for peace. Premier Tōjō supported me to an unusual extent. Thereupon, alternative (1) was dropped. The next stage was to make the great decision whether, in case of failure of the negotiations, Japan should with fortitude persevere through difficulties, or should decide immediately upon war.

Having served in Europe during the First World War, I had learned at firsthand the lesson of the consequences of a modern war not only to the defeated nations but to mankind as a whole. I had come to the conviction—clearly expressed in my study prepared for Foreign Minister Uchida in 1933 [3]—that a nation's development and progress should be grounded in the certainty

---

[3] "A Foreign Policy for Japan following Withdrawal from the League of Nations." See the Translators' Introduction, p. 19.

that the steps proposed were in the direction of healthy growth. I foresaw, moreover, that a war against Britain and America was very likely to end disadvantageously for Japan, considering our respective resources and standards of technique, as well as the crucial supply of steel and petroleum. From the time of my entry into the Cabinet I had therefore labored to the utmost of my ability to prevent war. Achieving this involved a threefold task. First, I had won over those who insisted that without more ado the negotiations should cease and Japan resort to action in self-defense, and had brought the Liaison Conference to agree to continuance of diplomatic efforts. Next, working to achieve the maximum possible concessions in Japan's proposals to the United States, I had succeeded in establishing not only the principle of withdrawal of troops from China within a fixed time— dissension over which had been the cause of the downfall of the Third Konoe Cabinet—but also that of immediate withdrawal from southern French Indochina, which the Army high command had vehemently resisted. With regard, finally, to the problem now in question, of the measures which Japan should take in case of failure of the negotiations, I contended to the last for forbearance, arguing that Japan should wait and see developments at least until the United States should have entered the European War.

The reasoning of the military spokesmen on this subject may be summarized thus. Considering Japan's consumption of essential materials, she would succumb to "gradual exhaustion" if the economic blockade was to be continued by America, Britain, the Netherlands, *et al*. With regard to petroleum in particular, they said, the civilian store would, despite complete wartime control of consumption, be drained dry by mid-1942, and the military reserve would be so depleted within a year and a half that the

Navy would be reduced to inability to function. In view of the burgeoning in the southern areas of the warlike dispositions of America, Britain and the Netherlands, Japan had to expect that these countries would bring still greater pressure to bear upon her if the negotiations ended in failure; a Japan with her supply of materials exhausted would have no power to resist any pressure, and would be forced to surrender totally, lacking the ability to fight even if she wished to. In such circumstances, they argued, Japan should decide on war while she still held the advantage. For strategic reasons, moreover, it was necessary—they said—that it be decided in favor of opening the war by the end of November.

In connection with this contention, we made an intensive examination particularly of the possibility of obtaining an adequate petroleum supply. It was agreed that the supply from Karafuto (Southern Sakhalin) was entirely insufficient to meet the demand. The potentialities of synthetic production were considered, but the Planning Board concluded that even if two billion yen were to be invested in facilities, production would lag far behind demand so long as output of armaments and other manufactures were to be maintained. It therefore appeared that even if synthetic-petroleum production had been projected at that time at the expense of cutting back other industries, not only would it have resulted in an irrational structure of industry generally, but it would not have served the purpose of providing the necessary supply of oil.

As the conclusion of these discussions, the general consensus of the Liaison Conference was for war if the negotiations failed, and therefore that we should carry on the negotiations with the expectation of going to war in case of their failure. To this consensus I could but continue in opposition; I felt, and argued, that it was premature to decide on war in the event of failure of negotiations yet to be commenced, and that to set a time limit on the negotiations would further diminish the possibility of their succeeding. The majority of the participants, however, continued to harp on their arguments of "gradual exhaustion," increased pressure by the United States if the negotiations failed, and the inadmissibility of further procrastination, considering developments since the decision of 6 September.

At this point I demanded that the high command give its forecast of the outlook for a war. The Chief of the Naval General Staff, Admiral Nagano,[4] said that the opportunity for war would be lost unless it was to be launched immediately if the negotiations were not consummated by the end of November; unless Japan fought Britain and America now, she would forever forfeit her opportunity, and would be driven to surrender to them. If, on the other hand, Japan fought now, the prospect for the initial stage of hostilities was certain; subsequent developments would be dependent largely on the national strength and international events, but—the Navy being confident in its strategy of "interception," or "ambushing," of the enemy—it was considered possible by occupying strategic points in the southern areas to establish an invulnerable position. The Army high command was even more optimistic, and echoed the demand that the decision to fight should be made instanter. I countered that a war against Britain and America would be a long one, and that Americans and Britons had inexhaustible tenaciousness, as well as commanding

---

[4] Admiral of the Fleet Nagano Osami (1880–1947) was Chief of the Naval General Staff from early 1941 to February 1944, when—despite his having been honored by being created in 1943 an admiral of the fleet—he was removed from office at the same time as Army Chief of Staff Sugiyama. Nagano had become known to the West as chief delegate to the London Naval Limitation Conference of 1935–36, from which Japan withdrew. After his dismissal as Chief of the General Staff, he held no further active office; put on trial at the IMTFE, he died of illness early in the proceedings.

abundant war potential, whereas Japan could count on no assistance from Germany or Italy, and the promised successes in the early stages should consequently not be too highly rated. It would be foolish, I pointed out, to decide on war on the strength merely of the prospects of its initial stage; after all, if one wins ninety-nine battles and loses the hundredth, one loses the war. I argued that we should not be serving our people faithfully if we threw the nation into a war without any assurance of final victory; and I pressed the soldiers for an avowal of their expectations for a war as a whole. The War Minister responded that victory was certain in the over-all view, and that I could put my fears at rest, trusting in the high command. The Navy Minister repeated that there was no need for pessimism. The Navy Chief of Staff reiterated his confidence in ambushing operations, and said that the Navy would sink the American fleet as it sailed north from the Central Pacific toward the area of the Mandates.

The participants in the conference of 1 November thus contended vigorously for the immediate decision for war in case the negotiations failed; some of them tried to persuade me in personal conversation, or even to intimidate me by hinting that "if the Foreign Minister opposes war, it is only a matter of replacing him." Nevertheless, I had serious misgivings because I felt that almost all the advocates of this course were failing to give due consideration to the ruinousness of war, and I continued unable to put full credence in the estimates by the Planning Board and the military representatives of our war potential. Above all, I could not conquer my reluctance to accept the prophecies of the high command as to the outcome of the war. I therefore declined —in company with Finance Minister Kaya, who had maintained a cautious attitude—to give immediate concurrence in the general opinion of the conference, and requested that the decision be deferred overnight to allow of thorough deliberation. It was finally so agreed, and the Liaison Conference adjourned.

It was then about two o'clock in the morning of 2 November, and I lost no time in reviewing the entire position. Having regard to the United States' uncompromising attitude, I could feel little optimism for the negotiations. At the same time, it was evident that Japan would face exhaustion of her petroleum supply, and it was not without reason that the Army and the Navy were anxious lest the United States in such an event bring increased pressure to bear upon Japan. The assurances of the military services did not appeal to me as quite reliable, but I was in no position to refute their assertions, having no information available to me concerning the size or condition of our armed forces or the state of our military science, all which were cloaked in secrecy. On the other hand, argument based on the international situation had been exhausted. I came to the conclusion that I had no alternative to taking on trust the services' assurances relative to the outlook for a war.

It remained only to consider whether I could influence the outcome by resigning the Foreign Ministership. Early in the morning of 2 November I called on former Premier Hirota,[5] a senior of the Foreign Ministry whom I had long worked under and whose counsel I had occasionally asked on important questions. Having been concerned as one of the Senior Statesmen with formation of the Tōjō Cabinet, Mr. Hirota was familiar with the general course of events; I explained to him the unexpectedly critical state of affairs and the danger of war, and told him that

[5] Hirota Kōki (1878–1948) was a diplomat whose career led through ambassadorial posts (Holland, the U.S.S.R.) to the Foreign Ministership (1933–36, 1937–38) and the Premiership (1936–37). For responsibility imputed to him as Foreign Minister for atrocities committed in the China Affair, and upon conviction of "conspiracy to wage aggressive war," Mr. Hirota was hanged in accordance with the verdict of the IMTFE.

if I could contribute to the preservation of peace by resignation, I should very much like to resign at that moment, when I was discouraged at finding conditions worse and Japan's own attitude less yielding than I had anticipated. Mr. Hirota urged me to remain in office to work for the success of the negotiations, saying that my resigning would result only in the recruiting of a more pliant Foreign Minister, who would espouse the cause of the war party.

I learned also that Finance Minister Kaya had already, early that morning, conveyed to the Premier his acceptance of the general opinion of the Liaison Conference. Such being the circumstances, I called on the Premier at noon and told him that I too would assent to the course of action proposed the preceding night. At the same time, however, I obtained from him several commitments.

Of these one was that in case the United States responded favorably to Proposal "A" or Proposal "B," the Premier would support me in persuading those concerned to make further concessions in order to bring about consummation of the negotiations. Another was the confirmation of an agreement already made at my request at the Liaison Conference—and concurred in by the high command—that all operational activities, at whatever stage of progress, would immediately be stopped and the original status restored upon conclusion of the negotiations. The third was the Premier's understanding to my warning that I might tender my resignation if the negotiations based on Proposals "A" and "B" ended in failure. Tōjō, however, responded to this notice that my resignation would in no event be necessary.

The gist of the decision of the Liaison Conference of 1 November thus was (1) to conduct negotiations with the United States on the basis of Proposals "A" and "B," and (2) to determine on war against the United States, Britain and the Netherlands if the negotiations should not be successfully concluded by the end of November. This decision was subsequently reported to the Cabinet and was ratified by it, after I had explained in detail the proposals and how the negotiations would be conducted.

The decision of the Liaison Conference was further submitted to an Imperial Conference on 5 November, and was adopted as its decision. This conference was attended by the Cabinet members, the two Chiefs and the two Vice-Chiefs of Staff, and as well the Chief Secretary of the Cabinet and the directors of the Military and Naval Affairs Bureaus; the President of the Privy Council was present by the special wish of the Emperor. Premier Tōjō outlined the decision of the Liaison Conference and how it had been necessary to arrive at it. I then spoke briefly in connection with the Japanese-American negotiations. The substance of my remarks was that the negotiations were at a precarious turning, with little room for diplomatic activity, and that we could, regrettably enough, not count very heavily on their succeeding; but that we would make every effort to conclude them on the basis of our new Proposals "A" and "B," which had been worked out to meet the desires of the United States so far as that was possible without prejudice to the honor or the security of the Empire. A few Cabinet ministers followed me with some explanations. President Hara of the Privy Council asked two or three questions, one of which was, "The statement has been made that the likelihood of success in the negotiations is slight; how slight is it?" Upon my stating that there was not more than a ten-per-cent chance of success, having regard to the attitude of the United States and to the content of our proposals, Premier Tōjō interjected that there was a forty-per-cent chance, as the United States would be desirous of averting a two-front war and should soon become aware of the condition of the distribution of Japanese military forces. President Hara said that he agreed with the Foreign Minister that there was little prospect of success of the negotiations, but that the conclusion reached was unavoidable in the circumstances, with the United States on the one hand maintaining a rigid attitude, and Japan on the other having to give consideration to her operational requirements. The Emperor retired without making any remark, and subsequently gave his sanction to the Liaison Conference decision.

The way was thus cleared for me to proceed with the negotiations with the United States for the sake of which I had taken office.

CHAPTER 5

The Negotiations in Washington

In view of the lateness of the hour, I had transmitted Proposals "A" and "B" to Ambassador Nomura on 4 November, prior to the Imperial Conference. Immediately after the Imperial approval had been given them, he was instructed to proceed with negotiations on the basis of Proposal "A."

In sending the proposals to Nomura, I had addressed to him the following long cable of instruction.

1. Strenuous efforts are being made day and night in order to adjust Japanese-American relations, which are on the verge of rupture. The government has held daily meetings of the Liaison Conference with the high command to examine the fundamental principles of our national policy. After long and exhaustive deliberation and discussions, the government and the high command have reached unanimous agreement on proposals in the Japanese-American negotiations (separate telegrams Nos. 726 and 727). These proposals, together with other basic policies, await final sanction of the Imperial Conference to be held on the 5th.

2. Conditions both domestically and internationally are extremely pressing and we cannot tolerate any procrastination. Out of the sincere intention to maintain peaceful relations with the United States, the Imperial government continues the negotiations after thorough consideration. The present negotiations are our final effort, and you must realize that these proposals are truly our last. If speedy conclusion of the negotiations is not to be attained even on the basis of these proposals, their breakdown

is unavoidable, however regrettable it may be. Relations between the two countries face rupture in such a case. The future of our country is profoundly involved in the outcome of the present negotiations, and the security of the Empire depends on it.

3. The Japanese-American negotiations have been protracted for over half a year. Our government has made concession after concession, in spite of difficulties, for the speedy consummation of an agreement, but the United States insists on the assertions with which she started, showing no response whatsoever to our attitude. There are not a few in this country who are suspicious of the real intention of the United States. In such circumstances, it is only out of our earnest desire to maintain the peace of the Pacific that we express our sincerity by offering to make still further concessions. These, unilateral on our part though they are, are not made because of any lack of power or of confidence in solving difficulties, as some Americans misunderstand them to be. There is a limit to our forbearance, and our existence and prestige must if necessary be defended, however great the cost. If the United States continues further to disregard our position, we can but say that there is no room for negotiation. Now that we make the utmost concessions in the spirit of complete friendliness for the sake of a peaceful solution, we hope earnestly that the United States will, on entering the final stage of the negotiations, reconsider the matter and approach this crisis in a proper spirit with the view of preserving Japanese-American relations.

4. The circumstances being as they are, the mission entrusted to you has great importance to the destiny of our country. We do well understand how difficult your task is, and we expect that you will do all that you can, bearing the above points in mind. We will let you know as soon as the Imperial Conference is over. You will thereupon see President Roosevelt and Secretary Hull and do your best to make them thoroughly understand our determination and to bring the negotiations to a speedy conclusion.

5. In view of the serious nature of the negotiations, I intend to carry on talks with the American Ambassador in Tokyo in parallel with those in Washington. It is therefore desired that we be informed of any appointment with the American authorities as soon as it is made; that the course of future negotiations be promptly reported; and that you keep close contact with us whenever you take new steps. In order to avoid any

contretemps, you are directed to abide strictly by your instructions and you are given no room for discretion.

Simultaneously with this instruction, Ambassador Nomura was informed that it was necessary in the circumstances to conclude an agreement by 25 November, and also was instructed to arrange with the United States its taking the necessary steps to have Britain and the Netherlands join in the agreement when it should be concluded, they being *de facto* parties to the current negotiations.

I was aware that not only Matsuoka, but equally Navy quarters, had been less than satisfied with the way Ambassador Nomura was conducting the proceedings in Washington. It was out of the question to replace our ambassador at that critical stage; but no more could I ignore the existence of a real problem. I therefore counseled the Ambassador in much detail about such things, unfamiliar to him, as the forms for agreement; and in view of the previous complaints of him I used in my instructions language which in other circumstances might have been unduly strong. Parenthetically, the State Department seems to have felt that my language showed that we had no genuine desire to reach a settlement; such phraseology in my instructions as "this is our final proposal," or "so-and-so is absolutely necessary," was played up by the prosecution in the IMTFE as if it had made a great discovery—that Japan was delivering an "ultimatum." This, of course, is absurd; even in ordinary commercial transactions a "final offer" is not inevitably the last proposal, and *a fortiori* the same is true in diplomacy. I had myself had the experience, while serving abroad and conducting negotiations, of receiving from Tokyo an instruction saying that I should bear in mind that the current proposal was the final one—then to have it followed by another, and another, in the same language.

This is, for those familiar with such dealings, only a matter of course.

Before turning to consideration of the negotiations in Washington, it will perhaps be well to explain the purpose and manner of the dispatch to the United States of Ambassador Kurusu, which was my own idea. From my assumption of office in October, I had been so busy with study of the history of the negotiations, with the establishment of new policies, and with almost daily attendance at the Liaison Conference, that I had had no time to make the visit to the Grand Shrine of Ise [1] which was customary for a minister of state newly assuming office, and it came to me that I was being censured in some quarters for my failure to observe the forms. The decision on Japan's new course being reached by the Liaison Conference on 2 November, I was for the moment without responsibilities of immediate urgency, and I promptly left Tokyo for Ise that same night. On 3 November, in the clear autumn sunshine of the national holiday of the Emperor Meiji's Birthday, I paid my respects at the Inner and Outer Shrines of Ise, then took an afternoon train back to Tokyo.

Despite my fatigue from the strain of the preceding strenuous days, while on the train I could not prevent my thoughts from recurring to the Japanese-American negotiations and the quest for ways and means of warding off a catastrophe. It was at this time that the idea of sending Ambassador Kurusu [2] to the United States occurred to me. The thought came to me partly because the activities of the Embassy in Washington were giving concern

[1] The most sacred shrine of the Shintō religion, at Uji-Yamada in the Kii Peninsula. Tradition required that report be made there, to the national gods, of all important events affecting the state or the dynasty.

[2] Kurusu Saburō (1886–1954), after a number of years in the consular service, had become Ambassador to Belgium in 1936. In 1939 he was promoted to the Berlin Embassy, where he remained until 1940; during this period he had represented Japan in execution of the Tripartite Pact. After repatriation from America in 1942 he lived in retirement.

in Tokyo, partly because Ambassador Nomura had long before requested that Kurusu be sent to assist him.

It was necessary to obtain Kurusu's consent, in view of the unpredictable misadventures which might befall him, going to America at a critical time when war might be destined to come. That same night, therefore, immediately upon my return to Tokyo, I asked him to call on me at my Official Residence. I explained fully to him that Japanese-American relations were on the verge of rupture; I told him that my utmost efforts had not been entirely successful, and that although I had managed to get approval for two proposals moderating Japan's stand to a considerable extent as compared with her previous position, the possibility of success in the negotiations must be acknowledged to be very slight. I then said that, it being my intention to probe to the bottom every possibility, I wanted him to go to Washington to convey a sense of crisis to Ambassador Nomura and, working in co-operation with him, to win over the United States. Mr. Kurusu was at first hesitant, but at length acceded to my request, on my stressing that duty demanded of us all at that moment the making of every effort for success in the negotiations, whatever the outcome.

I went on to tell Kurusu that I had tried so to contrive that it should not come to war even if diplomacy failed, but that the conclusion had been that war was unavoidable in such an eventuality, as Japan would otherwise be "gradually exhausted." I had therefore worked hard, I explained to him, to find a way to bring the negotiations to fruition, but had had to recognize that the only hope was to persuade the United States on the basis of Proposals "A" and "B"; if the United States responded favorably to these proposals, Japan could then consider some further concessions. I made it clear to Kurusu, however, that any efforts to solve the problem which deviated from the general outlines of these proposals would not be of service, and impressed upon him that he should make Ambassador Nomura understand that fact, as well as the inevitability of war if the negotiations broke down; and I concluded by saying that his primary mission was to go with a correct comprehension of conditions, and to impart it to Nomura. I emphasized this last point because from my long diplomatic experience I knew that it often happens that when negotiations have fallen into complication seemingly insoluble the ambassador abroad, instead of carrying out his duty of trying to convince the other party in accordance with the instructions worked out at home upon thorough consideration of all aspects of the case, will make recommendations of superficial opinions or impracticable proposals, which may only prolong and increase the difficulty. To avoid any such occurrence, I gave to Kurusu this explicit instruction. He having understood my intentions in general, I directed the Ministry officials in charge to provide him with the requisite information relating to the negotiations.

The next morning I spoke to Premier Tōjō, prior to the Cabinet meeting, about the dispatch of Ambassador Kurusu and requested him to obtain Imperial sanction for Kurusu's going, and I also asked Navy Minister Shimada to have him flown by naval plane to Hong Kong or to Guam, which he agreed to do. Simultaneously I sent my secretary to Ambassador Grew to bespeak the affording of facilities by the United States government for Kurusu's trip. This also was done, a Clipper being held up until he could reach Hong Kong to board it.

I received Kurusu again on the morning of the 4th, the day before his departure. He said somberly that his review of the negotiations, and what he had learned from other quarters, had impressed him with the imminence of war. He added that he hoped that I would look after his family during his absence should war break out, as it would be uncertain when he could then return home (I readily undertook to do this, of course). Kurusu asked me to let him be the one to present Proposal "B" to the United States, as he wanted to try whether he could conclude an agreement on the basis of it. I assented to this, and in the instruction conveying the proposal to Ambassador Nomura, sent him after the Imperial Conference, told him that it should not be presented without further directions.

On account of his going on this mission to Washington Mr. Kurusu was subjected to much unpleasantness in connection with the IMTFE, where he was threatened by the prosecution with "indictment." I, too, was no less annoyed as a result of Kurusu's trip, and—now that it has proved that all the effort in connection with it was wasted—I rather regret having arranged it. It was, for example, widely rumored that the dispatch of Kurusu was "camouflage." I cabled Nomura at the time, telling him that Kurusu carried no new instructions, but was being sent simply to bring him to date on conditions in Tokyo and to assist him with the negotiations at their climactic stage. I explained this frankly to the British and American Ambassadors in Tokyo, and so informed Nomura, instructing him to bear this in mind in his dealings with the press. The purpose of the sending of Kurusu, so far from being "camouflage," was to make the actual state of affairs known to the American government and to all those concerned. To refer to it as "camouflage" is the merest nonsense, despite whatever suspicion and malice may wish to believe.

In Washington, Ambassador Nomura recommenced negotiations, as instructed, by presenting Proposal "A" to Secretary Hull on 7 November. The Secretary, upon reading through the proposal, commented that the suggested provision for nondiscriminatory treatment in trade was to the interest of Japan as well. In connection with the problem of stationing of troops he inquired concerning the ratio of those to be withdrawn to those left; the Ambassador answered, as he reported, that the greater part would be withdrawn and only a small number would remain on. He further reported that Secretary Hull asked him—and requested him to inquire the opinion of his government—what Japan's reaction would be if the highest authority of China should pledge China's friendship to and confidence in Japan and should express the desire for the restoration of friendly relations. I promptly replied to this cable of Ambassador Nomura's that the Secretary's suggestion was welcomed as a constructive idea for promoting peace between Japan and China.

Ambassador Nomura met with President Roosevelt also, on the 10th, to make explanation of the new proposal. Before hearing what the Ambassador had to say the President, referring to a note, stated that the United States desired Japan to clarify her intention of following peaceful, rather than opposite, courses, and that the United States wanted to prevent expansion of the war and to establish a lasting peace. He added, according to Nomura's report, that he hoped to see the principle of non-discrimination in trade applied throughout the world. He also dilated on the meaning of the term *"modus vivendi."*

The report of the Ambassador indicated that the response of the United States to Proposal "A" was not entirely unreceptive. I therefore instructed him to develop Secretary Hull's suggestion into concrete terms, as well as to proceed with negotiation on the other points. At the same time I endeavored in Tokyo to expedite the negotiations; here I may digress to speak briefly of some of the steps I took.

Since becoming Foreign Minister, I had two or three times

taken occasion to say to Ambassador Grew that it was vital that Japanese-American relations be preserved from catastrophe. Now I specially invited him to call on me on the 10th, when I assured him of the earnestness of the Japanese government in its efforts to conclude the negotiations on an equitable basis. I explained Proposal "A" to him in detail, and strongly urged that he, too, do everything possible for achieving our common object. I urged also that the United States government should take measures necessary for the making of an agreement with Japan by the British government simultaneously with conclusion of the Japanese-American settlement. In the discussion which followed I pointed out that economic pressure could sometimes result more distressingly than military, and said, in connection with the China problem, that the Japanese nation could not accept any terms which should deprive it of the fruits of four years and a half of sacrifices. As our conclusion, I said, we could not consider the American government's understanding of the realities existing in the Far East to be sufficient, and I stressed the fact that the negotiations were at a very late stage. Prior to this time, and even thereafter, the proposals of the United States were all labeled "preliminary and tentative," or "without commitment"—even its culminating note of 26 November was marked "strictly confidential, tentative and without commitment." It seems that the United States wishes to say, on the ground of such labels, that even its last note was not a final proposal, but still left room for negotiation. It was because these terms were habitually used by the United States that I made plain to Ambassador Grew that the negotiations, when resumed in early November, were in their decisive stage. This point was repeatedly brought to the attention of the United States government, both in Tokyo and in Washington, so that there could be no mistake.

With the British Ambassador, Sir Robert Craigie, also, I discussed the negotiations. Since 1940 Britain, America, the Netherlands and China had on numerous occasions held military conferences relating to Japan and the tightening of their encirclement of her; the British Prime Minister and the American President had moreover assuredly discussed at their Atlantic Conference preparations for joint war against Japan. Britain and America could thus be regarded as virtual allies; nevertheless, since the major problem at issue in the Japanese-American negotiations was that of China, in which Britain was vitally interested, I thought it appropriate to have her participate directly in them. I pressed this idea upon Ambassador Craigie on 29 October and on other occasions thereafter, and I understood that he had made a recommendation to that effect to his government (he informed me later that the reply had been that it was not deemed necessary to participate directly in negotiations which had been entrusted to the United States government). When he called on me on 12 November I told him that I had already directed Ambassador Nomura to express to Secretary Hull our desire for a simultaneous conclusion of agreements by Great Britain and the Netherlands, as *de facto* parties to the negotiations. To Ambassador Craigie also I emphasized that the negotiations were approaching their denouement, and I asked if the British government would not do well to make itself acquainted with their contents and to co-operate in the effort to conclude them. He listened attentively as I spoke of the development of the negotiations; impressed—seemingly for the first time—with the gravity of the case, he promised to communicate his feeling to his government, and on his own part to make efforts for a solution.

It will be convenient here to refer to our relations with Germany at this period. As I have mentioned, Foreign Minister

Matsuoka had early made known to the German and Italian governments, through their Ambassadors in Tokyo, the fact that Japanese-American negotiations had been initiated; they had responded with protests. During the Third Konoe Cabinet, Foreign Minister Toyoda had maintained a negative attitude toward Germany and Italy, as Japan was taking the position that she should interpret and implement independently her obligations of aid to them against the United States. This position toward the Tripartite Pact continued unchanged under the Tōjō Cabinet. Japan therefore could not be said to be really faithful to the pact, but was nevertheless under the necessity of co-operating with Germany and Italy and keeping up the relation of alliance in case of failure to reach a settlement with the United States. In those circumstances we could not inform the German and Italian governments of the true state of affairs, and consequently I responded only in abstract terms to the repeated inquiries of Ambassador Ott. The Germans apparently felt a considerable dissatisfaction. At the same time I paid no heed to various German blandishments, made through Ott and otherwise, and there was no German influence whatever on the negotiations.

In Washington, meanwhile, the negotiations were in progress. On 12 November Secretary Hull handed two Oral Statements to Ambassador Nomura. One quoted the Japanese government's document of 28 August stating its position in regard to following peaceful courses, and requested a further declaration on the withdrawal of troops from Indochina and on our peaceful intentions toward the Soviet Union. The other was an amplification of Mr. Hull's earlier suggestion of a mutual exchange of pledges as a means to Sino-Japanese peace. Normura complained that the Secretary, without making any concrete commitment, merely said that the United States might be able to act in furthering the making of peace if the other issues, such as nondiscrimination in trade, were once settled. The Embassy were discouraged by Secretary Hull's attitude, which they found quite different from his and the President's at the previous meeting—discouraged the more, in that the Secretary's suggestion for attainment of peace between Japan and China had been taken to indicate that some constructive action could be expected from the United States. (One reason for this indifference we came to know of long afterward—that the United States was reading our correspondence, in garbled form.)

On 14 November Ambassador Nomura cabled a review of the outlook and his recommendations. America's war preparations were, he said, progressing, and her military operations in case of movement by Japan either north or south were being planned; now that the European War looked brighter for England, the United States was ready to fight Japan rather than compromise on fundamental principles. It being thus possible that the United States might go to war in the Pacific—to which there was less popular opposition than to entrance into the European War—he recommended that however critical relations and however wrought up the people of Japan, Japan should, if her domestic situation permitted, persevere to watch a little longer the line of development of the world war, rather than making the decision in a month or so.

On the 15th Secretary Hull, bringing up the Tripartite Pact question, told Ambassador Nomura that he wanted to see the pact abrogated or made a dead letter upon conclusion of a peaceful agreement with the United States; this was the first revelation of his real intention. At the same meeting he rejected, in an Oral Statement, Japan's proposal on nondiscrimination in trade, and in a proposed joint declaration on economic policy reiterated the earlier demands of the United States. He repeated also that Japan should declare whether she intended to "adopt peaceful courses."

I had previously at the Liaison Conference contended for perseverance, as recommended by Nomura, but had been overruled —as I have related—by opposition based mainly on the argument that Japan would be "gradually exhausted." I therefore instructed Ambassador Nomura in answer to his telegram of the 14th that after having thoroughly debated such considerations as those presented by him, we had with regret come to the conclusion that Japan could not wait in patience and watch the development of the war, but that it was necessary to complete the negotiations promptly by the end of November. Also, in answer to his report of the conversation with the Secretary of State, I directed him to apprise the Secretary of Japan's entire willingness to give confirmation of her peaceable intentions. The attitude of the United States concerning nondiscrimination in trade, however, was unjustifiable, and I instructed the Ambassador therefore to request the United States to withdraw the joint economic-policy declaration, which was considered as entirely disregarding Japan's interests. Explanations of our position on each of these points were included in the instruction.

Ambassador Kurusu arrived at Washington on 16 November, and the two Ambassadors were received by President Roosevelt on the 17th. At the interview Kurusu said to the President that Japan was striving earnestly for successful conclusion of the Japanese-American negotiations, but that her economic and military situation would deteriorate if diplomatic activities were protracted, and that she could not bear the total surrender to which she might be driven by longer delay. The President pointed out, in connection with the China problem, that the United States did not intend either to "intervene" or to "mediate," but only to "introduce." Regarding the Tripartite Pact, Kurusu went on to say, as Japan had made it clear that she would act in accordance with her own and independent opinion, an over-all understanding between Japan and the United States would naturally "outshine" the pact, and in such circumstances the United States' apprehensions would be dispelled. Here Secretary Hull, who sat in on the meeting, interjected a criticism of Hitler, and said that for the United States to provide against the danger to herself from Germany, while the British-German war was in progress, was simply self-defense.

On the 18th Secretary Hull took up new ground when he declared that the adjustment of Japanese-American relations was difficult so long as Japan remained tied to Hitler under the Tripartite Pact. Upon Ambassador Nomura's introducing the quite novel suggestion of withdrawal of troops from southern French Indochina and simultaneous rescission of the freezing of assets, the Secretary replied that such a makeshift was of no use when a disagreement over fundamentals was evident. As to the problem of nondiscriminatory treatment in trade, Mr. Hull said that it had been with the postwar state of affairs in mind that he had contended for the principle, and that Britain was coming to accept his views concerning Imperial preferences, to which he had long been opposed.

The attitude of the United States thus grew more uncompromising as the days went by. Contrary to the earlier reports of Ambassador Nomura that a meeting of minds had substantially been arrived at on points other than that of troop stationing, the United States was now requiring total acceptance by Japan of its position on all three of the major issues—its attitude concerning nondiscrimination in trade, for example, having stiffened in recent days. Agreement seemed remote; I saw no other possible course for the time being than to try to effect a *modus vivendi*, by arranging an accommodation on an essential minimum of items to remove the imminent threat of war. On 20 November I ordered the Ambassadors in Washington to present Proposal "B."

Having already observed that our Ambassadors were deviating from their duty of scrupulous carrying out of their instructions, I admonished them in strict terms that a breakdown of the negotiations would be unavoidable if Proposal "B" could not gain acceptance by the United States. About that time Premier Tōjō, too, having remarked to me that submission of private proposals by our diplomatic representatives was not welcomed, I made it abundantly clear to the Ambassadors that there was no solution, other than Proposal "B," which Japan could accept—and, I added, the Premier was of exactly the same opinion. The Ambassadors' departures from their instructions were unfortunate in their tendency to complicate and prolong the affair. In particular, it was absurd from the viewpoint of the technique of negotiation that the Ambassadors should have presented Proposal "B" to the United States piecemeal (its important new provision, for immediate withdrawal from southern Indochina, had already been disclosed to Hull on the 18th), thus blighting any prospect for acceptance of it; no negotiations could be consummated by such means. On the other hand, even if diplomatic relations are severed or war breaks out during an ambassador's service or his conduct of negotiations, he incurs neither blame nor responsibility therefor so long as he has faithfully observed his instructions.

The discussions based on Proposal "B" started, then, on the 20th. When the proposal was presented, Secretary Hull dwelt upon the difficulty of suspending aid to Chiang Kai-shek, and restated his previous position relative to the Tripartite Pact. Upon the Ambassadors' objecting that it was unreasonable for

161

the United States to continue its assistance to Chiang—an obstacle to the restoration of peace between Japan and China—when the President was to be an "introducer" in the Sino-Japanese peace, the Secretary evaded the point by answering that the President's offer was made on the assumption that Japan's policies would be fundamentally peaceful. He promised, however, that he would study the proposal sympathetically and would discuss it further with the Ambassadors.

On the 22d the two Ambassadors were informed by Secretary Hull that he had consulted with the British Ambassador and the Australian and Dutch Ministers concerning our proposal, and that their opinions were that their governments would willingly co-operate with Japan in such ways as the restoration of normal trade relations, if only Japan's intention was peaceable. However, he said, the tone of the Japanese press and of the speeches of her leaders was quite the reverse of peaceable. He said also that relaxation of the embargo should be brought about, if at all, only very gradually, in view of the remarkable increase in Japan's petroleum imports, owing to her Navy's stockpiling, prior to the freezing. The Secretary added that he would communicate with our Ambassadors upon receiving the replies of the other governments whom he had consulted. In response to inquiries by the Ambassadors, he said that although "it is little enough that we are actually doing to help China," the United States could not assent to the Japanese request to cut off its aid. In any event, Hull said, the time was not yet ripe for the President's introduction between Japan and China.

Upon receipt of the report of this conversation, I instructed our representatives in Washington that there could be no solution unless all the items of Proposal "B" were worked out, and that they should therefore do all within their power to persuade the

United States to conclude the agreement by 29 November. I made similar representations to Ambassador Grew, in Tokyo. At this time it appeared that some of the more intransigent elements in the Army high command were trying to embarrass the negotiations, for, despite the United States' reluctance to lift the petroleum embargo, they sent to the Foreign Ministry, for presentation to the United States upon entering into a settlement, a demand for an excessive quantity of oil. I ordered the document returned to the Army, and sent an instruction to the Ambassadors to the effect that the amount of petroleum which we would ask would be that of our imports as of the time of imposition of the embargo, in accordance with the basic idea of Proposal "B." To Washington also I sent some draft texts of agreement, to assist Nomura and Kurusu in their activities.

Secretary Hull had asserted on the 22d that the American aid to Chiang Kai-shek was less significant than the reports had it. But according to publications of the United States government after the war, it had even up to 1941 provided to Chiang a considerable total of credits, many aircraft and pilots, and a large quantity of munitions. In those days the United States government scouted also the idea that any encirclement of Japan was forming; but Ambassador Nomura was reporting that America's war planning had been accelerated since 1940, and that the military preparation against Japan was all but readied by the summer of 1941. It was published in the press that Anglo-American or Anglo-American-Dutch military conferences had been held in Washington and Singapore since January of 1941, and it was no secret that these conferences were aimed at Japan. The Congressional Pearl Harbor investigation committee established the fact that President Roosevelt had already, by the time of his "quarantine" speech in Chicago in 1937, come to the conclusion that the

United States would most probably, sooner or later, go to war against Japan; and it was proved that an over-all strategic plan—worked out at the Anglo-American joint staff conferences held from January to March and in April 1941—in case of war against Japan, Germany and Italy was approved formally by the War and Navy Secretaries and informally by the President.[3] In particular, the memoranda of 5 and 27 November, submitted to the President by the Army Chief of Staff and the Chief of Naval Operations, showed the encirclement of Japan to have been substantially completed, and expounded various war plans vis-à-vis Japan. An open advertisement of the war preparations was the reconnaissance flight of an American plane over the southern part of Formosa on 20 November.

The government of the United States began around this time to complain that Japanese leaders and press were agitating the public through the expression of "strong" views, and that this evidenced a lack of sincerity for peace. But at that same time, one of the American leaders, Secretary of the Navy Knox, went so far as to proclaim that the United States Navy was prepared to cope with any eventuality, and the American press was no less provocative. I could not but feel that, in taking exception to the attitude of the Japanese officials and press while aware that similar conditions obtained in the United States, the American government was seeking for pretexts. Accordingly, when the American Ambassador called my attention to a radical statement concerning the negotiations carried in the *Japan Times*, I immediately warned the paper (and received the assurance that it would be more circumspect thereafter); but at the same time I conveyed to the Ambassador the suggestion that the United States

---

[3] See the references given in Beard, *President Roosevelt and the Coming of the War, 1941,* 1948, pp. 442–9. T. S.

should on her part see to it that the American press also was prudent. As the old saw has it, "Who can tell the sex of a crow?" A most regrettable point was that our military people, being keen on "thought control," exerted maladroit but vigorous pressure upon the press through the Army and Navy publicity organs.

In Washington, meanwhile, from the 22d the Secretary of State was in frequent consultation with the Ambassadors and Ministers of Great Britain, the Netherlands, Australia and China. Various press reports of these conferences appeared. The statement was once carried by the wire services that it was planned to try to avert war by agreement on a *modus vivendi*. This comment being supposed to be based on Proposal "B," the news was heartening to us, and we entertained some slight hope of the negotiations—depending, of course, on the nature of the proposal which the United States might present; but as it began to be observable that in Washington opposition to the idea was gaining momentum, I thought it hardly conceivable that a *modus vivendi* if offered by the United States could possibly be one acceptable to Japan.

While things stood thus, I received from Ambassadors Nomura and Kurusu a telegram, sent on the 26th, in which they put forward a plan as an alternative to the collapse of the negotiations—which, they said, was assured as things were drifting. Their suggestion was to have President Roosevelt address to the Emperor a statement of his desire that the two countries cooperate for preservation of the peace in the Pacific, upon which the Emperor would return a personal message to the President— thereby clearing the air and gaining time for reaching a settlement—while proposing from our side creation of a neutralized zone comprehending French Indochina, the Dutch East Indies and Thailand. The Ambassadors requested that their plan be made known "at least as far as to Lord Keeper of the Privy Seal Kido," and that they then be instructed immediately. Here, I thought, was the beginning of those superficial recommendations which I had been apprehensive of. An ambassador conducting negotiations should exert all his personal influence and force to persuade the other party—but on the basis of instructions received. It should have been clear to our Ambassadors in Washington that the proposing of an impracticable plan which took no account of the determination of the other party, and which disregarded the extremity to which we were reduced, would serve no purpose. Particularly Kurusu, who had every reason to have comprehended fully these considerations, exemplified the proverb of the one who goes in search of mummies and himself turns into a mummy.

This telegram of the two Ambassadors arrived, as it chanced, after another of theirs of the same date reporting receipt by them of the "Hull Note" and giving the gist thereof. I lost no time in taking these telegrams for consultation with those interested. Their opinions coincided with mine; both Tōjō and Navy Minister Shimada considered that it would be utterly impossible to achieve a solution through any such scheme as this of the Ambassadors', and Lord Keeper Kido did not find it worth attention, commenting that "such a plan would result in rebellion." It is needless to point out that Japan could not tie her hands at that time without getting any assurance from the other party.

The Ambassadors were told on the 28th, therefore, that their plan had been made known in the quarters concerned, including that mentioned by them, but that none found it appropriate at the moment. The Ambassadors—apparently overwhelmed by the Hull Note, which had in the interim been handed to them—made no further reference to this recommendation of theirs. After receiving the Hull Note on the 26th, and before my message of the 28th had come to their hands, they cabled once more, saying that inasmuch as it could not be considered legitimate to resort to "freedom of action" without avowedly terminating the negotiations, notification of the termination—being intimately related to secrecy of military operations—would properly be given in Tokyo, but should concurrently be made in Washington as well.

Before concluding this chapter, I must refer to the mischief done by the intercepting and translating by the American authorities of the telegrams passing between the Foreign Ministry and the Embassy in Washington. The United States' discarding of Proposals "A" and "B" without according them serious consideration was, as attested by the evidence of Mr. Ballantine at the IMTFE, the result chiefly of the fact that, on the basis of knowledge of our diplomatic correspondence as intercepted by them, the American government had no confidence in the sincerity of Japan. I have already remarked that negotiation is meaningless if one party has no faith in the solemn promises of the other. Such a condition is particularly tragic when the lack of confidence is baseless.

By November 1941, with Japanese-American relations at the crisis in which they then stood, there was no room for technical maneuvering, and my endeavor in the negotiations was to realize a compromise between the two countries without resort to such tactics. All instructions sent by me being the forthright embodiment of our true intentions, the interception of our telegrams could not have embarrassed me so far as my actual language should have become known to the adversary. However, our messages intercepted by the American authorities were, for reasons beyond my comprehension, fantastically garbled in translation. The subject of these mistranslations was gone into thoroughly at the IMTFE, by my defense counsel, who exposed the errors contained in them and confuted the contentions of the prosecution and the testimony of Ballantine based on them. Those interested in the subject should refer to the record of the proceedings of the IMTFE, in which it is fully covered.[4] I shall quote only one example of the mistranslation—that of my instruction of 4 November explaining Proposal "A," which was of a peculiar importance in that it conveyed the basic idea of the negotiations to be conducted. Here are parallel excerpts from the two versions, the original and the intercepted:

Original	*Intercept*
This is our proposal setting forth what are virtually our final concessions	This proposal is our revised ultimatum
We make the following relaxation	We have toned down our insistence as follows
(Note) In case the United States inquires into the length of the "necessary period," reply is to be made to the effect that the approximate goal is 25 years	(Note: Should the American authorities question you in regard to "the suitable period," answer vaguely that such a period should encompass 25 years)
In view of the strong American opposition to the stationing for an indefinite period, it is proposed to dismiss her suspicion by defining the area and duration of the stationing	In view of the fact that the United States is so much opposed to our stationing soldiers in undefined areas, our purpose is to shift the regions of occupation and our officials, thus attempting to dispel their suspicions
You are directed to abide, at this moment, by the abstract term	We have hitherto couched our answers in vague terms. I want you

[4] IMTFE Record of Proceedings, pp. 43,607–21. T. S.

Original	*Intercept*
"necessary period," and to make efforts to impress the United States with the fact that the troops are not to be stationed either permanently or for an indefinite period	in as indecisive yet as pleasant language as possible to euphemize and try to impart to them to the effect that unlimited occupation does not mean perpetual occupation.

It is obvious at a glance that the "translation" of the intercepted telegram is no translation, but might well have been a malicious distortion of the message aimed at creating an impression of perfidy.

CHAPTER 6

The "Hull Note"

SECRETARY HULL'S NOTE, which proved to signalize the end of the Japanese-American negotiations, was handed to our Ambassadors, in Washington, on 26 November (an Oral Statement simultaneously delivered contained nothing new, merely summarizing previous developments). The full text of this "Hull Note" follows.

Strictly Confidential,
Tentative and Without
Commitment.   WASHINGTON, NOVEMBER 26, 1941.
OUTLINE OF PROPOSED BASIS FOR AGREEMENT BETWEEN THE UNITED STATES AND JAPAN

SECTION I

Draft Mutual Declaration of Policy

The Government of the United States and the Government of Japan both being solicitous for the peace of the Pacific affirm that their national policies are directed toward lasting and extensive peace throughout the Pacific area, that they have no territorial designs in that area, that they have no intention of threatening other countries or of using military force aggressively against any neighboring nation, and that, accordingly, in their national policies they will actively support and give practical application to the following fundamental principles upon which their relations with each other and with all other governments are based:

(1) The principle of inviolability of territorial integrity and sovereignty of each and all nations.

(2) The principle of non-interference in the internal affairs of other countries.

(3) The principle of equality, including equality of commercial opportunity and treatment.

(4) The principle of reliance upon international coöperation and conciliation for the prevention and pacific settlement of controversies and for improvement of international conditions by peaceful methods and processes.

The Government of Japan and the Government of the United States have agreed that toward eliminating chronic political instability, preventing recurrent economic collapse, and providing a basis for peace, they will actively support and practically apply the following principles in their economic relations with each other and with other nations and peoples:

(1) The principle of non-discrimination in international commercial relations.

(2) The principle of international economic coöperation and abolition of extreme nationalism as expressed in excessive trade restrictions.

(3) The principle of non-discriminatory access by all nations to raw material supplies.

(4) The principle of full protection of the interests of consuming countries and populations as regards the operation of international commodity agreements.

(5) The principle of establishment of such institutions and arrangements of international finance as may lend aid to the essential enterprises and the continuous development of all countries and may permit payments through processes of trade consonant with the welfare of all countries.

SECTION II

Steps To Be Taken by the Government of the United States and by the Government of Japan

The Government of the United States and the Government of Japan propose to take steps as follows:

1. The Government of the United States and the Government of Japan will endeavor to conclude a multilateral non-aggression pact among the British Empire, China, Japan, the Netherlands, the Soviet Union, Thailand and the United States.

2. Both Governments will endeavor to conclude among the American, British, Chinese, Japanese, the Netherland and Thai Governments an agreement whereunder each of the Governments would pledge itself to respect the territorial integrity of French Indochina and, in the event that there should develop a threat to the territorial integrity of Indochina, to enter into immediate consultation with a view to taking such measures as may be deemed necessary and advisable to meet the threat in question. Such agreement would provide also that each of the Governments party to the agreement would not seek or accept preferential treatment in its trade or economic relations with Indochina and would use its influence to obtain for each of the signatories equality of treatment in trade and commerce with French Indochina.

3. The Government of Japan will withdraw all military, naval, air and police forces from China and from Indochina.

4. The Government of the United States and the Government of Japan will not support—militarily, politically, economically—any government or regime in China other than the National Government of the Republic of China with capital temporarily at Chungking.

5. Both Governments will give up all extraterritorial rights in China, including rights and interests in and with regard to international settlements and concessions, and rights under the Boxer Protocol of 1901.

Both Governments will endeavor to obtain the agreement of the British and other governments to give up extraterritorial rights in China, including rights in international settlements and in concessions and under the Boxer Protocol of 1901.

6. The Government of the United States and the Government of Japan will enter into negotiations for the conclusion between the United States and Japan of a trade agreement, based upon reciprocal most-favored-nation treatment and reduction of trade barriers by both countries, including an undertaking by the United States to bind raw silk on the free list.

7. The Government of the United States and the Government of Japan

will, respectively, remove the freezing restrictions on Japanese funds in the United States and on American funds in Japan.

8. Both Governments will agree upon a plan for the stabilization of the dollar-yen rate, with the allocation of funds adequate for this purpose, half to be supplied by Japan and half by the United States.

9. Both Governments will agree that no agreement which either has concluded with any third power or powers shall be interpreted by it in such a way as to conflict with the fundamental purpose of this agreement, the establishment and preservation of peace throughout the Pacific area.

10. Both Governments will use their influence to cause other governments to adhere to and to give practical application to the basic political and economic principles set forth in this agreement.

Our Ambassadors reported that they told Secretary Hull, when his note was handed to them, that they found it unacceptable as discrepant with the tenor of the discussions thitherto, and that they could hardly bring themselves to transmit it to their government.

In considering the nature of the Hull Note, the sequence of events in Washington from 20 November to the delivery of the note, as I learned it later, is of interest. As I have mentioned, a *modus vivendi* had been under contemplation. According to Dr. Charles A. Beard [1] (who made a detailed study, on the basis of American sources, of the days leading to the outbreak of the Pacific War), Secretary Hull, in co-operation with the President and the highest military officials, had worked out a plan for adjusting relations, with the Japanese proposal as its groundwork. This was on 21 November and the days following. Secretary of War Stimson approved the plan in its final form, declaring that it would adequately safeguard the interests of the United States. Conferences were held also with the ambassadors or ministers of the other countries interested; but the Chinese registered pas-

[1] *President Roosevelt and the Coming of the War, 1941,* 1948, pp. 513–6. T. S.

sionate protests against any form of *modus vivendi*—Ambassador Hu Shih was very active in urging China's opposition, and Chiang Kai-shek sent numerous "hysterical" cables direct to several American leaders. Even Prime Minister Churchill intervened in support of the Chinese position, apparently causing no small embarrassment to Secretary Hull. Suddenly—for reasons which as Dr. Beard says are nowhere made explicit—after consultation with President Roosevelt, Hull discarded his proposed *modus vivendi*, and on the 26th handed to the Japanese Ambassadors the note printed above.

President Roosevelt, it will be remembered, had promised Prime Minister Churchill in August that he would try to delay war with Japan by one to three months. The three months had now run out. In the entry for 25 November in the diary of Secretary Stimson,[2] he records that there was held at the White House, from twelve to one-thirty of that day, a meeting of the "War Cabinet"—the President, Hull, Stimson, Secretary of the Navy Knox, Chief of Staff Marshall and Chief of Naval Operations Stark. The President, saying that a Japanese attack appeared imminent, posed the question what should be done. The dilemma thereby suggested was a serious one, since the problem as stated was to minimize the damage which would be inflicted by the attack which Japan was to be maneuvered into initiating. In the discussion which followed, Stimson said that since the President had served on Japan as early as August a caveat against her military aggrandizement, it was necessary now only to point out to the Japanese that an advance by them into Thailand would constitute a transgression. It was decided that the Secretary of State should draft such a communication. In his testimony at the Congressional hearings, Secretary Stimson admitted with refer-

[2] *Pearl Harbor Attack,* Part 11, pp. 5, 433–4. T.S.

ence to the decision reached on that day that, while it is not wise ordinarily when one knows that an enemy is going to strike to wait "until he gets the jump on you," they realized that by making Japan commit the first overt act—attended though that course was by some hazard—the government could gain the full support of the American people. The primary concern at this conference, it is obvious, was how it might be possible to jockey Japan into the position of firing the first shot; there was no atmosphere of working for consummation of the negotiations with Japan by means of the note to be handed to her the following day.

The evidence concerning activities in Washington following delivery to the Japanese Ambassadors of the Hull Note may also profitably be examined. The day after the handing over of his note, Hull, in telling Stimson (according to Stimson's record) that he had "broken off the whole matter," and that it was now "in the hands of the Army and the Navy," affirmed that war was certain. On the 27th also, the Army and Navy Chiefs of Staff alerted their Pacific outposts, informing them—after consulting with Hull—that negotiations with Japan were at or virtually at an end. Secretary Hull during those days told the British Ambassador that diplomatic relations with Japan were in effect ruptured, and to the Australian Minister, who on the 28th advanced the suggestion of Australia's essaying mediation between the United States and Japan, he said that he had no objection, but that the diplomatic phase was over and nothing could come of such a move. An abundance of evidence in the record of the Congressional Pearl Harbor Committee, and analyzed by Dr. Beard,[3] establishes these facts. And these facts speak beyond peradventure of mistake that the Hull Note was handed to Japan in

[3] *Op. cit.*, Chapter XVII.

the calculated expectation that it would by no possibility be accepted by her, and that the negotiations would be ruptured and the rupture followed by war—that the note had been studiously prepared, judging from the timing, with a view to forcing Japan to commit the first overt act. Of course, these data were not available to us in those days of the negotiations; but, having realized from the utterances of the American leaders and their increased war preparations as reported in the press the hardening of their determination to go to war, I could read their intention distinctly in the Hull Note itself. When I received our Ambassadors' cabled report of the gist of the note, and then the full text which followed on its heels, I was utterly disheartened, and felt like one groping in darkness. The uncompromising tone was no more than I had looked for; but I was greatly astonished at the extreme nature of the contents.

Concerning this point, it is instructive to compare the Hull Note with the earlier proposals of the United States. Leaving aside the fact that the Hull Note dropped not a few of the provisions, favorable to Japan, of the original Japanese-American Draft-Understanding of 16 April, we can make an illuminating comparison with even the American proposal of 21 June, to which the United States had clung throughout and on which Secretary Hull stated his Note to be based:

Hull Note	*21 June Proposal*
1. Multilateral nonaggression pact	[No equivalent]
2. Multilateral agreement concerning French Indochina	[No equivalent]
3. Unconditional withdrawal of all Japanese military, naval, air and police forces from China and Indochina	Timing and conditions of the withdrawal of Japanese forces from China to be studied in future (no reference to French Indochina)

Hull Note	21 June Proposal
4. Disapproval of regimes in China other than the Chiang regime	Friendly negotiations concerning Manchoukuo
5. Abrogation of the Tripartite Pact	Japan's commitment, in connection with the Tripartite Pact, that she would not act upon it in case of an act of self-defense on the part of the United States
6. Giving up of all extraterritorial rights and all rights and interests concerning international settlements and concessions and those under the Boxer Protocol	[No equivalent]

As this comparison clearly shows, the Hull Note injected into the negotiations demands which had not previously been raised. It was Mr. Hull's plea that these were but applications of the principles which the United States had consistently contended for; but there can be no doubt that the Hull Note in many ways went beyond what the United States had stood for in the negotiations.[4] It required no great perspicacity to deduce that the United States had deliberately made proposals of content known to be unacceptable to Japan, and in a form moreover rendering them impossible of acceptance.

By the time the Ambassadors' résumé of the Hull Note was received in the Foreign Ministry, the Army and Navy had received their reports from their attachés in Washington, and a meeting of the Liaison Conference was held without delay, on 27 November. All the participants expressed stupefaction at the attitude of the United States as revealed by the note. Some proponents of war among the military men seemed to experience

[4] Compare Beard, *op. cit.*, pp. 235–6, 556–9. T. S.

a sense of relief at this development, but it was evident that to most the feeling was one of discouragement. Upon receipt of the full text of the note, I had consulted specially with the Premier, the Navy Minister and the Lord Keeper of the Privy Seal, and all agreed that there was nothing further that we could do. The consensus was that the United States had advanced such demands —in disregard of the anterior development of the negotiations and the understandings thus far reached in them, going beyond the most extreme position which she had ever taken theretofore —because she had no sincere desire to make a peaceful settlement and was bent on forcing a complete surrender upon Japan, and that what the United States intended was to coerce Japan into abandoning her place as the strong Power in the Far East, indifferent to Japanese sacrifices in the preceding long years. On the one hand, to capitulate to such a demand was for Japan tantamount to suicide; on the other, the economic blockade and military encirclement of Japan, growing daily tighter under the management of the United States, were threatening Japan's existence. Japan therefore was driven to the conclusion that there was no alternative to making a stand at this point.

Our feeling concerning the American attitude as embodied in the Hull Note is expressed in my statement made on 1 December to the Imperial Conference called to consider our course at this juncture. After outlining the previous development of the negotiations, I recapitulated the contents of the note (including verbatim quotation of Part II thereof), then continued:

Regarding the above proposal, our Ambassadors pointed out its inequity, and remonstrated earnestly with Secretary Hull over it; but, they reported, the Secretary gave no evidence of concession. On the 27th the President, in an interview with our two Ambassadors, told them that though he still hoped for an amicable conclusion of the Japanese-American negotiations, he considered, on the basis of the latest information, that there was danger that cold water would be dashed upon the United States for a second time, just as had been done last July by the advance of Japanese troops into southern French Indochina. It would be futile, he added, to try to surmount the crisis by a *modus vivendi* if the fundamental policies of the two countries were not in accord.

The American proposal, it is true, contains some acceptable items; such are those relating to international trade (Paragraphs 6, 7 and 8) and the abolition of extraterritoriality rights in China (Paragraph 5). Such provisions, on the other hand, as those of Paragraphs 2 and 3 concerning China and French Indochina, and those relating to the nonrecognition of the National government of China [5] (Paragraph 4), disapproval of the Tripartite Pact (Paragraph 9) and conclusion of a multilateral nonaggression pact (Paragraph 1), are obnoxious to Japan. All in all, this proposal is unreasonable, constituting a marked retrogression from the earlier understandings, and wholly disregarding the course of negotiations of over half a year.

In short, the United States has persistently adhered to traditional ideas and principles, ignoring actual conditions in East Asia and attempting to force Japan to act on those principles, which the United States herself would not submit to. Throughout the present negotiations, continuing for the past seven months, the United States has receded in no particular from her original stand, despite the various and numerous concessions by Japan.

It has been a consistent policy of the United States to obstruct Japan's efforts toward establishment of the New Order in East Asia, which constitutes our immutable national policy. If we yielded to the present demands of the United States, Japan's international position would be inferior even to that which she occupied prior to the Manchuria Incident, and her very existence itself would be endangered. Specifically:

(1) China under the rule of Chiang Kai-shek would be more than ever disposed to dependency upon Britain and the United States, and Japan would be obliged to break her faith with the National government of China. Friendly relations between Japan and China would be precluded

[5] Both Chungking and Nanking governments denominated themselves "National Government of the Republic of China."

for years to come. Japan would be forced to withdraw entirely from the continent; the existence of Manchoukuo, accordingly, would inevitably be threatened; and we would, of course, be left without means of carrying through the China Affair.

(2) Britain and the United States would reign as leaders over these areas. Japan's authority, as well as her position as the stabilizing force in East Asia, would be wholly subverted, and the work of establishment of the New Order in East Asia would collapse midway.

(3) The Tripartite Pact would become a mere scrap of paper, and Japan would forfeit her national good faith.

(4) The design of restraining Japan by organization of a collective machinery of Powers, with the Soviet Union brought in as a new member, would intensify the menace to our northern frontier.

(5) As to such principles as that of nondiscrimination in trade, they are not necessarily to be rejected. However, it is only to attain their selfish aims that Britain and the United States propose application of these principles to the Pacific area exclusively, and Japan would have to contend with insuperable obstacles to the obtaining of essential goods and materials required by her.

All things considered, the above proposal is utterly intolerable for Japan, and we must recognize that unless the United States withdraws it almost in its entirety, there is no possibility of realizing our claims by negotiation. Upon the basis of the present proposal negotiation is impossible.

Since the end of the war various interpretations of the Hull Note have been offered, and criticisms made of the management of relations by the authorities of the two countries. A revolution may well change the standard of values; but a defeat in war cannot alter facts. A certain Japanese diplomat, in his report upon returning home from service abroad, said that it was extremely questionable that the United States was at that time really earnest in seeking a definitive adjustment of her relations with Japan, but that rather there was reason to conclude that she had been determined since July 1941 at latest that a war was unavoidable. The Roberts Commission Report,[6] he wrote, put it beyond doubt that the disaster of Pearl Harbor was not ascribable—as the propaganda was—to the treachery of Japan, but was invited by negligence on the part of the United States herself. This self-same diplomat now, after the end of the war, is saying that it is too hasty to assert that the United States had no intention whatever at that time of bringing the negotiations to a successful conclusion, but that quite conceivably the China problem and the other thorny issues might, if diplomacy had been persisted in, gradually have found their solution. The effect of this argument is to censure the then authorities of our government for failure to go on with negotiations. However, the United States having been resolved on war against Japan—as was stated in Ambassador Nomura's report on his repatriation, as well as in his telegrams—there was no doubt that Japan had the alternatives only of war or of total surrender, even though the United States diplomatically professed still to wish for a peaceful settlement, or not to purpose termination of the negotiations.

Japan at that time naturally could not prolong the negotiations out of mere hope of a solution, without concrete prospects—this at a time when the military men were insisting that even a month or two could not be let pass by, since the United States' policy, in anticipation of a turning of the European War in favor of the Allies, was based on the assumption that Japan would gradually come to suffer economic distress. It was equally obvious that Japan's position vis-à-vis the United States could not have been improved by deferring a solution; that divers proposals looking to delay at the last moment were rejected in Tokyo is, therefore,

---

[6] A five-man commission under the chairmanship of Mr. Justice Owen J. Roberts of the Supreme Court was appointed by President Roosevelt, on 16 December 1941, to investigate and report on certain aspects of the Pearl Harbor debacle. Its report, placing responsibility on the local commanders, was published on 24 January 1942.

181

not to be wondered at. An objective and precise study of the negotiations will bring conviction that their success depended not on resolution of one or two issues, not on the exceptionable character of speeches by Japanese leaders, or the like, but fundamentally on one thing and one thing only—whether Japan would truckle under to the United States. To do so would have entailed not only seeing all sacrifices made since before the Manchuria Incident suffered in vain, but submitting to expulsion from the continent; it would have been, in fine, to resign ourselves to Japan's being reduced to a state comparable to that of the present, after the defeat.

That Japan was at that time not prepared to endure this is beyond controversy. In any event, none—in the official or the nonofficial world—favored submission in surrender; neither the so-called liberal camp nor the Senior Statesmen's circles advocated acceptance of the American proposal *in toto*.

Since the end of the war there are, of course, those who assert that there was no reason that Japan could not approve the Hull Note. The argument goes that Japan need have withheld concurrence in the proposal of a multilateral nonaggression pact only because she was tainted by the ideology of aggression, that the principle of economic equality in French Indochina was a matter of course. The opposition to withdrawal of military and police forces from China, they say, was an idea peculiar to the Army, and without justification; and it would not necessarily have been a betrayal for Japan to undertake not to support the Wang regime by military, economic or political means. Japan could have promised that she would in no event go to war against the United States, because the purpose of the Tripartite Pact itself was to prevent the United States' entry into the war. Finally, there was all the more reason to subscribe to the Hull Note in

182

that it envisioned economic arrangements advantageous to Japan herself. However, the very person who is now the proponent of this argument was most ardent before the war for nullification of the Nine Power Treaty; he cried for highly preferential treatment for Japan in the southern areas, the Netherlands Indies in particular; and he was a leading promoter of the Anti-Comintern Pact, precursor of the Tripartite Pact. More, he wrote to Premier Konoe during the Japanese-American negotiations saying that— having, as the Premier knew, fought hard for the sake of the New Order in East Asia—he was chagrined that Japan should make concessions to the United States in this respect. Japan's obligations under the Tripartite Pact, he added, involved her honor, and repudiation of it would stain the virtue of the Emperor; it would be an act of suicide internationally for Japan to adjust her relations with the United States by entering into an agreement whereby to evade her treaty obligations. One hardly knows which to believe, this man's acts before or his words after the war.

Now, after the defeat, those who were not informed of the facts relating to the coming of the war may well question whether there was no way to prevent it; it is for this reason that I have written in such detail. But it cannot be said to be in good taste for those who were in the thick of affairs, or were otherwise familiar with the circumstances, to indulge now in empty argumentation, oblivious of what they have done or said previously.

I must advert to a few more points for clarification of the contemporaneous situation. It is evident that the Hull Note was an implementation of the concept underlying the Nine Power Treaty and the Stimson Doctrine, with the addition of exactions of assurances concerning the Tripartite Pact and economic affairs. So far as concerns the Nine Power Treaty, it is still fresh in the memory of the public how nonofficial as well as official Japan struggled with that treaty—that revision of it was longed for even by those who accepted its premises, not to speak of those urging its abrogation, is notorious. On a strict interpretation of the Nine Power Treaty, the independence of Manchoukuo or the subsistence of the Nanking government is, certainly, unjustifiable; but who in Japan in those days deprecated the existence of those governments? Search of the records of the Diet proceedings, scrutiny of the newspapers, will provide a plethora of evidence that none did.

The primary objective of the Nine Power Treaty was to guarantee the territorial and administrative integrity of China, for the ostensible sake of which objective the Pacific War came about. But did Britain, the United States and their allies conclude this treaty and wage the Pacific War purely for the sake of peace, or for the sake of the integrity of China? If so, how to explain Britain's and America's consenting at Yalta on 11 February 1945 to an exclusive control of Manchuria by the U.S.S.R., in negation of the whole concept of the Nine Power Treaty? And why could they not have admitted for Japan what they were thus willing to approve for Russia? As I pointed out to the American Ambassador during the negotiations, it was inequitable that the United States should censure Japan's stationing of troops in China, the while offering no protest against that of the U.S.S.R. in Outer Mongolia; such is not the way of fidelity to a principle. If a nation acts upon a given principle differently as its convenience of the moment may dictate, it cannot be heard to assert that it is motivated by attachment to justice or the passion for peace; it is then acting only on caprice. Is it strange that Japan could not yield so submissively to a demand of such a nature?

What was intended by Mr. Hull's proposed multilateral nonaggression pact was to require Japan to commit herself to abstaining from war against the Allies. Clause 9 of the Hull Note would then have had the effect of making the Tripartite Pact a dead letter, by preventing Japan from entering the European War even when the United States might become a participant in it; and Clause 4, obligating Japan to disown the Manchoukuo and Nanking governments, would have committed her for the future in accordance with the multilateral pact. No nation can bow to a demand, made in the name of peace but capricious, requiring it to give up what for over a decade it has with all its energies striven for as vital to its national interests; only a visionary with no experience of actual politics could suppose that it would.

The language of the Hull Note relating to French Indochina need not be dwelt upon, as it contemplated only the extension of the provisions of the Nine Power Treaty to that area. With respect to the requirement of withdrawal of troops from China, I had of course no objection, having from the beginning insisted on withdrawal; but opposition to it prevailed, as I have explained, not only in the Army but in other quarters also. And, as to the charge that, in rejecting the Hull Note and breaking off negotiations, we were embarking on a war without hope of victory, it must be borne in mind that the military authorities then offered a quite different prediction.

In connection with economic equality, it was proposed to secure application of the principle in China (Indochina being separately provided for) by means of the Nine Power Treaty. It is, however, incomprehensible why the principle could not have been put into practice in China simultaneously with that application uniformly throughout the world which Secretary Hull asserted would be realized in the near future (as it has turned out, of course, there is no free trade now, after the war, despite

185

Mr. Hull's advocacy). To enforce in China alone a principle which does not operate in other areas of the world is to accord to China a colonial treatment which amounts to a derogation from her sovereignty; if the sovereignty of China is to be respected, why should she not be at liberty, if she so wishes, to conclude preferential-tariff agreements or even to enter into customs unions?

Some may wish to dwell upon the supposed benefits which Japan would have realized by acceptance of the Hull Note. It is incontrovertible that any such benefits would have been minuscular by comparison with the detriments which I have mentioned. Indubitably, with the fiat of the Hull Note enacted, Japan's position would have been roughly the same as that at present, the consequence of her defeat. But he who argues that Japan would nevertheless have been in better case by bowing to the American dictate, and thus escaping the ravages of war, while plausible, is wholly sophistical, for he fails to allow weight to either the honor or the prestige of the nation. Entirely aside from the question whether Japan had or had not long been engaged in aggression, had or had not invaded foreign rights and interests, it has to be remembered that she was then struggling to maintain her status as a Great Power, and that the soldiers—who alone were qualified to pronounce an informed judgment—were confident that she would not be defeated in a war.

It was the force of such circumstances as I have here set out which assured even the American leaders that Japan could not submit to their demands as formulated in the Hull Note. The contemporaneous recognition by President Roosevelt, Secretary Hull and other authorities in Washington of that fact is confirmed by every objective opinion formed at the time or afterward. We may sample those opinions. Ambassador Grew, then in

Tokyo, later said [7] that when the note of 26 November was sent the button which set off the war had been pushed. On the 26th and 27th Secretary Hull held special press conferences at which he gave a full account of the Japanese-American negotiations; the American press responded by reporting almost unanimously that it was Japan's choice whether to accept the Hull Note or go to war. Later—in wartime—an American chronicler wrote that even a Monaco or a Luxemburg would have taken up arms against the United States if it had been handed such a memorandum as that which the State Department presented to the Japanese government.[8] In June 1944, Captain Oliver Lyttelton, Minister of Production and a leading member of the British War Cabinet, created a celebrated incident when he declared in an address to the American Chamber of Commerce in London that it was a distortion of history to say that the United States had been driven into war with Japan, the truth being that the United States had challenged Japan to the point that Japan was finally compelled to stand and fight. It is, lastly, even recorded in the written report of my then secretary, Kase, on his call on Ambassador Craigie at the latter's departure for home on 29 July 1942, that the Ambassador told Kase that he had first read the Hull Note in the press after the war had begun, and had then realized that the rupture of the negotiations had been inescapable, the note having wholly disregarded the national feeling of Japan.

It is therefore no longer arguable at this time of day that the American authorities, having made all necessary preparations in the expectation that the negotiations would break down and a war ensue, delivered the Hull Note anticipating that Japan would reject it, thus compelling her to elect between total surren-

---

[7] *Pearl Harbor Attack,* Part 39, p. 137, T. S.
[8] Albert Jay Nock, *Memoirs of a Superfluous Man,* 1943, p. 249. T. S.

der and war. Indeed, remembering that the question of how to insure that Japan should fire the first shot had been in the forefront in the War Cabinet's discussions in Washington, it seems not unwarrantable to construe the note as going beyond the forcing of a choice—it is not too much to say that it was the throwing down of a challenge to Japan, or at the least constituted an ultimatum without time limit. This we knew in Tokyo—though we could not then know of the words and acts of the high American officials which confirmed our deduction—from the drastic terms of the note and the inclusion among them of conditions never theretofore suggested. Our interpretation was confirmed by the reaction to Hull's disclosures by the American press—which played up, as if at the urging of the governmental authorities, the choice between the terms of the Hull Note and war—and by the plainly visible tightening of the encirclement of Japan.

So far as concerns my own state of mind upon receipt of the Hull Note, I can never forget the despair which overpowered me. I had fought and worked unflaggingly until that moment; but I could feel no enthusiasm for the fight thereafter. I tried as it were to close my eyes and swallow the Hull Note whole, as the alternative to war, but it stuck in the craw. In contrast to my dejection, many of the military men were elated at the uncompromising attitude of the United States, as if to say, "Didn't we tell you so?"—they were by no means easy to be patient with.

With the catastrophe of war, betraying the hopes with which I had taken office, foreshadowed, my thoughts again turned to resignation. I asked Mr. Satō, Adviser to the Foreign Ministry, and some others, whether they could see anyone who, replacing me, could lead the development of events away from war. I was advised by them all by all means to remain in office, as no one could be expected to achieve more. Even would resignation by me have brought about that of the entire cabinet, the position would have remained unchanged; in the conditions of November 1941 it was unthinkable that a cabinet which would capitulate abjectly to pressure of the United States could be established. Far less would my resigning individually have had meaning, however much it might have insured my personal safety and enabled me to evade responsibility. I therefore made up my mind to remain in office to try to obtain the United States' reconsideration, to fight for peace to the last moment, and if war did come to devote myself to working for its early termination, for the sake of Japan and of the world.

It was at this stage a matter of time only. It being then to the interest of the United States, and to the detriment of Japan, to prolong the prevailing uncertainty, what was needful was to clarify the situation. The doing of this may be said to have been the sole achievement of the Tōjō Cabinet.

As I have said, the Hull Note was laid before the Liaison Conference of 27 November. It was considered also at a Cabinet meeting on the 28th, and at other conferences which I shall detail in the next chapter. In the Liaison Conference there was no extended discussion, all being of the same mind; the conclusion reached by the conference, on the 30th, was as follows. The United States intended by the Hull Note to drive Japan from the continent, and it was to be expected that unless Japan would wholly withdraw, war with the United States and Great Britain must come sooner or later. Since the military estimate was that the United States would intensify its pressure upon us after having defeated Germany and Italy—by which time Japan, having been gradually exhausted, would have no strength to resist— Japan should, accepting the American challenge, fight now while she had still the resources and while the outlook was not entirely unpropitious. If the Dutch East Indies were to be occupied by the United States and Britain, as suggested in Ambassador Nomura's telegram, Japan's emergency supply of petroleum would be cut off, involving her national survival. The encirclement of Japan had been daily extended, the American and Australian forces having been reinforced in the Philippines and the Netherlands Indies and a powerful British fleet having seemingly been hastily dispatched to Malaya. Japan should now promptly decide on war, as she would contribute to her own destruction by merely leaving events to develop in their present direction. It was recognized that Japan could not utterly abandon her continental policy; and the consensus was that as the United States had, despite Japan's utmost efforts to succeed with the Japanese-American negotiations, challenged Japan by delivery of such an ultimatum as the Hull Note and by application of military pressure, there was for Japan no alternative to fighting in her self-defense.

In this connection, a few words should be added on the scope of the right of self-defense. The definition of the right as arrived at by the international law based on opinions of scholars and precedents had limited it to cases in which the territory of a nation was actually invaded, or peril was of such immediacy as to admit of no pausing for consideration. In the Japanese-American negotiations, however, the United States had defended a different thesis, asserting that her right of self-defense extended to resisting whenever and wherever—within or without her territory—her interests might be threatened. The United States government, obstinately standing its ground, took no heed of Japan's repeated objections to so broad an interpretation of "self-defense." Since in diplomacy there are always two parties, Japan could not fail to take the American contention into account, whatever the academic theory.

It often occurs that international law is acknowledged to have undergone change owing to such arbitrary action of the Great Powers. Thus, it had become the accepted practice to extend "recognition" to a newly established government once its permanence had been demonstrated; but recognition has developed into a political act since President Wilson's withholding of it from the Soviet regime. With respect to neutrality, again, established practices of international law were violated in many ways during the First World War, and the United States' infractions of a neutral's obligations after the beginning of the European War in 1939 were flagrant; the United States, who during the First World War had stood for freedom of the seas and had attempted to restrain Britain's excesses, gave little care to the matter during the Second World War, when she had strong naval and air forces. Few countries undertook to make an issue of the United States' contraventions of international law, and the extent of present-day recognition of the legal requirements pertaining to neutrals remains unclear.

International law being thus at the mercy of arbitrary action of one or a few Great Powers, Japan quite naturally, in connection with the right of self-defense, took the American interpretation into consideration at least in so far as concerned her dealing with the United States. The United States further postulated that each nation for itself is to determine, conclusively, whether its action falls within the ambit of self-defense. But any principle or rule of law which is to be applied to one country has to be applied equally to others; and by the United States' own reasoning, Japan's determination that it must act in self-defense cannot be called in question as going beyond the scope of its legal right.

After receipt of the Hull Note, I instructed our Ambassadors in Washington that they should point out to the American authorities that the absence of any response to Japan's co-operative attitude, adopted at great sacrifice, rendered negotiations extremely difficult, and to ask reconsideration. The United States, however, while thereafter complaining that a speech of Premier Tōjō's had been very radical, or that Japanese forces were apparently being moved south, manifested no intention whatsoever of reconsidering the issues in the negotiations, continuation of which thus was impossible. The Foreign Ministry could not, however, itself discontinue them until that step should have been decided upon by an Imperial Conference; this was pointed out to our representatives, and they were instructed that they should do nothing to suggest abandonment of the negotiations.

CHAPTER 7

War Begins

THE OPINION in the Liaison Conference, as well as among the Cabinet, was that at this point war was inevitable. The Emperor, however, wished to learn the opinions of the Senior Statesmen before giving his sanction for war, and at the Liaison Conference of 28 November Premier Tōjō raised the question of the explanation to be made to them. Some said that it was not necessary that they be informed in any detail, since their authority to advise the Emperor was—by comparison with that of the Genrō of former days—very limited. I argued, however, that now that the nation was on the verge of a great crisis, it was appropriate that as many people as possible be made conversant with the facts; and especially, as the Emperor was desirous of hearing the opinions of those veteran statesmen of the nation, the government should provide them with all the particulars in its possession, to help them to a clear understanding of conditions. It was decided as I had proposed, and the following morning was appointed for explanations by the Cabinet members to the Senior Statesmen, prior to their being received in audience by the Emperor.

On the 29th, therefore, the Premier first told the Senior Statesmen of the reasons which compelled us to go to war, after which I recounted the development of the Japanese-American negotiations; some questions were asked by Baron Wakatsuki [1] and Mr. Hirota, and I answered fully. There was no one who suggested accepting the proposal of the United States. There followed various questions responded to by others, on problems of supply (as of shipping, aircraft and petroleum), public finance, foodstuffs, the views and morale of the people and the like. The discussions took so long that the Emperor's luncheon to the participants was delayed beyond the scheduled time.

In the afternoon the Senior Statesmen were received in audience, and the Emperor invited each of them to give his opinion. Prince Konoe expressed his appreciation of the efforts of the government in the Japanese-American negotiations; but, he said, while the negotiations had, seemingly, proved abortive in view of the latest American proposal, he wondered whether it might not be possible nevertheless to persevere at this moment, to wait and see the unfolding of events. The Premier replied, "This has all been threshed over and over until it makes my head ache, but the conclusion always is that war is unavoidable." The exploration of this question developed no further. Two or three of the Senior Statesmen expressly stated their view that there was no alternative to war; a few voiced apprehension concerning the prospect of a war. Tōjō answered each of them; some of his answers I recall as curt and brusque, but at any rate the discussion remained calm.

The decision for war was made at the Liaison Conference held on the following day, the 30th, when it was decided also to hold an Imperial Conference on 1 December, and the agenda therefor

---

[1] Baron Wakatsuki Reijirō (1866–1949), after a bureaucratic career, had become Premier in 1926–27. In 1930 he was chief delegate to the London Naval Conference, and in 1931 emerged again as Premier from April to December, his government being forced out by the upsurge of jingoism attendant upon the Manchuria Incident. He had been an outstanding figure in the struggle to free civil government from military domination.

was deliberated on. A draft of the Imperial Rescript to be promulgated immediately after the opening of hostilities was submitted to the Liaison Conference about this time, and much thought was given to it. Our reply to the Hull Note, however, had not yet been presented to the conference; this reply had been under preparation by the bureau of the Foreign Ministry responsible, but the answer returned to my repeated requests for prompt submission of it was that the drafting had been delayed by the necessity of going through many hands for co-ordination with Army and Navy. There was thus no discussion at the Imperial Conference of 1 December of the reply to the Hull Note.

The agenda of the Imperial Conference consisted of two propositions:

The negotiations with the United States have finally failed of consummation.

Japan will commence hostilities against Great Britain, the United States and the Netherlands.

The Conference was attended by all members of the Cabinet, the Chiefs and Vice-Chiefs of Army and Navy General Staffs, the Chief Secretary of the Cabinet, the Directors of the Military and Naval Affairs Bureaus, and President Hara of the Privy Council, attending at the special desire of the Emperor. The Premier opened the conference with the following statement:

With His Majesty's permission, I shall manage today's proceedings. On the basis of the Imperial Conference decision of 5 November, our Army and Navy have devoted themselves to completion of preparations for their operations, while the government has made all possible efforts to readjust diplomatic relations with the United States. The United States, however, not only does not recede a step from its former contentions, but has now begun to demand unilateral concessions by us, in adding such new requirements as unconditional and wholesale military evacuation from

China, withdrawal of recognition of the Nanking government, and abrogation of the Japan-Germany-Italy Tripartite Pact. If we submit to these demands, not only will the honor of the Empire be lost and any prospect for successful conclusion of the China Affair vanish, but our very existence will be threatened. It is therefore clear that we cannot gain our contentions by diplomatic means. On the other hand, the United States, Great Britain, the Netherlands and China have recently further increased their economic and military pressure on us; this, in consideration of the state of the national strength as well as of strategy, has resulted in a condition in which we cannot passively watch developments. Things having reached this point, we have no recourse but to go to war against the United States, Great Britain and the Netherlands, in order to surmount the present crisis and to preserve our existence.

It is extremely regrettable that His Majesty must be troubled by the outbreak of this great war, when the China Affair has already gone on for four years and more. When we think, however, that our national strength has several times multiplied since before the China Affair, with the people drawn closer together and with the spirit of the fighting men of our Army and Navy higher and more vigorous than ever before, it is beyond doubt that this crisis will be survived by the whole nation's contributing, as one man, its life to the country.

Now, therefore, I should like to have discussion by the participants of today's agenda, as shown on the paper before you. As to diplomatic negotiations, operational matters and other points, explanation will be given you by the Ministers responsible and the military staffs respectively.

Following the Premier, I narrated the development of the negotiations and how the United States' latest proposal rendered their continuation impossible; the concluding part of my statement has been given above, at page 178. The Agriculture and Forestry and Finance Ministers and, in his capacity as Home Minister, Tōjō again, also made statements, as did the Chief of the Naval General Staff. President Hara asked a few questions, after which he said, "It having come to this, I think that there is no alternative to resorting to arms." The propositions of the agenda were unanimously approved, and the decision made. Tōjō informed me later that the Imperial sanction was subsequently given.

The war decision was thus made, and various problems which would arise with the opening of the war were submitted to meetings of the Liaison Conference. One thing which—needless to say—was not discussed in the Liaison Conference was operational aspects of the impending hostilities. It was disclosed at the IMTFE that the naval task force under Admiral Nagumo had sailed from Hitokappu Bay on 26 November under orders to strike Pearl Harbor, and in its judgment the tribunal made the absurd finding that the scheduled attack was freely discussed at the meeting of the Liaison Conference on 30 November. We had, of course, no knowledge of the plan; it was the invariable practice of the high command not to divulge to civilian officials, such as us, any scrap of information bearing on these highly secret operations, and anyone familiar with the system will readily understand our total lack of knowledge of them. (This condition is sufficiently well illustrated by the fact, which I have mentioned elsewhere, that Tōjō told me that it was only at the IMTFE trial itself that he first learned any operational details of the Pearl Harbor attack; a mass of additional evidence was adduced at the trial showing that the civilian members of the Cabinet had no prior knowledge even of the existence of the plan to attack Hawaii.)

The Imperial Rescript of declaration of war was submitted to the meeting of the Liaison Conference immediately following the Imperial Conference. At this meeting I had the feeling that the members from the high command were unwontedly carefree in attitude, by contrast with their previous intenseness concerning an early commencement of the war. Finding this attitude strange

197

—and also because there remained to be settled the matter of notification of the declaration of war—I inquired of them when the hostilities were to begin. Army Chief of Staff Sugiyama replied vaguely that it would be "around next Sunday." This deepened the suspicion which I already felt of the high command, and I therefore pointed out that naturally we should give notice of the commencement of hostilities through usual procedures. To this, however, the Navy Chief of Staff, Admiral Nagano, retorted, "We're going to make a surprise attack," and the Vice-Chief, Admiral Itō, followed by saying that the Navy wanted to leave the negotiations unterminated until hostilities should have begun, in order to achieve the maximum possible effect with the initial attack.

I then understood what the carefreeness in the attitude of the high command had meant. I was equally astonished at the proposal of a surprise attack by a Navy which had professed such confidence in its interceptive operations, and discouraged over the future of the war, as the proposal amounted to an admission that the Navy had no expectation of success, even in the initial phase of the war, unless it could achieve surprise. At any rate, I stressed that notification of a declaration of war was absolutely necessary from the point of view of international good faith. I pointed out that the action proposed by the Navy was entirely unallowable, being in contravention of accepted procedure, and that it would be inauspicious for Japan at the opening of the war to commit irresponsible acts which would be hurtful to the national honor and prestige. In further proof that my position was the natural and normal one, I recalled to them that Ambassador Nomura had urged the necessity of terminating the negotiations before resorting to "freedom of action," and of giving such notification in Washington. I was so disgusted with the high command over these tactics of starting to insist, after the decision for war had been made, on their surprise attack and to try to lure me into consenting to it, that I took the initiative in adjourning the meeting, quitting my seat on the plea of a previous engagement.

As I arose to go, Vice-Chief Itō came to my place and pleaded with me to indulge the wish of the Navy, and asked me whether at least the notification of termination of negotiations, if one was essential, could not be served in Tokyo, on the American Ambassador, rather than in Washington. Feeling a certain insecurity over the plan, I rejected it, and at that we separated. I judged, however, that the Navy recognized that it would have to agree to the service of some form of notification, whether in Tokyo or in Washington.

At the beginning of the following meeting of the Liaison Conference, Admiral Itō spontaneously stated that the Navy had no objection to delivery in Washington of notification of termination of the negotiations. It should be served, he said, at 12:30 P.M., 7 December, Washington time. All the other participants in the meeting approved the proposal. When I demanded of Itō, "Will there be a proper interval between notification and attack?", he assured me that there would be; and I accordingly assented to his request, and it was so decided. I considered that I had succeeded through this controversy in confining the Navy's demand within the ultimate limits of legitimacy as recognized by international law.

The notification to the United States was submitted to the Liaison Conference for the first time on 4 December. It had been drawn—as was testified by Bureau Director Yamamoto, who was the draftsman—on the basis of the discussions of the Liaison Conference, and amended in accordance with the views of the

199

Army and Navy officials concerned. When it was brought before the Liaison Conference, copies were submitted to all participants, and it was approved by the conference.

This notification, after setting forth the views of the Japanese government on the maintenance of peace, summarized the negotiations of the past months. The United States' assertions were adverted to, and it was pointed out that the final American note, constituting a threat to the existence of Japan and flouting her prestige as a Great Power, was unacceptable to her. It was noted that Great Britain, Australia and the Netherlands stood in the same case as the United States, and were at one with it in ignoring Japan's position. The hope "to preserve and promote the peace of the Pacific through co-operation" of Japan and the United States, therefore, was declared finally to have been lost; and it was concluded that the negotiations could now only be terminated. The document in full follows.

1. The Government of Japan, prompted by a genuine desire to come to an amicable understanding with the Government of the United States in order that the two countries by their joint efforts may secure the peace of the Pacific Area and thereby contribute toward the realization of world peace, has continued negotiations with the utmost sincerity since April last with the Government of the United States regarding the adjustment and advancement of Japanese-American relations and the stabilization of the Pacific Area.

The Japanese Government has the honor to state frankly its views concerning the claims the American Government has persistently maintained as well as the measures the United States and Great Britain have taken toward Japan during these eight months.

2. It is the immutable policy of the Japanese Government to insure the stability of East Asia and to promote world peace and thereby to enable all nations to find each its proper place in the world.

Ever since China Affair broke out owing to the failure on the part of China to comprehend Japan's true intentions, the Japanese Government has striven for the restoration of peace and it has consistently exerted its best efforts to prevent the extention [*sic*] of war-like disturbances. It was also to that end that in September last year Japan concluded the Tripartite Pact with Germany and Italy.

However, both the United States and Great Britain have resorted to every possible measure to assist the Chungking régime so as to obstruct the establishment of a general peace between Japan and China, interfering with Japan's constructive endeavours toward the stabilization of East Asia. Exerting pressure on the Netherlands East Indies, or menacing French Indo-China, they have attempted to frustrate Japan's aspiration to the ideal of common prosperity in cooperation with these regions. Furthermore, when Japan in accordance with its protocol with France took measures of joint defence of French Indo-China, both American and British Governments, wilfully misinterpreting it as a threat to their own possessions, and inducing the Netherlands Government to follow suit, they enforced the assets freezing order, thus severing economic relations with Japan. While manifesting thus an obviously hostile attitude, these countries have strengthened their military preparations perfecting an encirclement of Japan, and have brought about a situation which endangers the very existence of the Empire.

Nevertheless, to facilitate a speedy settlement, the Premier of Japan proposed, in August last, to meet the President of the United States for a discussion of important problems between the two countries covering the entire Pacific area. However, the American Government, while accepting in principle the Japanese proposal, insisted that the meeting should take place after an agreement of view had been reached on fundamental and essential questions.

3. Subsequently, on September 25th the Japanese Government submitted a proposal based on the formula proposed by the American Government, taking fully into consideration past American claims and also incorporating Japanese views. Repeated discussions proved of no avail in producing readily an agreement of view. The present cabinet, therefore, submitted a revised proposal, moderating still further the Japanese claims regarding the principal points of difficulty in the negotiation and endeavoured strenuously to reach a settlement. But the American Government, adhering steadfastly to its original assertions, failed to display in the

201

slightest degree a spirit of conciliation. The negotiation made no progress.

Therefore, the Japanese Government, with a view to doing its utmost for averting a crisis in Japanese-American relations, submitted on November 20th still another proposal in order to arrive at an equitable solution of the more essential and urgent questions which, simplifying its previous proposal, stipulated the following points:

(*1*) The Governments of Japan and the United States undertake not to dispatch armed forces into any of the regions, excepting French Indo-China, in the Southeastern Asia and the Southern Pacific area.

(*2*) Both Governments shall cooperate with the view to securing the acquisition in the Netherlands East Indies of those goods and commodities of which the two countries are in need.

(*3*) Both Governments mutually undertake to restore commercial relations to those prevailing prior to the freezing of assets.

The Government of the United States shall supply Japan the required quantity of oil.

(*4*) The Government of the United States undertakes not to resort to measures and actions prejudicial to the endeavours for the restoration of general peace between Japan and China.

(*5*) The Japanese Government undertakes to withdraw troops now stationed in French Indo-China upon either the restoration of peace between Japan and China or the establishment of an equitable peace in the Pacific Area; and it is prepared to remove the Japanese troops in the southern part of French Indo-China to the northern part upon the conclusion of the present agreement.

As regards China, the Japanese Government, while expressing its readiness to accept the offer of the President of the United States to act as "introducer" of peace between Japan and China as was previously suggested, asked for an undertaking on the part of the United States to do nothing prejudicial to the restoration of Sino-Japanese peace when the two parties have commenced direct negotiations.

The American Government not only rejected the above-mentioned new proposal, but made known its intention to continue its aid to Chiang Kai-shek; and in spite of its suggestion mentioned above, withdrew the offer of the President to act as so-called "introducer" of peace between Japan and China, pleading that time was not yet ripe for it. Finally on November 26th, in an attitude to impose upon the Japanese Government those principles it has persistently maintained, the American Government made a proposal totally ignoring Japanese claims, which is a source of profound regret to the Japanese Government.

4. From the beginning of the present negotiation the Japanese Government has always maintained an attitude of fairness and moderation, and did its best to reach a settlement, for which it made all possible concessions often in spite of great difficulties. As for the China question which constituted an important subject of the negotiation, the Japanese Government showed a most conciliatory attitude. As for the principle of non-discrimination in international commerce, advocated by the American Government, the Japanese Government expressed its desire to see the said principle applied throughout the world, and declared that along with the actual practice of this principle in the world, the Japanese Government would endeavour to apply the same in the Pacific Area including China, and made it clear that Japan had no intention of excluding from China economic activities of third powers pursued on an equitable basis. Furthermore, as regards the question of withdrawing troops from French Indo-China, the Japanese Government even volunteered, as mentioned above, to carry out an immediate evacuation of troops from Southern French Indo-China as a measure of easing the situation.

It is presumed that the spirit of conciliation exhibited to the utmost degree by the Japanese Government in all these matters is fully appreciated by the American Government.

On the other hand, the American Government, always holding fast to theories in disregard of realities, and refusing to yield an inch on its impractical principles, caused undue delay in the negotiation. It is difficult to understand this attitude of the American Government and the Japanese Government desires to call the attention of the American Government especially to the following points:

1. The American Government advocates in the name of world peace those principles favorable to it and urges upon the Japanese Government the acceptance thereof. The peace of the world may be brought about only by discovering a mutually acceptable formula through recognition of the reality of the situation and mutual appreciation

of one another's position. An attitude such as ignores realities and imposes one's selfish views upon others will scarcely serve the purpose of facilitating the consummation of negotiations.

Of the various principles put forward by the American Government as a basis of the Japanese-American Agreement, there are some which the Japanese Government is ready to accept in principle, but in view of the world's actual conditions, it seems only a utopian ideal on the part of the American Government to attempt to force their immediate adoption.

Again, the proposal to conclude a multilateral non-aggression pact between Japan, United States, Great Britain, China, the Soviet Union, the Netherlands and Thailand, which is patterned after the old concept of collective security, is far removed from the realities of East Asia.

2. The American proposal contained a stipulation which states—"Both Governments will agree that no agreement, which either has concluded with any third power or powers, shall be interpreted by it in such a way as to conflict with the fundamental purpose of this agreement, the establishment and preservation of peace throughout the Pacific area." It is presumed that the above provision has been proposed with a view to restrain Japan from fulfilling its obligations under the Tripartite Pact when the United States participates in the War in Europe, and, as such, it cannot be accepted by the Japanese Government.

The American Government, obsessed with its own views and opinions, may be said to be scheming for the extension of the war. While it seeks, on the one hand, to secure its rear by stabilizing the Pacific Area, it is engaged, on the other hand, in aiding Great Britain and preparing to attack, in the name of self-defense, Germany and Italy, two Powers that are striving to establish a new order in Europe. Such a policy is totally at variance with the many principles upon which the American Government proposes to found the stability of the Pacific Area through peaceful means.

3. Whereas the American Government, under the principles it rigidly upholds, objects to settle international issues through military pressure, it is exercising in conjunction with Great Britain and other nations

pressure by economic power. Recourse to such pressure as a means of dealing with international relations should be condemned as it is at times more inhumane than military pressure.

4. It is impossible not to reach the conclusion that the American Government desires to maintain and strengthen, in coalition with Great Britain and other Powers, its dominant position it has hitherto occupied not only in China but in other areas of East Asia. It is a fact of history that the countries of East Asia for the past hundred years or more have been compelled to observe the *status quo* under the Anglo-American policy of imperialistic exploitation and to sacrifice themselves to the prosperity of the two nations. The Japanese Government cannot tolerate the perpetuation of such a situation since it directly runs counter to Japan's fundamental policy to enable all nations to enjoy each its proper place in the world.

The stipulation proposed by the American Government relative to French Indo-China is a good exemplification of the above-mentioned American policy. Thus [that] the six countries,—Japan, the United States, Great Britain, the Netherlands, China and Thailand,—excepting France, should undertake among themselves to respect the territorial integrity and sovereignty of French Indo-China and equality of treatment in trade and commerce would be tantamount to placing that territory under the joint guarantee of the Governments of those six countries. Apart from the fact that such a proposal totally ignores the position of France, it is unacceptable to the Japanese Government in that such an arrangement cannot but be considered as an extension to French Indo-China of a system similar to the Nine Power Treaty structure which is the chief factor responsible for the present predicament of East Asia.

5. All the items demanded of Japan by the American Government regarding China such as wholesale evacuation of troops or unconditional application of the principle of non-discrimination in international commerce ignored the actual conditions of China, and are calculated to destroy Japan's position as the stabilizing factor of East Asia. The attitude of the American Government in demanding Japan not to support militarily, politically or economically any régime other than the régime at Chungking, disregarding thereby the existence of

the Nanking Government, shatters the very basis of the present negotiation. This demand of the American Government falling, as it does, in line with its above-mentioned refusal to cease from aiding the Chungking régime, demonstrates clearly the intention of the American Government to obstruct the restoration of normal relations between Japan and China and the return of peace to East Asia.

5. In brief, the American proposal contains certain acceptable items such as those concerning commerce, including the conclusion of a trade agreement, mutual removal of the freezing restrictions, and stabilization of yen and dollar exchange, or the abolition of extraterritorial rights in China. On the other hand, however, the proposal in question ignores Japan's sacrifices in the four years of the China Affair, menaces the Empire's existence itself and disparages its honour and prestige. Therefore, viewed in its entirety, the Japanese Government regrets that it cannot accept the proposal as a basis of negotiation.

6. The Japanese Government, in its desire for an early conclusion of the negotiation, proposed simultaneously with the conclusion of the Japanese-American negotiation, agreements to be signed with Great Britain and other interested countries. The proposal was accepted by the American Government. However, since the American Government has made the proposal of November 26th as a result of frequent consultation with Great Britain, Australia, the Netherlands and Chungking, and presumably by catering to the wishes of the Chungking régime in the questions of China, it must be concluded that all these countries are at one with the United States in ignoring Japan's position.

7. Obviously it is the intention of the American Government to conspire with Great Britain and other countries to obstruct Japan's efforts toward the establishment of peace through the creation of a new order in East Asia, and especially to preserve Anglo-American rights and interests by keeping Japan and China at war. This intention has been revealed clearly during the course of the present negotiation. Thus, the earnest hope of the Japanese Government to adjust Japanese-American relations and to preserve and promote the peace of the Pacific through cooperation with the American Government has finally been lost.

The Japanese Government regrets to have to notify hereby the American Government that in view of the attitude of the American Government it cannot but consider that it is impossible to reach an agreement through further negotiations.

It will be evident that this notification is in form different from a declaration of war—it became in form a notice merely of termination of negotiations, as contrasted with the declaration of war which I had originally suggested, but in conformity with the decision of the Liaison Conference. That it was, at all events, tantamount in the circumstances to a declaration of war is sufficiently betokened by the fact that the President of the United States upon first reading it (even lacking the last part) declared, "This means war!" [2] and that General Marshall, interpreting it as an announcement of the taking of hostile action by Japan, immediately issued war warnings to American outposts in the Pacific.[3]

The question of notification of declaration of war, which has been so much mooted in recent years, arises from the Third Hague Convention, of 1907.[4] But at the Hague Conference at which the convention was adopted, General Porter, the American delegate, declared that it was the interpretation of his government that the provision of the convention should not apply in cases of war of self-defense—from which view the delegates of the other nations participating voiced no dissent. If Japan believed the war to be one of self-defense, therefore, she needed not, in accordance with the assertion of the American delegate, give any notification.

Examples abound moreover, to show that nations have not in

[2] Testimony of Commander Lester R. Schulz, *Pearl Harbor Attack,* Part 10, pp. 4,659–62. T. S.

[3] Testimony of General of the Army George C. Marshall, *Pearl Harbor Attack,* Part 3, pp. 1,108–12. T. S.

[4] The pertinent language of the convention is: "It is recognized that hostilities should not be commenced between the parties without prior notification."

practice observed the suggestion of the convention [5]—in the most recent instance, the French note to Germany upon going to war in 1939 stated merely that France would carry out her obligations to Poland, and was not in terms a notification of commencement of hostilities. The Japanese memorandum not only conformed to the precedents of notification of declaration of war, but it left no slightest doubt in high quarters of the adversary nation that it meant war. It being clear from the data of American origin which I have referred to in the preceding chapter that the United States schemed to make Japan fire the first shot, her conduct can be characterized only as provocation of Japan. Morally, it is hypocritical, malicious and cowardly to take the position that one is free with impunity to provoke one's adversary as far as one wishes, so long only as one refrains from striking first. Such a position is indefensible not only by Oriental morality, but as well by Western ethics, with its emphasis on motives.

I must now recount the subsequent history of the note which constituted our declaration of war. It had been decided in the Liaison Conference, as I have mentioned, to make delivery to the United States government at 12:30 P.M., 7 December, Washington time. On 5 December, however, Tanabe and Itō, the Vice-Chiefs of Staff of Army and Navy, called on me at the Foreign Ministry, and Itō told me that the high command had found it necessary to postpone presentation of the document thirty minutes beyond the time previously agreed upon, and that they wanted my consent thereto. I asked the reason for the delay, and Itō said that it was because he had miscalculated; Tanabe added that the Army also was an interested party, as its operations would commence after the Navy's had begun. I inquired further what period of time would be allowed between notification and

[5] See Summation for the Defense, IMTFE Proceedings, pp. 42,417–9. T.S.

attack; but Itō declined to answer this, on the plea of operational secrecy. I persisted, demanding assurance that even with the hour of delivery changed from twelve-thirty to one there would remain a sufficient time thereafter before the attack occurred; this assurance Itō gave. With this—being able to learn no more—I assented to his request. In leaving, Itō said, "We want you not to cable the notification to the Embassy in Washington too early." I replied that I must cable it so that it would without fail be communicated to the United States at the designated time.

The change in the time for delivery was reported to the Liaison Conference by Vice-Chief Itō, at the meeting of 6 December; nobody objecting, it was approved. At this meeting Chief of Staff Nagano suggested that our Ambassadors should be instructed to hand the note to the Secretary of State personally, in view of its extreme importance. I pointed out that, it being a matter of Sunday noon, the Secretary might have a luncheon engagement which would render it impossible for the Ambassadors to make personal delivery to him, but promised that I would instruct them to do so if possible. The Ambassadors were so instructed.

The Third Hague Convention prescribes no minimum period of time which shall elapse between prior notification and attack. Being aware that some authorities of international law had therefore held that even one minute's notice would suffice, I thought that in modern times, with our highly developed communications, one hour's allowance certainly would amply fulfill the requirement of the convention. It was therefore with satisfaction at the correctness of my reasoning that I later learned that the American authorities estimated the time required for telecommunication to their Pacific installations at thirty to forty minutes. It is worth noting that even the IMTFE chose in its verdict, despite the emphasis placed by the prosecution on the problems raised by the Third Hague Convention, not to go deeply into them, but rather conceded the defectiveness of the convention.

At the IMTFE the prosecution treated the contents, as well as the time of delivery, of our notification to the United States as crucial points in establishing guilt of "war crimes." It is my intention in this narrative to refrain so far as possible from discussion of the IMTFE proceedings, and to confine myself to chronicling the events of those days on the eve of war. I therefore merely mention, without going into detail, the fact that this position of the prosecution led more than one of the defendants concerned, who had actually participated in the Liaison Conference discussions of the subject, to undertake to improve his situation by asserting that he had not attended those meetings, that he had not seen the documents, or that otherwise he had had nothing to do with these matters. Some unpleasant occurrences ensued in the course of the trial; but I leave these controversies with the precise factual analysis and conclusive refutation of my adversaries contained in the final summation by my defense counsel.

Another unpleasant incident, however, I cannot escape considering—the delay in delivery of our final note. The time of presentation having been decided at the Liaison Conference, I instructed the bureau director in charge, and the Chief of the Cable Section, to use the utmost care to take measures such that our Ambassadors in Washington might without fail have the notification for delivery at the designated time. That those measures were in fact taken pursuant to my instructions is clear if we retrace the steps in the process. The sequence of events was as follows. The Foreign Ministry transmitted to the Embassy in the afternoon of 6 December the instruction that as soon as it should have received the long note which would follow, it should make all necessary preparations, documentary and otherwise, so that it could serve the note on the United States government at any time upon receipt of further instructions. The text of the note was divided for transmission into fourteen parts, of which all with the exception of the fourteenth, consisting of the last several lines of the note, were dispatched from the Tokyo Central Telegraph Office between 6:30 A.M. and 10:20 A.M., 6 December (this and all following times are for convenience stated as Washington time). The fourteenth part was cabled between 3:00 A.M. and 4:00 A.M. on 7 December; to insure safe receipt, it was sent by two routes. Finally, the instruction to make delivery of the note at 1:00 P.M. on the 7th was dispatched at 3:30 A.M. of that day, also by two routes. All these telegrams duly arrived at Washington and were received by the Japanese Embassy there. That there was a sufficiency of time for deciphering and typing was established by the investigation later conducted in the Foreign Ministry, and by a plenitude of evidence presented to the IMTFE.[6] Notwithstanding this, the typing was not completed until after the designated hour of delivery, by reason of the negligence of the staff of the Embassy—negligence in delaying to decipher the cables which arrived in the early hours of the 7th, and in having failed earlier to type immediately those parts of the text which had arrived during the preceding evening.

The Ambassadors made an appointment with the Secretary of State for 1:00 P.M., as directed. As it proved, however, by the time the note was finally typed and they arrived at the State Department it was after two o'clock, and they met with Secretary Hull only at 2:20 P.M., which was an hour after the attack on Pearl Harbor. The culpability of the Embassy staff for this result is not open to doubt. In accordance with our training of many years in the Foreign Ministry, it was standing procedure that in

[6] See Summation for the Defense, IMTFE Proceedings, pp. 43,711-8.

a period of such emergency a few of the staff remained on duty throughout the night, and all telegrams were immediately deciphered and submitted to the chief of the mission, even in the dead of night. Meanwhile—while our Embassy was taking its responsibilities thus lightly—each part of the text of our final note was being intercepted, deciphered and delivered to the American military authorities, the Secretary of State and even the President. The President had already, upon reading as far as the thirteenth part, declared that "This means war!"; did not the Japanese Ambassadors read during the 6th the major part of the note, which is known to have been deciphered in their Embassy by the late evening of that day? Or can they have failed to realize its gravity, what it imported, even after reading it?

The United States wasted no time in utilizing for its propaganda the fact of the delay in delivery of our note. The President, addressing Congress on 8 December, announced that the United States had been attacked by the Japanese Army and Navy, an attack sudden and carefully planned, and launched when negotiations, entered into with Japan at her solicitation, aimed at the maintenance of peace in the Pacific, were still continuing. Only an hour thereafter, he stated, did the Japanese Ambassadors hand to the Secretary of State the Japanese reply to a recent message of the United States—and, he said, that reply contained no threat nor hint of belligerent act. The President in his speech naturally condemned also the content of the Japanese note to the United States; his condemnation, however, was in the same sense as his characterization of Japan's commencing hostilities as unexpected—when he had induced Japan to fire the first shot, and had anticipated, by his knowledge of the contents of our intercepted telegrams, all that was to come. Nevertheless, it was of course true that the negotiations had not been formally terminated when the hostilities commenced, and it was not to be wondered at that the President made the most of the turn of events, which must have been far more advantageous than had been looked for. It is most unfortunate that Japan's cause should have been prejudiced by the contretemps of this delay in delivery of our note.

Learning from American radio broadcasts immediately after the beginning of the war that it was being extensively publicized by the United States that Japan had attacked her while negotiations were still pending, I told Tōjō about it. Tōjō was much astonished, and said, "I wonder if the United States didn't purposely delay transmission of our telegram?" I answered that I had no idea what might have caused such an occurrence, and that to investigate it we would have to await the return of Ambassador Nomura and his staff. I reported the American propaganda also to the Emperor, telling him that it would be necessary to prosecute an inquiry; and I instructed the Vice-Minister and the Chief of the Cable Section to do so. When Councilor Iguchi arrived home in August 1942, immediately before the return of Ambassador Nomura, bringing with him the text of the report which the Ambassador was to make to the Emperor, I asked him the reason for the delay in service of the note. Iguchi evaded my question, saying that he had not been in charge, and did not know the facts. I had intended to make direct inquiry of the Ambassador, but I resigned from the Ministership soon thereafter without having had an opportunity to talk with him, other than casually at my garden party welcoming home those repatriated on the exchange ship. I had, however, occasion to learn the circumstances from Kurusu later.

As I have said, I had been giving to the German Ambassador no substantial information concerning the Japanese-American negotiations, feeling that to do so would militate against their success. With receipt of the Hull Note, however, there remained no prospect that the negotiations could succeed. On 30 November, therefore, after having obtained concurrence of the Liaison Conference, for the first time I instructed the Japanese Ambassadors in Berlin and Rome that they should give the respective governments to which they were accredited a general outline of the negotiations. They were to inform those governments that the United States and Great Britain had adopted a challenging attitude and had been reinforcing their forces in the Far East, and that if a war broke out, Japan expected Germany and Italy to join in it immediately, and considered it appropriate that the three countries enter into an agreement not to make peace separately. The result was the No-Separate-Peace Treaty, signed on 11 December.

A word concerning Thailand. When war became inescapable, I had instructed Ambassador Tsubogami there to request of the Thai government facilities for the passage of Japanese troops, and the taking of measures to prevent any clash of Japanese and Thai forces. The Ambassador communicated this request to Premier Phibun in the early morning of the 8th, and the agreement for transit of Thai territory by the Japanese forces was signed at 10:30 A.M. The Japanese-Thai Alliance was concluded on the 11th.

Although the Imperial Conference decision was to declare war upon the Netherlands also, it was agreed subsequently at the Liaison Conference not to do so, it not being necessary—acquisition of the Dutch East Indies intact, moreover, being desirable. However, war was promptly declared on us by the Netherlands, on the 8th.

I may explain one further point in connection with the declaration of war—the relation to England. It has, I believe, been made abundantly clear that Great Britain and the United States were united in the relation of allies. Not only were they allies; Prime Minister Churchill had announced that Britain would declare war on Japan "within the hour" if the United States became engaged in hostilities with her. In connection with the procedure for opening hostilities, I had fought in the Liaison Conference against the high command until they had capitulated to the extent of conceding the necessity of serving a notification of termination of the negotiations. Britain, however, was not formally a party to the diplomatic conversations, and it would therefore not have been appropriate to notify her directly of their termination. On the other hand, we having repeatedly pointed out to the United States that Britain was considered by us a *de facto* participant in the negotiations, the United States was in a position to inform her immediately they were broken off. In such circumstances, it was not necessary legally—in view of the international precedents— for Japan to declare war on Great Britain.

I had interviews with the American and British Ambassadors in the morning of the 8th. The purpose of these meetings was not to serve the declaration of war upon them—it was served formally in Washington, and copies were merely handed to the Ambassadors in Tokyo, as I told them, for their information. The state of war between Japan and the two countries was to have arisen at 3:00 A.M., 8 December, Tokyo time, with the notification in Washington; my intention was to see Grew and Craigie to express personally my appreciation for their past efforts and to present them copies of our final note to clarify Japan's position, and I had instructed my secretary to arrange the interviews for the early hours of the 8th. (I had also to see the American Ambassador in connection with the President's telegram to the Emperor, which

215

I shall come to presently.) The Ambassadors, however, called on me rather late, because the Metropolitan Police Board had already cut off their telephones by the time my secretary tried to call them.

Meanwhile, my subordinates reported to me before the arrival of the Ambassadors that there had been a radio broadcast telling of the commencement of war against the United States and Britain and Japan's attack on Hawaii, and I naturally supposed the Ambassadors to know of this broadcast when they called on me. Thinking it, then, unnecessary that I mention painful subjects, I greeted them on the basis of taking the commencement of the war as an accepted fact. Incidentally, the prosecution at the IMTFE made these interviews a ground of accusation against me; my friendly sentiments toward the Ambassadors having turned out to be a cause of misunderstanding, I now think that I should rather not have seen them at all.

My interviews with the Ambassadors having been delayed, I was unable to attend the Cabinet meeting in the early morning of the 8th, and arrived only belatedly at the meeting of the Examination Committee of the Privy Council,[7] which opened at 7:30 A.M. I understood that few questions were put at this meeting; I had, of course, frequently reported to the Privy Council on the development of the Japanese-American negotiations. The committee reported in favor of the proposal to declare war on the United States and Britain, its recommendation later being unanimously approved at the formal meeting of the Privy Council. The Imperial Rescript proclaiming the war was promulgated at 11:40 A.M., 8 December.

---

[7] In the Privy Council, as the "supreme advisory body to the Emperor," was vested power to pass upon treaties, amendments to the Constitution, and other matters of fundamental importance to the state, as well as upon questions affecting the Imperial Household.

A remaining point to be spoken of is the telegram addressed by President Roosevelt to the Emperor. This message attracted much attention when the prosecution at the IMTFE pressed it into service for making great propaganda of President Roosevelt's earnestness for peace, and played it up as having a high significance. Even recently, there are still some who argue that the war might have been averted if this telegram had arrived a little earlier—and usually they claim the credit as begetter of it. In view of these circumstances, a detailed explanation is in order, to clear away any misapprehensions.

I saw this telegram for the first time at 12:30 A.M. on 8 December, when Ambassador Grew called upon me with a copy of it. Before I speak of the treatment of it, I should like to deal with some of the circumstances surrounding its dispatch. It was a long message; recalling the ancient friendship between Japan and America, and America's earnestness in the preceding several months of the Japanese-American negotiations, it referred to recent heavy reinforcement of Japanese military and naval forces in southern French Indochina, and offered the undertaking that if Japan would withdraw her forces from Indochina not only would the United States not invade the area, but it would be possible to obtain similar assurances from the governments of the Netherlands East Indies, Malaya, Thailand and China as well. This suggestion of withdrawal from Indochina—the only concrete subject touched upon in the President's message—was, as has been seen, not a new one; at the time of Japan's move into Indochina, in July, Roosevelt had made the proposal of neutralization of the area, in response to which the Japanese government had on 5 August made a detailed counterproposal. The President's telegram was thus not novel in content.

As to the idea itself of a personal message from the President to the Emperor, I have already mentioned that this, too, had been proposed, on 26 November, by Ambassadors Nomura and Kurusu. Their plan had been rejected after consultation among those concerned in Tokyo, and they themselves had seemingly abandoned the idea, as they made no subsequent reference to it. Ambassador Kurusu, in his report rendered after his return, mentioned that there had been two groups—one around Senator Thomas, another in religious circles around a Father Jones—working to interest the President in plans of this nature, but that of course the Embassy had no way of knowing the actual facts concerning the decision to send the telegram.

Later, during the Congressional investigation of Pearl Harbor, those facts were to an extent made known. At another meeting of the "War Cabinet," on 28 November, it appeared, Secretary Stimson had first proposed that the United States should forthwith attack Japan without further notice, she having defied the warning of 17 August. Stimson's suggestion of course attracted no support from the meeting, the viewpoint being that it was more advantageous to make Japan commit the first overt act. The President then proposed a plan of addressing a message of monition to the Emperor; this, however, Stimson opposed, saying that the President should rather address himself to the Congress and the nation, making known to them the danger and what would be done to meet it if it materialized. In the end, the President requested Hull, Stimson and Knox to draft these documents.[8] The message to Congress, however, was not sent; and as to a personal communication to the Emperor, Secretary Hull told the President on the 29th that such a telegram would serve little purpose except for the record, and might even—as he and Stimson had argued the preceding day—"cause complications." The view of these

[8] See Stimson's Diary, *Pearl Harbor Attack*, Part 11, pp. 5,435-6. T. S.

high officials that the message to the Emperor would be futile was confirmed by the testimony at the IMTFE of Mr. Ballantine of the State Department, to the effect that the Department entertained slight expectations of it.[9] In this atmosphere, and despite the opposition of the Secretaries of State and War, the President ordered his message transmitted to the Emperor by the State Department, which was done on 6 December, at 6:00 P.M., Washington time.

The fact of the dispatch of this telegram, then, became known to me on the 7th when I received from Ambassador Nomura the report that the American press was carrying the news, released by the State Department, that a Presidential communication had been sent. Since such a telegram, being a personal message, would require most careful treatment, I ordered my private secretary, in spite of its being Sunday, to maintain close contact with the Ministry of the Imperial Household, to which it was to be supposed that the telegram would be addressed. When nothing had been received by evening at either the Foreign Ministry or the Imperial Household Ministry, we surmised that perhaps the plan had been dropped in Washington.

At ten-fifteen that night, however, my secretary had a telephone call from the American Embassy saying that the Ambassador had received an urgent telegram which was then being deciphered, and wished to see me as soon as he could be ready with the document. I answered that I would be awaiting him. Finally, at about 12:30 A.M. on the 8th, Ambassador Grew called on me at my Official Residence. He told me that he had received a personal telegram from the President to the Emperor, and asked me to arrange an Imperial audience. I answered that, it being so late at night, preparations would have to be made for the audience,

[9] Record of Proceedings, p. 10,969. T. S.

and I asked what were the contents of his message. The Ambassador handed me a copy of it, repeated his request for an audience, and left.

Upon perusing the President's communication and finding its contents to be as I have outlined them, I considered it appropriate to report the views of the government to the Emperor with the message—this having regard to the fact that a similar proposal had been turned down in July by the Third Konoe Cabinet, and that although time was now extremely pressing, the President made no mention of the issues in the Japanese-American negotiations other than the proposed neutralization of Indochina, and offered neither any guarantee nor concessions calculated to contribute to the averting of a crisis. I first got into touch with Imperial Household Minister Matsudaira to ask about being received by the Emperor. He referred me to Lord Keeper Kido, and I then telephoned to Kido, telling him of receipt of the Presidential message and asking him to arrange an audience for me. Kido answered that Ministers of State would be received in audience at any time, even in the dead of night if there was urgent business, and promised to be at the Court by the time I should arrive there.

As soon as the translation of the telegram was ready, I went to see the Premier and reported to him the visit of Ambassador Grew, going over in detail the contents of the message. Tōjō inquired only, "Isn't there any concession from them, in addition?", and said that such a proposal could achieve nothing. He suggested that I report the matter to the Emperor; and we then discussed the reply to be sent by the Emperor to the President. Upon my saying to him jocularly, on our separating, "It's a pity to run around disturbing people in the middle of the night," he responded, "It's a good thing the telegram arrived late. If it had

come a day or two earlier we would have had more of a to-do."
Leaving the Premier, I hastened to the Palace. Kido being already
there, I told him the contents of the President's message in the
brief space of time before my audience. He said laconically,
"That's no use, is it? What's Tōjō's opinion?" "The same as
yours," I answered. At that point, the time for the audience having come, I was received by the Emperor. I read to him the full
text of the message, then made explanation of the events connected with the similar proposal advanced by the President in
July. I presented the draft of his answer to the President which,
in consultation with Tōjō, I had prepared, the Emperor gave his
approval to the answer, and I withdrew from his presence at
three-fifteen. Returning to the Official Residence, at 4:30 A.M.
I was informed by telephone from the Navy Ministry that the
Navy had successfully attacked the American fleet at Pearl
Harbor.

In my interview with the American Ambassador on the following morning, I told him of having reported to the Emperor the
Ambassador's receipt of the President's personal communication
and the contents thereof, and that the Emperor had expressed his
appreciation of the message and had instructed me to transmit
his reply. That reply, which I then delivered orally and later sent
in writing, was:

In regard to the recent inquiry of the President concerning the circumstances of the augmentation of Japanese forces in French Indochina, I
have instructed the government of Japan to reply. The withdrawal of
Japanese forces from French Indochina constituted one of the subjects
of the Japanese-American negotiations; on this also, I have directed my
government to state to the United States government its views. I therefore
hope that the President will kindly refer to this reply. The establishment
of peace throughout the Pacific, and thence throughout the world, has
been my cherished desire, for the realization of which I have to the pres-

ent caused my government to exert its best efforts. I trust that the President is fully aware of this fact.

In the course of the proceedings of the IMTFE I learned for the first time—and with great astonishment at the extremes gone to by the Army General Staff—that the delivery to the American Embassy of the President's telegram had been held up for over ten hours by the Tokyo Central Telegraph Office, at the demand of an officer of the General Staff that all foreign cables be so delayed. Apparently even military men like Tōjō were not aware at the time that the General Staff was taking such measures. As to Tōjō's remark, quoted earlier ("It's a good thing the telegram arrived late. If it had come a day or two earlier we would have had more of a to-do"), he commented to me one day after the commencement of our trial that he had meant by it that if the telegram had arrived earlier some would surely have asserted—despite ultimate failure's being evident—that further negotiations should be attempted, causing thereby unnecessary complications; he had never imagined, he said, that a solution could be reached by means of such a message. So much should have been clear to anyone; as has been seen, the President proposed only the neutralization of Indochina, with no mention of other problems in the pending negotiations, of a basis for further discussions, or of concessions to be made by the United States. The neutralization of Indochina would, certainly, have been advantageous for the United States, in removing the threat posed by the Japanese troops there; but it would in no way have altered the position for Japan, who thought that she had no alternative to making a stand for her self-defense and her existence. It was therefore with absolute correctness that the highest American officials—not to mention those of Tokyo—had judged that such a message from the President could achieve no purpose, and the dispatch of the telegram was correctly characterized by them as an action taken with the awareness that it would serve only to make a record of peaceful intention.

Before closing this chapter I must say something of my feelings in that night of the war's beginning. Retiring from my audience, deeply moved by looking upon the countenance of the Emperor and there reading his noble feeling of brotherhood with all peoples, but seeing also his unflinching attitude even when receiving me on the very brink of war, I passed solemnly, guided by a Court official, down several hundred yards of corridors, stretching serene and tranquil, of the midnight Palace. Emerging at the carriage entrance of the Sakashita Gate, I gazed up at the brightly shining stars, and felt bathed in a sacred spirit. Through the Palace plaza in utter silence, hearing no sound of the sleeping capital but only the crunching of the gravel beneath the wheels of my car, I pondered that in a few short hours would dawn one of the eventful days of the history of the world; and various thoughts moved me. Having labored with heart and soul through the preceding month and a half for the sake of mankind and my country, I felt the conviction that our course, taken only when it had become a certainty that there could be no alternative, must find approval in the ultimate judgment of Heaven.

In my public life I have experienced many memorable moments. As fields of combat by disputation, there were the violent controversy with Litvinov, from the winter of 1939 to the following spring, over renewal of the fisheries-concessions in Russian waters; heated conflicts with the militarists in the prewar days, especially that continuing from the night of 1 November 1941 into the small hours of the 2d; and my three hours' altercation with Tōjō, after the commencement of the war, at the Cabinet meeting of 1 September 1942. Among other scenes of profound interest, there come to mind my conversation with Hitler at the mountain villa at Berchtesgaden, and the toast to the New Year of 1940 which I drank in the Kremlin at the close of an all-night conference. But on two occasions—on my return home from the Imperial Palace on the verge of war, and again at the close of the Imperial Conference of 14 August at the end of the war—was I filled with the assurance that, having participated in a momentous event, I had exhausted all my powers and my abilities in the conviction that Heaven knows a heart true to country and to mankind. Even now, thinking of those times, I feel the tears come to my eyes.

THE AUTHOR AFTER RETIREMENT
AS FOREIGN MINISTER OF THE SUZUKI CABINET
SEPTEMBER 1945

Part Two

IN QUEST OF PEACE

CHRONICLE OF EVENTS LEADING TO THE
END OF THE PACIFIC WAR
[*Far Eastern events expressed in East Longitude dates*]

1943

September 3	Italy surrenders
November 23–25	Cairo Conference
November 28– *December 1*	Teheran Conference

1944

July 18	Tōjō Cabinet resigns
July 22	Koiso Cabinet formed
October 20	American forces land on Leyte

1945

January 9	American forces land on Luzon
February 5–11	Yalta Conference
February 19	American forces land on Iōjima
April 1	American forces land on Okinawa
April 5	U.S.S.R. gives notice that Neutrality Pact will not be extended beyond April 1946
	Koiso Cabinet resigns
April 7	Suzuki Cabinet formed
May 7	Germany surrenders
July 13	Japanese request for Soviet mediation made in Moscow
July 26	Potsdam Declaration promulgated
August 6	Atomic bomb dropped on Hiroshima
August 9	The U.S.S.R. attacks Japan
August 9–10	Imperial Conference approves acceptance of Potsdam Declaration
August 14	Imperial Conference approves acceptance of American reply concerning maintenance of national polity
August 15	Imperial Rescript ending the war promulgated
	Suzuki Cabinet resigns

226

CHAPTER 1

Wartime Diplomacy

THE IMPERIAL RESCRIPT proclaiming the war was promulgated at 11:40 A.M. of 8 December 1941. I was informed that attacks or landing operations of our forces had commenced prior to that hour at Pearl Harbor and the Kota Bharu area of Malaya, and thereafter at Shanghai and Hong Kong. In the afternoon of that day I received the German and Italian Ambassadors and told them of the declaration of war and of the negotiations for a no-separate-peace treaty being carried on in Berlin and Rome. I summoned the Soviet Ambassador, also, for an interview, and, explaining to him the developments which had compelled Japan to declare war against the United States and Great Britain, stated our intention of faithfully observing our obligations under the Neutrality Pact and our expectation that the U.S.S.R. would do likewise.

The Japanese people in the early days of the war were generally intoxicated with victory, and the feeling was widespread that the years of suffering could be permanently consigned to oblivion. Not a few who have now after the war turned out to be proponents of "liberalism" were in those days congratulating me in person or by letter on the war successes. I even learned that there were those (some of them connected with the Foreign

Ministry) who were trying to make trouble for me by spreading reports that I had opposed the war. When such reports came to my ears, I pointed out that it was only natural that a Foreign Minister should endeavor to preserve peace, and it was certainly a fact that I had done my best to avert war; but that on the other hand even a Foreign Minister would stand and fight when the honor and the existence itself of his nation were threatened.

The Liaison Conference met less frequently after the commencement of the war. There was little diplomatic business of importance remaining with the conclusion, early in the war, of the No-Separate-Peace Treaty with Germany and Italy and the Treaty of Alliance with Thailand; and after the grueling efforts of the preceding weeks, I felt somewhat at loose ends. The atmosphere was such that the opinion could be heard, not only among the general public but even within the Foreign Ministry, that there was no place in wartime for diplomacy—an opinion resulting, patently, from the optimism born of victories of an unlooked-for magnitude, with a resultant feeling that an early peace would be disadvantageous for Japan rather than the contrary. Observing the popularity of this viewpoint, I took the occasion of the ceremonies on New Year's Day of 1942 to speak to the staff of the Foreign Ministry in the vein above indicated, concerning the relation of the Foreign Minister's position and war, and the importance of wartime diplomacy. It was, I admonished them, the duty of the Ministry to be making preparations now for terminating the war, lest the opportunity when it came should not be taken advantage of.

On the afternoon of the same 1 January, General Mutō, Director of the Military Affairs Bureau, called on me for New Year's greeting. After discussing the developments of the war in general, he said to me that it was his hope that I would work for a prompt

ending of the war, as the sooner it ended the more advantageous
for Japan; and, he added, for that purpose it was necessary to
replace Tōjō as Premier. When he left me, he announced that he
was going to visit Admiral Okada [1] to tell him the same things.
(Not long after, it was rumored that, Tōjō having heard of the
views that Mutō was expressing, he was to be transferred from
the ministry to a post in the South—which in fact occurred.)
Mutō himself, it is true, had responsibility for the militarists'
activities; but he was one of those among them possessed of relatively good political sense.

Meanwhile, the triumphant advance of our armies continued.
On 11 January our troops landed at Tarakan in the Netherlands
East Indies, Singapore fell on 15 February, the oil fields of
Sumatra and Borneo were seized. Not only the soldiers at the
front, but all classes in Japan, were filled with the exhilaration of
victory, felt that Japan was invincible. There was no thought now
but of destruction of the enemy, and it was asserted ever more
truculently that no diplomacy was wanted during the war. World
history affords many instances of the ultimate betrayal, by the
enhanced influence of military men in wartime, of a nation's
cause; this was true in an exaggerated degree in Japan, where
the high command had already its paramountcy. At the time of
the Russo-Japanese War of 1904–05, Japan found among her
military leaders such men of insight as Generals Ōyama and
Kodama and Admirals Yamamoto and Tōgō,[2] who did not over-

---

[1] Admiral Okada Keisuke (1868–1952) had during his active service been Commander in Chief of the Combined Fleet and Navy Minister. After his retirement,
he became Premier in 1934, his Cabinet falling as a result of the terrorist plot of
26 February 1936, in which he was to have been the chief victim but by good
fortune escaped injury. His moderate attitude had been demonstrated particularly
by his support of the London Naval Limitation Treaty of 1930.

[2] In the Russo-Japanese War, Field Marshal Prince Ōyama Iwao was concurrently
Chief of the Army General Staff and Commander in Chief of Expeditionary
Forces in Manchuria; General Baron Kodama Gentarō was Chief of Staff in

look preparing for an early end to the conflict. As such states-manship could hardly be looked for in the military community of my time, I suggested to the Imperial Household Minister and others that Court circles should be on guard against the development in our wartime Japan of a state of affairs which should threaten danger to the nation.

The intoxication with victory was no less apparent in the Diet, as an incident will illustrate. In February 1942, at a meeting of the Budget Committee of the House of Representatives, Representative Uehara demanded a statement of the attitude of the Foreign Minister toward the peace. I replied that it was equally natural and necessary to stop war and re-establish peace, and that I was consequently fully prepared and resolved to that end. This drew protests from members that, the purpose of war being to destroy the enemy, the Foreign Minister should not be heard to say that he was preparing for peace, and they demanded that I retract my statement. I refused, on the ground that no retraction was called for, what I had said being but axiomatic. Nevertheless, even within the Cabinet there was opinion that the Representatives were right—Japan might well, if she kept on at the present pace, occupy Washington, they said—and the Premier suggested that a compromise be somehow found. It was finally decided to strike my statement from the record of the Diet proceedings—a practice not infrequently resorted to in those days.

Immediately after the fall of Singapore a rumor gained currency that Great Britain had made an offer of peace. The same story was spread again in some quarters at the end of the war, and since there are apparently those who credit it still, I want to

---

Manchuria. Admiral Count Yamamoto Gombei was Minister of Navy during the war, and later twice Premier. Tōgō Heihachirō (no relation of the author), Admiral of the Fleet and Marquis, victor of the great naval battle of Tsushima Strait, was the war hero par excellence.

leave no room for doubt that the Japanese government received no such offer at that time. A negative can be proved only circumstantially, but the utter implausibility of this rumor is, I think, rendered sufficiently clear by the fact alone of the British government's having throughout the Pacific War fallen in completely with the designs of the United States—in view of this it is impossible to believe that she should have tried to make a separate peace with Japan. The following episode, moreover, will, I believe, serve to evidence the absence of any ground for the rumored British peace offer. When Ambassador Craigie was leaving for home, some time after the commencement of the war, I sent my private secretary to convey to him my regret that the Japanese-American negotiations had ended in failure and the war had ensued. I sent him also the message—asking that, if he thought appropriate, he communicate it to the British government—that now that war had come it was to the advantage of both parties to end it whenever either side should have lost the hope of victory. It was reported to me that the Ambassador answered that he could not convey my suggestion to his government at the moment, when the war was going unfavorably for Great Britain, but that he was appreciative of the intention of the Japanese Foreign Minister. I thought at the time that the Ambassador's words were quite a natural expression of the indomitableness of the Englishman.

The successes in the initial stage of the war were, as I have indicated, spectacular. The review at the Liaison Conference in February 1942 showed that in the diplomatic field all had proceeded smoothly and according to plan—the No-Separate-Peace Treaty had been concluded with Germany and Italy and the Treaty of Alliance with Thailand, and the U.S.S.R. had given assurance that it would continue neutral relations. In the military conference, Navy Vice-Chief of Staff Ōnishi [6] burst into the room, and with great emotion appealed to the two Chiefs of Staff, saying that whether the American reply was satisfactory was a minor point; the fundamental issue was that the armed services had lost the confidence of the Emperor, their Commander in Chief. Therefore, "it is necessary to submit to the Emperor a plan to gain the victory, and to ask his reconsideration"; and he cried that we would not be defeated if we resolutely risked the lives of twenty million Japanese as a "special-attack corps." As not even the chiefs of staff would comment on this, Ōnishi, turning to me, demanded, "What is the Foreign Minister's opinion?" I replied, "If only we had any real hope of victory, no one would for a moment think of accepting the Potsdam Declaration; but winning one battle will not win the war for us."

I took my leave of them, and dropping in at the Foreign Ministry on the way back went through the telegrams from the overseas offices and the records of foreign broadcasts, which bore in upon me the growing gravity of our peril. I pondered, in the car returning home, that even if we offered the sacrifice of twenty million Japanese lives, they would but fall easy prey to machines and gunfire. We could bear anything, if it promised a return; the arrows and bamboo spears of which the military men were prating promised none. The soldiers' ignorance of the nature of modern warfare was beyond my understanding. In any event, no further delay could be tolerated, and it was, I thought, absolutely necessary that a final decision be reached on the morrow, as planned by the Premier.

---

[6] Vice-Admiral Ōnishi Takijirō (1891–1945), Commander of the 1st Air Fleet in the Philippines, 1944–45, and Vice-Chief of the Naval General Staff from May 1945, was reputed the originator of the idea of "special-attack corps" of suicide planes. At Japan's surrender Ōnishi, himself a pilot, flew out to sea in a fighter plane and disappeared.

ices not only had not returned the requisitioned vessels, but on the contrary were clamoring for more. The civilian participants in the Liaison Conference, including myself, insisted that the original understanding should be carried out, as otherwise food and clothing supply would fall short, and production even of military necessities would eventually be jeopardized. In the face of the strong military persistence in their demands, however, it was finally decided to have the subject studied by the Ministry of Transportation jointly with the authorities of the Army and Navy, and it thus left our hands.

Meanwhile, the question of prisoners of war and alien residents came to the fore. The subject had first arisen when, shortly after the beginning of the war, the American and British governments—through Switzerland and Argentina, the Protecting Powers for their interests respectively—made inquiries of the Japanese government whether Japan would observe the Convention Relative to the Treatment of Prisoners of War concluded at Geneva in July 1929. Japan had signed the convention, but had not ratified it. When the inquiries came to me, I knew that while there had been some rumors of indiscipline of Japanese troops in the Siberian Expedition, prior to that—during both the Russo-Japanese War and the Ts'ingtao campaign of 1914—the Japanese forces had won the admiration of the world for their humanitarian treatment of prisoners of war. If for that reason alone, Japan must not during this war be guilty of conduct for which she would incur the world's censure; but in addition, there were several hundred thousands of Japanese residing in enemy territories, and it could be expected that if Japan should be delinquent in discharge of her duty to enemy nationals under her control, those Japanese abroad would suffer accordingly. It was with these considerations in mind that I instructed Director Matsumoto of the Treaty Bureau to arrange with the military authorities for application of the Geneva Convention with necessary modifications—*mutatis mutandis*—with a view to insuring fair treatment of prisoners of war and interned aliens held by us.

In response to my request, the Army and Navy Vice-Ministers advised the Foreign Vice-Minister that the Army and the Navy had no objection to *mutatis mutandis* application of the prisoner-of-war convention, nor to giving due consideration to national customs of prisoners in connection with the supply of food and clothing to them. The United States and Great Britain were duly notified of this. We further notified them, after consultation with the military officials, that the principles of the convention would so far as possible be applied *mutatis mutandis* to the treatment of interned noncombatants as well. It was reported to me at the time by the section chief in charge that neither Army nor Navy Ministry offered the slightest objection to humanitarian treatment.

Soon, however, I received from the United States an inquiry and protest concerning the treatment of its nationals, prisoners of war and internees, in Guam. I passed this on without delay to the Navy; a protest from Great Britain alleging atrocities in Hong Kong was similarly transferred to the Army. Then I learned that in Parliament Foreign Secretary Eden had taken occasion to censure Japan's treatment of prisoners of war. I went directly to Premier Tōjō and reported the fact to him, requesting that stricter supervision be exercised over the treatment of prisoners. Tōjō made no difficulty about assenting to my request, and I learned shortly thereafter that Secretary Eden had stated that conditions in Hong Kong had improved considerably. Nevertheless, as I regarded the treatment of prisoners of war and internees as an important problem of humanitarianism, deserving of utmost care, I instructed Vice-Minister Nishi to give personal attention to it, and simultaneously asked Adviser Satō to keep in close touch with the representatives of the Powers protecting enemy interests. Despite the precautions taken by me, there had been several protests, before I left office in September, alleging maltreatment of prisoners of war in various areas. This rather astonished me, in view of the attitude of the Army as the Foreign Ministry knew it from our contact with them, and in transferring the protests to the military authorities as they were received I urged them to make prompt investigation and replies. The question of the visiting of prisoner-of-war camps by the International Red Cross representatives also coming up during this time, I instructed my subordinates concerned to negotiate with the War Ministry to the end of being able to offer all possible conveniences for visits. It was reported to me at the time that the Red Cross representatives were satisfied with the way Japan was treating prisoners of war under her control. In any event, I was not able to think that there had been any serious cases of atrocities committed up to September, while I remained in office, and all protests which did come to my attention were promptly acted on by the Foreign Ministry. The ministry, of course, knew nothing of such incidents as the Bataan "Death March," the killing of survivors of torpedoed vessels by submarine crews or the working of prisoners on construction of the Burma Railway; neither was any protest referring to them received while I was in office. I naturally could not imagine the occurrence of such atrocities.

The bombing of Tokyo by the Doolittle planes on 18 April 1942 produced a serious shock in Japan, as it proved the falsity of the military assurances of the inviolability of the Imperial capital. It came to my knowledge that two of Doolittle's planes had landed in China, and that their crews had been captured and the high command wanted to impose heavy penalties on them. On learning this, I pointed out to Army Chief of Staff Sugiyama that it was necessary in any event that regard be had to the requirements of international law—aside from which, punishment would serve only to enhance, rather than to diminish, the determination and the fighting spirit of the Americans. Subsequently, the Foreign Ministry section in charge was informed by the Army that it would punish the crews on its sole responsibility, but wished to have the opinion of the Ministry concerning public disclosure of the disposition of the case. I instructed my subordinates to reply in the sense in which I had spoken to Chief of Staff Sugiyama. The punishment of the crews seems not to have been carried out during my continuance in office.

At the outbreak of the war the governments of Spain and Switzerland had undertaken protection of Japanese interests and nationals in the United States and Great Britain respectively. The latter nations, however, soon proposed repatriation, on a reciprocal basis, of their diplomatic and consular personnel and as many as possible of their resident nationals, and I heartily agreed to the proposal. However, there was a large number of Japanese resident in the United States, and not only would it have been impossible to repatriate all of them, but many had no desire to return to Japan. The arrangement was therefore made that not only American and British nationals, but also other Allied nationals residing in Japan—as well as in Manchoukuo, China, French Indochina and Thailand—would be returned while a roughly equivalent number of Japanese was sent home. The execution of the project was placed under the charge of Ōta Saburō, Chief of the Third Section of the European-Asiatic Bureau. It was a complex and difficult task; the high command, especially the Navy, had no enthusiasm for the proposed exchange, as the ships engaged in carrying it out would pass through areas of operations, and also the military services did not want to divert vessels for the purpose, the demand for shipping being heavy at the time. I had to negotiate frequently with the Chief and Vice-Chief of the Naval General Staff to obtain allocation of the ships. The Emperor was much concerned over this exchange, and repeatedly instructed me to expedite it. At last, the Navy having been induced to withdraw its final request —to delay the exchange as long as possible—it was decided that we would return by the *Asama-maru* and the *Conte Verde* the first group, and by the *Tatsuta-maru* and the *Kamakura-maru* the second, between 25 June and 10 August 1942. The vessels were to sail to Lourenço Marques in Portuguese East Africa, the point of transshipment, with repatriates embarked at Yokohama and Kōbe, Shanghai, Hong Kong, Saïgon and Singapore.

There were among the enemy nationals involved some against whom criminal charges had been lodged and whose cases were still pending, and it was not simple to procure their release for repatriation; as the judicial authorities concerned were not willing to free them, I had to raise the question with the Minister of Justice direct to get them released. Still another complication was introduced by the United States' threatening at the last minute to retain two Japanese nationals scheduled for return. After all this trouble, however, I was able to receive at my Official Residence, in August immediately before my resignation, the first group of repatriates, including Ambassador Nomura. I had no opportunity to greet the second party. The arrangement had been to continue the exchanges, but, I understand, only one more was carried out after my leaving office, when the *Teia-maru* took a group to Goa in Portuguese India in September 1943.

I repeatedly instructed the Ministry officials in charge to see that enemy aliens, and especially diplomatic personnel, were accorded proper amenities, and to maintain liaison with the military, Home Ministry and other organs concerned with the view to assuring that this would be done. When I did learn at first of some complaints of the protection, the rationing or other treatment of the American and British diplomatic missions, I lost no time in ordering necessary remedial action taken. Thus during my first Foreign Ministership I had hardly any further reports of complaints from any quarter.

From the beginning of the war, the government of Manchoukuo had expressed the desire to participate. I endeavored to persuade it to give up the idea. Not only was it preferable that it stand out to avoid complicating its relations with its neighbors, the U.S.S.R. and China, but I thought it proper for the cause of humanity and of prompt ending of the war to minimize the number of nations involved. The external affairs of Manchoukuo, however, had long been managed in Tokyo by the Manchuria Affairs Bureau, an organ under the jurisdiction of the War Minister with which I had nothing to do, and I could not prevent Manchoukuo from becoming a belligerent. The only foreign affairs of Manchoukuo which were left to the Japanese Foreign Ministry were negotiations with the U.S.S.R.; in this field, May 1942 saw the completion at last of the demarcation (under Japanese and Soviet auspices) of the disputed Manchoukuo-Mongolia boundaries by an exchange of notes between those countries. This was a solution the aftermath of the Nomonhan Incident, which as Ambassador to the U.S.S.R. I had settled in 1939. There was no other diplomatic business worthy of mention in connection with Manchoukuo, its relations with the U.S.S.R. after the outbreak of the war remaining tranquil.

Between Japan and Germany, also, after conclusion of the

No-Separate-Peace Treaty there were no major items of diplomacy, and general relations were satisfactory. There was a small problem—some of those who had surrendered themselves to the optimistic delusion that Japan's initial victories assured her of ultimate triumph seemed to look upon Germany as a potential rival, and were reluctant to supply her with the tin and quinine from the South Seas, tungsten from China, and other materials desired by her. I instructed our representatives in Nanking and elsewhere that they should see to it that Japan did not create friction with her current ally for the sake of this groundless optimism.

A far more serious question, one which occupied a large part of my thoughts during this time in office, was that of the U.S.S.R. and its relation to the war. The United States and Great Britain had been providing to the U.S.S.R. large-scale aid, and in May 1942 a treaty of alliance was concluded with her by Britain to strengthen the relationship of mutual assistance between them, entered into the year before. From the beginning I felt no small apprehension concerning Germany's military prospects, and I was never free of the fear that the war would end for her as had the war of 1914–18. In particular, I considered that the diplomatic battle in the present conflict lay in getting Russia on one's side—this battle I looked upon as destined to be the diplomatic Waterloo of the Second World War. Further, so long as Russia stood between Japan and Germany, with Germany and the U.S.S.R. at war, Japanese-German mutual assistance could be no more than nominal. To win the U.S.S.R. to Japan's side while she was at war with Germany would obviously be difficult, but to do so was essential to victory in our war. In order, moreover, to bring about an early termination of the war, it would be necessary to introduce peace from this quarter. It was for these reasons that, when the question of schemes for ending the war if it should come had been under deliberation at the Liaison Conference in the middle of November 1941, I had successfully maintained that it was Japan's task in the field of international diplomacy to endeavor to bring about peace between Germany and the U.S.S.R. When Soviet Ambassador Smetanin was leaving Tokyo for home in January 1942, I asked him to say to Foreign Commissar Molotov that the current Russo-Japanese relations in the midst of a world at war were as a beam of sunshine striking through a rainstorm, and it was my hope to see this sunlight extended over the whole world, and that if in future the Soviet government should entertain the desire for peace Japan would be ready to do all within her power by way of mediation.

But a Russian-German peace could be brought about only when German arms were in the ascendant and Russia receptive to the idea of truce, or vice versa. I therefore proposed at the Liaison Conference that we should stimulate Hitler to make peace before the summer offensive of 1942; but most of the military representatives were very sanguine of a German victory, and were even planning, against that event, an attack upon the U.S.S.R. from the east, and the Chief of the Army General Staff said that we should tender such counsel to Germany only if her summer offensive should have ended in failure. The Japanese representatives in Berlin had recommended against any efforts for Russo-German peace, and this my opponents at the Liaison Conference took advantage of to defeat my proposal.

At this stage of affairs, the Germans in July requested Japan to undertake joint operations against the U.S.S.R. The proposal was rejected by Japan, the ground assigned being that we were neither prepared for nor capable of two-front warfare, and that driving into European Russia from the east was no simple assignment. From my point of view of international politics, however, the reason for declining the German proposal lay in the consideration that Japan should work to restore peace between Germany and the U.S.S.R., as the most promising method of approach to a general peace, rather than herself joining the war against the Soviet Union. At about that time, I instructed Ambassador Satō —then evacuated, with others of the diplomatic corps, from Moscow to Kuibyshev—to visit Moscow from time to time to prepare the ground so that he could undertake mediation immediately upon receipt of instructions to that effect. Ambassador Satō replied that he was confident of being able to maintain neutral relations between Japan and the U.S.S.R., but not of bringing about mediation by us between the U.S.S.R. and Germany. I felt, however, that unless Russo-Japanese relations should without delay be adjusted, their maintenance on a footing of neutrality would itself become precarious if the fortune of war should turn against Japan. It was, accordingly, clearly necessary for Japan to do her utmost to bring about peace between Germany and Russia, Japanese-Russian relations being inseparable from German-Russian. I cabled further in this sense to Ambassador Satō, and at length he agreed with me.

The problem of peace between the Soviet Union and Germany was, as I have suggested, one of much difficulty for both sides. Its significance to the prosecution of our war was, none the less, plainly evident when it was considered that from the beginning of the Russo-German war the United States had been giving large-scale assistance to the U.S.S.R. to augment its capacity for resistance, and that the American Secretary of State and the British Foreign Minister had gone to the length of visiting Moscow to win Russia's good will. It was therefore essential that Japan prod Germany—and, so far as that was possible, try to compel her—to make peace with Russia. In July, immediately before our communicating to Germany our rejection of her request that we enter the war against the U.S.S.R., I had reported our decision to the Emperor. The Emperor than reiterated to me that he wished the war ended as soon as possible, and instructed that our rejection should be imparted to the German government not only through the Japanese Ambassador in Berlin but also via a more reliable channel. When ambassador in Berlin, I had learned from the Italian Ambassador there, Attolico, that Mussolini worried over Hitler's insouciance where Russia was concerned; and since only Mussolini, if anyone, could influence Hitler, I now thought it important that we send a special ambassador to Italy to try to obtain her co-operation in working for peace between Germany and Russia. I selected for this purpose Admiral Kobayashi Seizō, retired, and through Navy Minister Shimada I requested him in August to go to Europe. Shimada told me, however, on the morning of 1 September—the day of my resignation—that Kobayashi had declined the mission; and I thus left office before any step had been taken to realize the plan for a Russo-German peace or a general peace by that means.

The problem of China was one more complicated than those of Europe. Some years earlier there had been established the Asia Development Board, with authority over all political, economic and cultural matters relating to China, there being left to the Foreign Ministry only the field of "pure diplomacy"—queer phrase!—and the business of protection of Japanese residents in China and other consular functions. The Premier was president of the board, the local organs of which were authorized to negotiate with the Chinese regional regimes, and the Ministers of War, Navy, Foreign Affairs and Finance were vice-presidents. The influence of the Foreign Minister as vice-president of this board can be readily conceived, in the light of the fact that the board had been established precisely because, the Foreign Ministry's liberal attitude toward foreign countries being anathema to the militarists, they desired to remove China affairs from the Ministry and confide them to an organ under their control. But just as the Japanese forces stationed in China had difficulty in maintaining order and security, so did the Asia Development Board fail to function successfully. In particular, the board was much criticized for its commandeering of materials in China, and there were reports of complaints by the Chinese over the purchase of foodstuffs by the garrisons there. I pointed out to Tōjō —concurrently War Minister and president of the board—that the failure of the Army and the board to satisfy the Chinese even in such spheres would itself render it impossible for Japan to carry out successfully her general policy toward China, and that adequate budgetary provision should be made for such funds as those required for the purchase of provisions, in order to avoid creating ill will on the part of the Chinese. Tōjō told me that appropriate plans were in fact projected in Tokyo, and that the malfeasance was that of the field organs, whom he promised to instruct.

The state of the occupation in China was most unsatisfactory. I felt that the China problem, at least, should be solved, even despite the outbreak of the larger war, and I proposed to the Liaison Conference in March 1942 that we consider how to do this; now that Japan had achieved great operational successes and the Chungking regime was in difficulties, I said, it was opportune to settle the China Affair on a reasonable basis. Those supporting the permanent stationing of troops in China, or wishing continued the carrying on of profitable enterprises under military protection, opposed my suggestion on various grounds, but finally at my instance it was decided to determine on measures vis-à-vis the Chungking regime. The subject was further developed to search for means of applying increased military pressure on Chungking, or if none could be found to try to see how we could effect a compromise in the absence of them. As the conclusion, it was decided that the Army high command would study the possibilities and that the deliberations would thereafter be continued.

There was another disquieting aspect of the jubilance over our triumphs and its attendant feeling that Japan was invincible and had no cause for anxiety. This was the launching of such long-range programs as enterprise-readjustment and revision of the educational system, and the use of precious materials in the construction of plants which could come into operation only after ten years—the viewpoint being that the war against the United States would be a long one, and Japan must be incubating fighting power for twenty or thirty years hence. When the plans for revision of the educational system and for readjustment of enterprises were submitted to the Cabinet, I opposed them, saying that such undertakings should be ventured upon only after the war was over, that now we must concentrate on winning the war, as otherwise we should certainly lose it. The Premier and the other ministers, however, did not listen to me.

The Diet convened, composed of Representatives—elected at the "Recommendation Election" [3]—who did little else than cheer the victories. The Council for Establishment of Greater East Asia was formed, and, in the name of study and recommendation of projects other than those related to military and diplo-

[3] The general election of 1942 was in effect a single-party election, it being stigmatized as unpatriotic to vote for any candidates other than those "recommended" by the new totalitarian "political party," the Imperial-Rule Assistance Political Council.

matic affairs, promoted various superficial and self-seeking resolutions based on plans worked out by interested groups. Premier
Tōjō proposed the adoption as Cabinet decisions of many of
these resolutions as they stood, but I opposed on the ground
that the Cabinet should decide on policies which it could have
a reasonable expectation of being able to carry out, while most
of these plans seemed unrealizable. The underlying idea of these
resolutions was the extension of the system of the Asia Development Board throughout the entirety of Greater East Asia, with a
permanent organization envisioned for this purpose. Upon my
objecting to adoption of the resolutions as decisions of the Cabinet, they were debated upon only for reference; but it was from
about this time that a part of the Cabinet, as well as the Asia
Development Board, began to work for the establishment of a
Greater East Asia Ministry, which soon developed into a serious
difference over policy, and led to my quitting office.

As to my hope for solution of the China Affair, mentioned
above, I repeatedly called upon the Army authorities for a report
of their promised study, but the Chief of the Second Division—
Intelligence—of the General Staff apologized for the delay,
pleading that the report had not been completed because the
military aspect alone of settling with Chungking was very complex. While decision was thus in abeyance, Ōta Tamekichi, a
former Ambassador to the U.S.S.R., reported to me that in the
course of a trip to China he had received in Nanking, from Wang
Ching-wei, a suggestion of immediate cessation of hostilities and
general peace between Japan and China. I felt (and told Ōta)
that now that we were at war with the United States and Great
Britain, it would be difficult for operational reasons to withdraw
immediately all Japanese troops from China, but that practicable
means for a withdrawal could be worked out. I accordingly en-

deavored to expedite the settlement of the China Affair by having this possibility studied together with the agendum of the Liaison Conference to which I have previously referred. Tōjō did not specially oppose me in these efforts, but as the Army General Staff resisted the idea of withdrawal of troops, any plan involving it was turned down, and it was impossible to make headway toward a solution. For this reason, there was no development during my first Ministership. As the later plan of the Greater East Asia Ministry originated from this state of affairs, it was not by accident that when that plan was submitted to the Privy Council for deliberation the government's China policy was one of the points coming in for criticism, and that the Emperor, in approving the bill for establishment of the Ministry, warned that due consideration should be given to relations with China. The government as a result made a decision to improve its previous policies toward China; but this was after I had quit my office.

Areas of Greater East Asia other than China gave rise to little diplomatic business. As the only transaction of any importance in connection with French Indochina, there was concluded with her on 9 December 1941 a military agreement; with this, however—it being the work of the Army commander on the spot—the Foreign Ministry had nothing to do. As to the Philippines, Japan had declared in January 1942 that she was prepared to offer them independence. This step represented discharge of the legacy of America's promise of Philippine independence; my support of the policy, however, was at the same time motivated by the intention of emphasizing that Japan had no territorial ambitions in the South, and simultaneously of telling the Filipinos that Japan's policy toward them was identical with that of the United States, thereby removing obstacles to future efforts for peace between Japan and America.

CHAPTER 2

The Greater East Asia Ministry

IT WILL BE CLEAR from what I have said that my East Asiatic policy was founded on allegiance to the principle of establishing relations of amity and neighborly friendship with the countries of East Asia, with mutual respect for sovereignty and economic co-operation the keynote. Japan, as an advanced nation of East Asia, was to assist in the development of the other nations and the territory of this area, thereby bringing about through peaceful means the prosperity of all. This idea of mutual assistance left no room for any thought of control by military force. My foreign-policy speech to the Diet, on 21 January 1942, clarifying Japan's war aims, was an expression of these principles, as well as of Japan's intention not to exclude but to co-operate with non-Asiatic states in the development of East Asia. Naturally, in preparing my speech I had to give due consideration to the wartime atmosphere in Japan—it was a wartime speech—and to the views of my fellow cabinet members; but certainly the thoughts expressed by me conformed neither to the philosophy of military dominance nor to the concepts of bloc economy or of *Lebensraum*. It is clear that my position was discordant with the idea of a New Order in East Asia based on the idea of "living space," and accordingly with the designs for the Greater East Asia as then professed by Tōjō and his adherents.

I had noticed this discrepancy in our East Asiatic policy soon after entering the Cabinet, but the divergence naturally widened continually as the proponents of the New Order became increasingly drunk on the military successes. Tōjō himself, however, was rather cautious for some time, even after the war had actually begun. Thus, shortly after its outbreak the high command proposed to decide at once the future status of the Southern areas, for the convenience of military government of those areas after their occupation. When I objected that a decision of such importance should not be made when the war was still being fiercely fought and the situation fluid, Tōjō supported me, and the Liaison Conference decided in accordance with my contention.

There being these two currents of thought on East Asiatic relations, I had to endeavor to prevent the leadership in policy making from falling into the hands of those instigating establishment of the New Order. To this end, it was essential to keep management of those relations within the jurisdiction of the Foreign Ministry. Around May or June of 1942, however, I began to hear that there was under contemplation the creation of a new ministry, to be placed in charge of administration of the Greater East Asia area. With the passage of the days, the outlines of the scheme emerged. It contemplated that all overseas organs in that region (excluding only Korea, Formosa and Sakhalin) were to be directed and supervised by the new Greater East Asia Ministry; all political, economic and cultural affairs—everything but what was called "pure diplomacy"—relating to Manchoukuo, China, Thailand, French Indochina, and other areas (including the Kwantung Leased Territory and the mandated islands of the South Seas), were to be under the jurisdiction of the new ministry. The Manchuria Affairs Bureau, the Asia Development Board and the Ministry for Overseas Affairs would be abolished. The concept underlying this plan was said to be the treating of the East Asiatic countries as brothers, and the general mobilization of the material power of Greater East Asia, thus contributing to successful prosecution of the war.

Upon hearing of this, I told Tōjō that I was opposed to any such plan on the ground that the urgent thing was to mobilize our entire strength for carrying on the war and establishing ourselves in an impregnable position, and it was no time for play with organizational manipulation. I objected further that the plan as I had learned it not only would exclude the Foreign Ministry from the most important parts of the diplomacy of Japan—thereby impairing the unity of our diplomacy—but would injure the pride as independent nations of the East Asiatic countries, rendering it impossible to maintain co-operative relations with them. Tōjō promised me to give careful consideration to my views.

Before I heard anything more about the Greater East Asia Ministry, bad news of the war came—it was disclosed that in June our Navy, which had been boasting of its invincibility, had suffered a defeat at Midway. Although the Navy high command reported to the Liaison Conference that the losses were small, I soon learned in confidence that the damage included loss of several aircraft carriers which we could hardly hope to be able to replace. Even more than theretofore, I became mistrustful of the Navy, and began to feel still more somber apprehensions over the future of the war, apprehensions which the enemy's landing on Guadalcanal shortly thereafter, evidencing the vigor of their counteroffensive, did nothing to lessen.

Then on 29 August, Hoshino, the Chief Secretary of the Cabinet, called on me at the direction of the Premier and showed me a draft of a proposal for establishment of a Greater East Asia Ministry, which Hoshino said it was the intention of the Premier to have adopted at the Cabinet meeting of 1 September. After glancing through the document, and seeing that the plan accorded in general with what I had earlier heard rumored as its contents, I inquired of Hoshino the meaning of the "pure diplomacy" which was to be retained by the Foreign Ministry; he answered that it comprehended international protocol and the formalities of concluding treaties. I told him that I considered the plan altogether improper, and requested that submission of it to the Cabinet be postponed till 5 September, to allow time for study of it. Hoshino left, but later returned to report that the Premier wanted to have a decision made without fail on the 1st. Meeting Tōjō after a dinner party on 31 August, I stated to him my grounds of objection to the plan, and requested postponement of the decision by the Cabinet, but Tōjō refused to agree to any delay.

The Greater East Asia Ministry plan was accordingly submitted to the Cabinet meeting of 1 September. For three hours at the meeting, from 10:00 A.M., I carried on an altercation over it, with Tōjō chiefly, no agreement, however, being reached in the end.

My opposition to the plan was based on five grounds:

1. According to this plan, Japanese diplomacy was to be placed under the jurisdiction of two independent ministries—one for East Asia and the other for the rest of the world—making it impossible to conduct a unified and consistent diplomacy.

2. The concept of "pure diplomacy" was extremely odd; but the very fact that "pure diplomacy" had to be left to the Foreign Ministry proved the plan to have serious legal defects.

3. The East Asiatic countries being treated differently from nations elsewhere, they would lose trust in Japan and come to entertain suspicion of her motives, and their pride would be affronted. The plan thus contravened the idea of respect for the independence of those nations.

4. It was evident that the activities of the Asia Development Board, having aroused the antipathy of the Chinese, had proved a failure. But the Greater East Asia Ministry plan looked not only to perpetuation of the board but to the elaboration of its organization and the extension of its activities permanently throughout the entire East Asiatic area, and its failure was therefore foreordained.

5. The pressing task confronting Japan was to build up her military potential and establish an impregnable position. Japan could not afford to waste time with such schemes as administrative reorganization.

The gravamen of Premier Tōjō's argument, in the course of our long controversy at this Cabinet meeting, was that the countries of East Asia should be treated differently from other countries, as being Japan's kin. General Suzuki, President of the Planning Board, kept protesting that, contrary to my contention, the Asia Development Board had by no means been a failure; I retorted to this that the failure of the board was notorious. Among the others, Overseas Affairs Minister Ino and Navy Minister Shimada argued in favor of the plan, and I took issue with them also. The Cabinet meeting recessed without coming to an agreement.

During the recess of the meeting Tōjō suggested to me that I should resign. I refused, saying that it was the Premier and the advocates of the reorganization who should reconsider their plan and, if there were to be resignations over it, should resign. The

most serious ground of my opposition to the Greater East Asia
Ministry—that suggested by the first of the points stated above—
had been my fear that Japan's policy toward the countries of
East Asia would, under the proposed ministry, be formulated by
proponents of the Greater East Asia Co-Prosperity Sphere, a
"New Order" based on a bloc economy, thereby conflicting with
my policy for foreign relations. Going beyond this narrow
ground, however, I thought it necessary to make a stand to force,
if possible, the resignation of the entire Tōjō Cabinet. The spec-
tacle was exhibited of a government headed by a Premier who,
with such principles of war direction as has been seen, labored
mightily at advertising the initial successes of the war but was
guilty of flagrant nonfeasance in carrying out urgently needed
moves for increasing fighting power; under such a Premier ultimate victory in the war was not to be hoped for.

When I had returned to my Official Residence after the recessing of the Cabinet meeting, Finance Minister Kaya called on me
and asked in a friendly way whether I could find no room for
reconsideration. Thereafter, General Satō and Admiral Oka,
Directors of Military and Naval Affairs Bureaus respectively, together came with the same request, saying that establishment of
the new ministry had the support of both Army and Navy. I rejected all these overtures. Finally, Navy Minister Shimada came
to tell me that he had been summoned to the Court, and that it
was the Emperor's wish that some compromise be effected, as the
Court did not desire a change of cabinet at that moment. In view
of this statement, I proposed to Shimada a compromise; this was
in substance that the proposed ministry be abandoned, and while
management of economic affairs only of Greater East Asia
should be confided to a new organ, that organ should be preferably a ministerial committee. I was even willing that it be a

ministry, with this limited function, if that was believed better by a majority of our colleagues in the Cabinet; control of diplomatic affairs of the Greater East Asia area should, however, remain with the Foreign Ministry. Shimada left to report my suggestion to Tōjō, but returned shortly to say that the Premier would not agree to my proposal, nor was any form of compromise acceptable.

Although the Cabinet had not concluded its discussion at the recessing of the meeting, it had been evident that the general opinion favored establishment of the new ministry. Feeling that I could do nothing more to block it, and concluding that I should not cause anxiety to the Emperor by further complicating matters, I submitted my resignation. I left office that day, 1 September, and on the same day the Cabinet approved Tōjō's plan. On the following day I outlined the course of events to the staff of the Foreign Ministry, in the presence of Tōjō, who had taken over the Foreign portfolio temporarily in succession to me.

This controversy over the Greater East Asia Ministry has been alleged by some of little political understanding to have been a mere jurisdictional jealousy of the Foreign Ministry. That it was not so is evidenced by many facts. Thus, Shimada's report of the desire of the Court that there should be no cabinet change is proof that the question was one of basic national policy—the overthrow of cabinets is not threatened by mere jurisdictional disputes. Other clear evidences are the Emperor's expression of his wish, in connection with the deliberation at the Privy Council of the plan for the new ministry, that special consideration be given to our policy toward China, as well as the course of the discussion by the Privy Council, as mentioned below.

I learned that Tōjō and his faction took no small pains over the treatment of my resignation; they made apologetic explana-

tions in high places of the development, and even announced
that I had resigned for personal reasons. Meanwhile, the draft
of the Imperial Ordinance for establishment of the new ministry
was promptly submitted to the Privy Council, and it was intended, subject to the approval of the council, to open the ministry on 1 October. My resignation had, however, so aroused
public opinion that the Privy Council delayed even considering
the subject until after that date. There were some who wanted
me to continue working to thwart Tōjō's general arbitrary conduct of government; I decided, however, to abstain for the time
being from all such activities, the direct reason for my quitting
office having been this specific, limited question of policy. Those
in the Foreign Ministry who were fervent in their disapprobation
of the new ministry urged me to provide to the members of the
Privy Council materials for promoting opposition to it; but I told
them to abandon the idea of such schemes, and I myself escaped
further annoyance by retiring to Karuizawa.

Nevertheless, the government's plan encountered sharp antagonism and provoked considerable controversy at the Privy Council, some members even calling upon the government to withdraw
it—Admiral Suzuki, vice-president of the Privy Council and
chairman of its Examination Committee, in fact said, "This
proposal is based not on justice, but on sheer force." In the end,
the attitude of Tōjō was so uncompromising that the majority
supported the plan; it failed, however, to obtain the customary
unanimous approval of the council at its formal session, Councilors Ishii and Minami voting against it. The reason given for the
majority's action was that if they persisted in opposition there
would have to be a cabinet change, and that it was not desirable
that the Privy Council intervene in politics—a reason not entirely
convincing; the ultimate approval of the plan seems to have been

given reluctantly, and from various considerations. In view of
the circumstances, the Emperor, in sanctioning the creation of
the new ministry, directed that special attention be devoted to the
China policy. After these delays, the Greater East Asia Ministry
was opened in November.

====== CHAPTER 3 ======

Private Citizen

AFTER MY RESIGNATION from the Tōjō Cabinet, I held no public office, except for having a seat in the House of Peers, and until my entry into the Suzuki Cabinet in April 1945 I mainly rusticated in Karuizawa. During this time I made several visits to my old mother in my birthplace in Kagoshima, and especially at the end of 1944 I visited there to mourn her death. But with the intensification of air raids and the shortage of food making travel increasingly difficult, I came to confine myself to dividing my time between Tokyo and Karuizawa only.

Although but a private citizen, I watched the development of the war with inevitable interest. The Americans had landed on Guadalcanal in August 1942 to launch their first offensive operation. I had then felt that my recommendations, so often made, of prompt strengthening of Japan's fighting power had been justified, and had again reiterated my contentions to Tōjō, but he had paid little attention. The high command seemingly judged at first that the invasion of Guadalcanal could be easily repelled; but our operations met with unvarying frustration, and on 31 December it was decided to withdraw from the island. Thereafter the chronicle was one of retreat following retreat. The reasons for our reverses were plain enough. It was because the military authorities had underestimated the enemy that at the Battle of Midway in June 1942 Japan lost four of her six large carriers, together with many trained fliers; it was because they took for granted an ability to obtain sufficient transports that they distributed ground forces over many far-distant islands outside the orbit of Japan's operations—the perimeter, the result of many years' study of strategy, which they had expounded to us prior to the commencement of the war. Not only, however, did the enemy take full advantage of the developments of science in aircraft, radar, submarine sound ranging and like fields; its advance was scientifically planned, and slowly but surely overwhelmed our forces. I considered that the root of the failure on the Japanese side was that, having been spoiled by the initial success at Hawaii, our military services placed their reliance in moves of a headlong rashness based on mere personal bravery.

After September 1942 I was not in a position to receive official reports on developments of the war or on our strength, and had no way of knowing specific facts in detail, except that I had a means of access to the figures on shipping losses. The question of shipping I had studied earnestly at the Liaison Conference before the war, and I had come in the end to believe that the key to victory in the present war would prove to be tonnage of transports rather than numbers of men mobilized; I therefore followed with close attention the figures on our losses. Down to September 1942 these had conformed to the original estimates of the military authorities; but from October they tended to increase, confounding the earlier assumption to the contrary. I was gravely concerned over this, and took an opportunity in the summer of 1943 to call the attention of Naval Chief of Staff Nagano to it, despite the occasion's being a social one. Much later, in Karuizawa, Prince Konoe told me that on the way back from Nagoya, whither in the autumn of 1944 he had gone for the funeral of Wang Ching-wei, Tōjō had told him that the reason for the unfavorable state of Japan's war was that she could no longer obtain materials from the South, which in the beginning he had thought assured. I could not understand why Tōjō, to whom the statistics of these shipping losses suffered since late 1942 were available, should have continued to think the Southern resources secure. In any event, the war during 1943 was fought out mainly in the areas around Rabaul, the enemy counteroffensive was not rapid, and it was thought that it would take years for the Americans to approach the Japanese mainland by their island-to-island operations. Not only did the general public remain optimistic about the war, but the authorities made no serious efforts for the strengthening of fighting power or the renovation of international relations.

In Germany's war, our ally seemed to have lost the initiative. Field Marshal Rommel, in Africa, had once gained such victories that it looked as if he would occupy Cairo and strategic Suez; but with the landing of Eisenhower in Morocco and Algeria in November 1942 the prospect of his operations became very dubious. As to the Russo-German war, I have mentioned previously that the Japanese government had in July 1942 declined the German request for joint participation by Japan, and that I had around that time commenced preparations for making peace between the combatants. On the day before my resignation, however, the German troops had pushed their way into Stalingrad. Hitler's strategy behind this move was, instead of advancing toward Moscow in the north—in which he had failed the year before—to occupy Stalingrad and move southward into the Caucasus, to secure the oil fields of Baku, and to reach the Persian Gulf, opening the way to a junction with Japan (it was reported that the Japanese naval attaché in Berlin had presented requests to the Germans on this last point). The Soviet forces, however, stubbornly defended Stalingrad against the invaders, and finally a quarter of a million German troops under Field Marshal Paulus suffered annihilation as a fighting force on 31 January 1943, adumbrating the general defeat of the German armies.

After the dropping of the proposal for mediation for peace between Germany and the U.S.S.R., at the Liaison Conference in May of the preceding year, my opinion had been that we should urge Hitler to make peace before the success or failure of the second offensive should have become apparent, then should propose the peace to Moscow. When turning over my office to Tōjō as my successor I had spoken of this to him in detail, and during the ensuing winter I frequently talked with officials of the Foreign Ministry in the same sense. Nothing was done, however. I had dwelt upon the folly of losing the best opportunity to bring about a change in the general complexion of the war; but inasmuch as solution of this problem could be undertaken only if there was exceptional earnestness, and it could not be treated in a mere routine way—results being dependent on the person who dealt with it—I could only regret that the officials concerned would not work at it, and that consequently nothing ever came of the idea. The failure was especially to be deplored in that, as I later learned, at the time of the defeat at Stalingrad, when Hitler had been completely discouraged and had even been reluctant to go on with the war, the Japanese military attaché had exerted himself to encourage him. The German retreat continued thereafter, culminating in September in the withdrawal from the Bryansk region, in central European Russia. Meanwhile, the coming collapse of Italy was apparent; on 10 July the American forces landed on Sicily, and invasion of the mainland was evidently imminent. The Fascist Grand Council on the 25th resolved the expulsion from office of Mussolini, and on 3 September, simultaneously with the Allied landings in Italy, the new head of the government, Marshal Badoglio, surrendered to the Allied commander.

The United States and Great Britain seized the opportunity of this time of military advantage to launch a diplomatic offensive, and a meeting of the chief executives of those countries and the U.S.S.R. was bruited. Judging from President Roosevelt's previous line of action, I considered it natural to expect him to pay any price to win Russian favor, and I therefore contended that Japan should press her own diplomatic designs in advance of the meeting of those three heads of the Allied states, after which there would be no scope for our activities. President Roosevelt did in fact, on this occasion of the Italian capitulation, persuade Prime Minister Churchill in November 1943 first to meet with Chiang Kai-shek at Cairo to take resolutions looking to the defeat of Japan, then even to journey to Teheran, at the back door of Russia, for a meeting with Stalin. Such was his catering to the Russians. In October 1943, when Japan had finally proposed to Moscow the dispatch of a special envoy, the proposal was rejected; it was easy to see that the Russians could not have accepted then, with the meeting of the three chiefs of state in the offing. I understand that the suggestion of sending a special envoy was renewed, once again during Tōjō's time and later by the Koiso Cabinet, but was each time turned down by the U.S.S.R. A leading official concerned with this problem confided to me that although it was recognized that Japan must pay the stiff price which would be necessary for purchasing adjustment of relations with the U.S.S.R., no conclusion could ever be reached when it came to the question of the actual amount of the compensation which could be paid. At any rate, the spring of 1945 arrived before there were any negotiations with the Soviet Union. During 1943 things were going badly on the Pacific fronts. The military authorities, undertaking an over-all study of the position, decided on an ultimate defense perimeter which the enemy would not be permitted to breach; this was, as I heard, submitted to an Imperial Conference for approval on 30 September 1943. I understood that the perimeter ran from the Kurile Islands through the Inner South Seas, the Marshall Islands, western New Guinea, Java, Sumatra and the Andaman and Nicobar Islands to Burma. However, since learning that shipping losses had been increasing after October 1942, I had been convinced that Japan's defeat was a certainty if things went on as they were going. In the autumn and winter of 1943 I impressed upon some of the Senior Statesmen that defeat was inevitable unless drastic changes could be realized, and that for this purpose the overthrow of the Tōjō Cabinet was essential. In answer to my earnest contentions, Count Makino [1] disagreed, on the ground that there was no one else who could keep the Army under control; Prince Konoe fully agreed with me, but said that nothing could be done, because Kido would not move; and Admiral Okada said that I was right, but that we were powerless. Imperial Household Minister Matsudaira's view was that he, being in the Court service, must not become involved in the affairs of the government. I insisted that he should recognize that the circumstances differed from the ordinary case, since defeat would naturally involve the question of the Throne; Matsudaira, however, took no action.

With 1944, things became worse, in both East and West. The

---

[1] Count Makino Nobuaki (1861–1949) was not strictly a "Senior Statesman," not having been Premier; but as a former Lord Keeper of the Privy Seal for many years (1925–35) he was accorded treatment as in some wise a member of the group.

Germans withdrew from Odessa in early April; Russian forces had reached the border of Czechoslovakia on the 8th; and the combined armies of America and Britain landed on the Normandy beaches in June. On 20 July occurred the attempted assassination of Hitler in Munich, and by August or September almost the entire Balkan area had slipped from the German grasp. In the Pacific theater, Hollandia in New Guinea fell in May 1944—the enemy thereby intruding within the ultimate defense perimeter; many vessels and supplies were lost in the engagements in the Solomons, and the Battle of the Marianas likewise was ending in our defeat, by the close of June. The high command had counted on destroying the enemy by deploying northward the fleet based on Singapore, as well as by consolidating our available air power, but inferiority of our equipment resulted in serious attrition of our strength, and on 7 July Saipan fell to the American assault forces. The island proved to be a formidable stronghold for the Americans; from it, as a base, their attacks on traffic on our seaways were intensified, severing our supply lines to our outposts while interdicting our obtaining of materials from the South. Conditions were exceedingly grave for Japan, with hardly any prospect of recovery. The Tōjō Cabinet was finally obliged by these developments to give place, and it resigned en bloc on 18 July, to be succeeded by that of General Koiso.[2]

Despite my expectation that the Koiso Cabinet would, in view of our unbroken series of military reverses, work for a general peace, it seemed to be doing nothing in that direction, nor did it make any definite move in connection with Russian relations. I

---

[2] General Koiso Kuniaki (1880–1950) retired from the Army in 1938, becoming Minister for Overseas Affairs in 1939, and filling the post of Governor General of Korea, 1942–44. He was convicted by the IMTFE of conspiring to wage aggressive war, and was sentenced to life imprisonment, dying in prison.

therefore, impotent, resigned myself sadly to the conclusion that Japan's defeat was but a question of time; and, staying in Karuizawa through the autumn and winter of 1944, I occupied myself with study of the history of defeat, in particular the recent examples of Russia and Germany in the First World War.

It is commonly the case that a people's morale is high at the start of a war and while the war continues favorable, but that dissatisfaction develops in the course of two or three years as shortages of food, clothing and fuel begin to make themselves felt. Unless this condition is properly dealt with it leads then, when defeat is suffered, not only to political but to social revolution. With the ending of a war, the mass of the people experiences liberation, equally whether in victory or in defeat, and at that stage it is only to be expected that surviving remnants of feudalistic customs, institutions and prerogatives will be drastically curtailed and the power of the common people enlarged. In the case of Japan, however, it is necessary by all means that the national polity of the Emperor system be preserved; hence I thought it imperative to achieve peace at the earliest possible moment, and desirable to secure a peace comparable in general to that granted to Germany in the last war.

The United States had from long before adhered to the fundamental policy of driving Japan from the Asiatic mainland; the Hull Note had been an expression of this policy, and the Cairo Declaration clearly reiterated it. It was, therefore, naturally to be expected that if she defeated Japan the United States would insist on Japan's complete expulsion from the continent, whatever the aftermath of the withdrawal; but it was essential that for the sake of her eighty million people Japan's industry should be maintained intact, and any system for recovery of reparations should represent a different approach from that imposed upon

263

Germany after the First World War. If these points could be gained, the expenditures which in the past had gone for armaments could in the postwar era be appropriated to such general governmental purposes—especially welfare, education and economic development—as would improve the national well-being. That Japan should in future eschew war went without saying; the Constitution should be amended to eliminate the concept of independence of the high command, and further to insure restraint of the rampancy of the military services the ideas of international co-operation and peaceful development should be cultivated.

These were my main conclusions from my study of history. It is obvious that once a country has suffered defeat in war, external pressure is increased; in particular, it was to be expected that pressures from the east and the north would entail conflicts within Japan. Once, in the autumn of 1944, I talked over these problems for hours with Prince Konoe. What I said to him was in essence that it was necessary that the Japanese take a fresh start from the concept of respect for human rights—the concept, born of the Renaissance culture, of respect for human personality, one's own as well as that of others. This being essential, defeat would be the opportunity to arouse our people to restore themselves, without dependence on foreign benevolence or assistance, thus strengthening the spirit of independence by rejection of foreign intervention while at the same time cultivating the morality of co-operating in peace with other nations. What concerned me, here, was that the recent trend of international society allowed of no optimistic outlook for some time to come of safety and security for Japan in a postwar world in which would prevail the free trade prophesied by Secretary Hull during the Japanese-American negotiations. It was rather to be anticipated that, more and more, intercourse between nations would tend to emphasize political—rather than economic or legal—relations; security organizations would suffer nullification or destruction by the political demands of a great Power or a group of Powers, or even merely by force of circumstances; and the ideal of free trade would prove unrealistic. Such a state of affairs, nevertheless, I considered as unavoidable, being beyond the control of a Japan in defeat—and a Japan which, defeat aside, is painfully poor in natural resources.

As the war progressed, the hope of victory for Japan receded. The American offensive arrived at Leyte, in the Philippines, in October 1944. I was told by the high command that they would do all possible to restore the position, and of course I hoped that they could succeed; but our defenders were overwhelmed by the superior air power of the enemy; we lost many vessels and our operations met with no success. The expectations which had been entertained of the new Cabinet were dying out. The American forces landed in quick succession on Luzon, the main island of the Philippines, at the beginning of 1945, on Iōjima on 19 February, and on Okinawa on 1 April, and the assault on our mainland appeared imminent. As we entered 1945, also, the air raids on Japan proper were intensified, very serious damage being inflicted on transportation and production.

Although our strength had progressively declined, the people at large still had faith in victory, and patiently endured privation and hardship. On 10 March, the Diet session having just closed, I took train from Ueno Station for Karuizawa. It was the morning after the indiscriminate bombing of Tokyo, and the train was filled to overflowing with victims, carrying suitcases or cloth-wrapped bundles. Many of them, apparently having been separated from husbands, wives or children, or being in search of their families, were on their way to relatives in the country. It was a pitiful sight. I heard many say that even though they had been burned out, having managed to escape Tokyo with their lives they would not complain if only Japan could win the war. The gallant spirit was touching, and I could not keep the tears from my eyes at thought of this pathetic nurturing of confidence in a victory which the inexorable march of events had already put beyond the pale of hope. Such scenes were to be witnessed frequently at that time; but the purest and most glowing patriotism could not contend with material forces, and our soldiers were obliged to continue unendingly, step by step, their bitter retreat before the advancing enemy.

In February 1945, President Roosevelt, despite ill health, made the long voyage with Prime Minister Churchill to confer with Stalin at Yalta in southern Russia. After a week's conference, they three issued a communiqué reciting the policies which they had agreed upon taking vis-à-vis Germany. As later became known, they had reached agreement also that within three months after the defeat of Germany the U.S.S.R. would go to war against Japan, and would be rewarded by the return of Southern Sakhalin and bestowal of the Kurile Islands, as well as the grant of concessions in southern Manchuria.

President Roosevelt died suddenly on 12 April, and Vice-President Truman succeeded to the office. The condition of Germany's war rapidly deteriorated, and the Soviet armies entered Berlin on 21 April. On the 30th Hitler committed suicide in his chancellery, and on 7 May, Doenitz, Commander in Chief of the Navy and Hitler's designated successor, ordered signed at Reims the instrument of unconditional surrender to the United States, Great Britain and the U.S.S.R. Five years and eight months of the European War had ended.

I have previously referred to the probability that as Japan became debilitated the U.S.S.R. might abjure neutral relations. Toward the end of 1943 it had begun to appear that the Russians had arrived at a decision on the point, and when, in his speech on the 1944 anniversary of the November Revolution, Stalin branded Japan as an aggressor, side by side with Germany, it was an unmistakable warning that Japan must exercise great caution. I understood that when Foreign Minister Shigemitsu [3] instructed Ambassador Satō to make inquiry of the Soviet authorities concerning the Yalta Conference, Foreign Commissar Molotov stated, on 26 February 1945, that there had been no discussion of Japan at Yalta. Nevertheless, Russia's entry into the war had been arranged, as I have said, at that conference. On the same occasion, Molotov evaded questions directed to the status of the Neutrality Pact; and he refused thereafter to receive our Ambassador, on the ground that he was too busy.

On 5 April, however, Molotov requested Ambassador Satō to call on him, and when the Ambassador did so he was told that prolongation of the Russo-Japanese Neutrality Pact had become impossible, inasmuch as Japan was giving aid to Germany's war against the U.S.S.R. and was at war with the United States and Great Britain, nations which were allies of the U.S.S.R. It was therefore the intention of the Soviet government, Molotov said, not to extend the pact after the expiration of its term in April of the following year, 1946.

This was the day of the fall of the Koiso Cabinet.

[3] Shigemitsu Mamoru (1887–   ), a professional diplomat, was Vice-Minister of Foreign Affairs in 1933–36, and Ambassador to the U.S.S.R. in 1936–38 and to England in 1938–41. Following the outbreak of the war, he was Ambassador to the Nanking government, in 1942–43, and Foreign Minister in the Tōjō and Koiso Cabinets, 1943–45, and again in the Higashi-Kuni Cabinet at the surrender. After trial and conviction by the IMTFE for vicarious responsibility as Foreign Minister for atrocities, he served his sentence (seven years), and emerged to become Foreign Minister and Deputy Premier in the Hatoyama Cabinets of 1954 to the present.

CHAPTER 4

Foreign Minister Again

AT THE CLOSE of the Diet session in March 1945 I had quitted Tokyo, then under heavy air attack, for Karuizawa. There on the morning of 7 April the governor of Nagano Prefecture called me on the telephone, saying that Admiral Suzuki Kantarō [1] was forming a Cabinet and wished me to come to Tokyo immediately. A little later the governor called in person, said that Admiral Suzuki wanted me to become Foreign Minister in his Cabinet, and asked what reply he should make. I told him to say that I would not join the Cabinet until I should have talked with the Admiral and reached an agreement of views. I took a train for Tokyo, and shortly after 10:30 P.M. met Admiral Suzuki, who was at the Premier's Official Residence after having finished with the investiture of the new Cabinet (he himself having temporarily taken the Foreign portfolio).

I had known Admiral Suzuki, but our relations had by no means been intimate. While Foreign Minister in the Tōjō Cabi-

[1] Admiral Baron Suzuki Kantarō (1867–1948) as a junior officer gained distinction in the Russo-Japanese War, and thereafter rose to occupancy of many of the most important posts in the Navy before his retirement in 1929. His later career was one of direct service to the Emperor, as aide-de-camp, Grand Chamberlain, Privy Councilor. Being regarded as an unduly moderate influence, he had been attacked and seriously wounded in the 26 February 1936 Incident.

net, I had had no occasion to meet him on a personal basis, but I had from time to time encountered him at the Privy Council, of which he was then Vice-President. When the proposal for establishment of the Greater East Asia Ministry, the direct cause of my resignation, had been before the Privy Council, Admiral Suzuki had—so he told me at the time—agreed with my position and strongly opposed Tōjō's scheme.

Now the Admiral said to me that although he was a sailor and not qualified for political office, the weighty responsibility as Premier had been imposed on him, despite his age (he was then over seventy-seven) and in circumstances making it impossible for him to escape it. Having had no experience in diplomacy (among other fields of politics) he wanted me without fail, he said, to come into his Cabinet as Foreign Minister. I responded to this invitation by first remarking that I assumed that he had taken office with some fixed resolution, since it would be anything but easy to manage national affairs now, with the war effort reduced to the last extremity. I proceeded to say that, having made great exertions to avert this war, I should be gratified to try to end it as soon as possible; but that, as termination and direction of the war alike had to be dealt with in accordance with changing conditions, I should like to hear the Premier's opinion of the prospect of the war, before giving my answer whether to accept office under him. Admiral Suzuki replied, "I think that we can still carry on the war for another two or three years." I answered to this that in view of the fact that the decision in a modern war turns predominantly on consumption of materials and the ability to increase production, I was convinced that continuing with the war would be exceedingly difficult, and that Japan could not carry it on for as long as another year. I therefore declined the Foreign Ministership, saying that even if I felt able to accept the grave responsibility of our diplomacy, the Premier and I would be unable to co-operate effectively so long as we held divergent views on the prospects of the war. The discussion continued for a while, but as it was late at night and the Premier seemed tired, I left him, asking him to reconsider his views.

On the following day, the 8th, I called on Admiral Okada, with whom I had occasionally discussed the ending of the war, and who I supposed would have played a considerable part in the formation of the Suzuki Cabinet. I told Admiral Okada in detail of my conversation of the preceding night with Admiral Suzuki. He strongly encouraged me to enter the Cabinet; "We can't suppose," he said, "that Admiral Suzuki's policy for prosecuting the war is necessarily fixed, and you should join his Cabinet and help to mold it. Besides, the Suzuki Cabinet will be in very difficult straits if you don't join it." On my way back I called on two of my seniors in the foreign service, Imperial Household Minister Matsudaira and former Premier Hirota, to discuss the problem with them; both earnestly advised me to take the Foreign portfolio and find a way out of the impasse.

From various other sources pressure was put on me to take the office. Chief Cabinet Secretary Sakomizu called on me that afternoon to try to persuade me to accept. He said, referring to my conversation with Premier Suzuki, that it was impossible for the Premier to speak of an early peace—such language, coming from one in the Premier's position and in the circumstances, might have undesirable repercussions; but I should, he thought, read the Premier's real intention, and take the Cabinet post. I did not find this convincing; it seemed to me that if the Premier was of the same opinion as I, there was no reason that he should not have confided the fact to me in a tête-à-tête. If he had not that

270

much confidence in me, we could hardly expect to achieve the co-operation which the critical days ahead would demand.

The following day, Marquis Matsudaira, chief secretary to Lord Keeper Kido, called on me to add his persuasions. "I don't think that Premier Suzuki's views on the war are unalterable," he insisted, "and you should correct them after entering the Cabinet. Anyway, I believe that you needn't worry too much, because it seems that the Emperor is considering the ending of the war." He telephoned me, also, that afternoon to say that he had reported our conversation to the Lord Keeper, and that Kido too was of the opinion that it was vital that I accept the portfolio. Afterward, Sakomizu again came and asked me at least to see the Premier once more, and I therefore did so, calling on him at the Official Residence. In the course of our conversation this time the Premier very frankly said, "So far as the prospect of the war is concerned, your opinion is quite satisfactory to me; and as to diplomacy, you shall have a free hand." I spoke to him then about some details of the Foreign Ministry personnel and some other points, and he approved my ideas. Finding that we were at one in our views, I told the Premier that I would undertake the Foreign Ministership.

By the time of my becoming Foreign Minister for the second time, the Philippines had already fallen into the hands of the enemy, as had Iōjima; enemy landings had been made on Okinawa, and heavy fighting was in progress there. The immediate task facing the Suzuki Cabinet was to increase production of munitions, and at daily meetings of the Cabinet or of groups of ministers this and the related problems of food, transportation, public finance and welfare were exhaustively reviewed. The position in Okinawa, however, grew worse; air raids on Japan proper were stepped up; shipping wasted away; and each fresh report of

271

the responsible ministers made it more certain that a debacle was approaching. Communication with the continent became daily more difficult, and it appeared that the complete cessation of supply of materials therefrom was but a question of time—a short time. The currency in circulation in Japan expanded daily, and the growth of inflation could not be ignored. I had high appreciation for the earnestness with which the ministers concerned, especially those in charge of economic affairs, struggled with these difficulties; but there was no means of turning the tide, and with the increase in destructivity of the air raids and the general paralysis of production, the continuation of the war was obviously becoming impossible.

My first duty in the Suzuki Cabinet was the conduct of the Greater East Asia Ambassadors' Conference, in April. Notwithstanding that I had resigned the Foreign Ministership in September 1942 on the ground specifically of the Tōjō Cabinet's insistence on establishment of the Greater East Asia Ministry, I took that portfolio concurrently when I became a member of the Suzuki Cabinet, my purpose being to arrange the abolition of the Ministry as soon as pending business could be settled. Already by April 1945 that ministry had very little to do. Its jurisdiction over the occupied areas comprised not administrative affairs, but merely the training of officials for dispatch to those areas. In Burma—as well as in the Philippines, which had been granted independence a few months before—the military commanders exercised not only military control but also administrative guidance, which was inseparable from the conduct of the war. Therefore, although our ambassadors to those countries carried on diplomatic affairs under the direction of the Minister for Greater East Asia, the local commanders as well had a concurrent jurisdiction. The same limitations restricted the ambassador to French

272

Indochina—the administrative arrangements differed somewhat, but the ambassador there equally could do nothing which did not conform to the opinion of the commander of the occupation forces. Such being the actualities, one found it difficult to understand why Tōjō and his coadjutors had made such a to-do over establishing the new ministry. Aside from this, the progress of the war had rendered it impossible for our ambassadors to remain in some countries; in Burma, for example, part of the territory occupied had been recaptured, and the ambassador had had to evacuate from Rangoon into the interior, whence there was scarcely any communication with Tokyo. The Philippines also had been recaptured, and our ambassador there had been obliged to return home.

I have said that I had purposed the abolition of the Greater East Asia Ministry after disposing of pending business. It had already been planned before I came into office to assemble the representatives of the Greater East Asia countries for a conference. In November 1943, under the Tōjō Cabinet, the initial Greater East Asia Conference had been held in Tokyo, on which occasion the establishment of the Greater East Asia Co-Prosperity Sphere had been proclaimed, but misunderstanding of Japan's war aims had nevertheless still persisted in various quarters, and required clearing up. There was also the necessity of counteracting the plan of the enemy Allies to gather at San Francisco to make large-scale publicity of their war aims. For these reasons a second Greater East Asia Conference had been planned; but since from many of the countries concerned representatives could no longer come to Japan, the arrangement had had to be altered to one for a conference of their ambassadors stationed in Tokyo.

The conference was held, after preliminary consultations with the countries involved, on 23 April 1945, the ambassadors in

Tokyo of Manchoukuo, China, Burma, Thailand and the Philippines participating under special commission of their respective governments. Pledges of sincere mutual co-operation were renewed, and the following resolution was adopted as the act of the conference.

1. The fundamental basis of the international order to be established should be sought in the idea of coexistence and co-prosperity which, embodying the principles of political equality, economic reciprocity and respect for individual cultures, aims at the removal of all discrimination based on racial prejudice or similar antagonisms, and the securing of mutual friendship and co-operation.

2. Political equality will be guaranteed to all countries, regardless of their respective national power, and equal opportunities will be allowed to all for their prosperity and growth. The forms of their respective governments shall be decided in accordance with their own will, and shall not be subjected to any interference of other countries.

3. Peoples in colonial status shall be emancipated and established in their rightful place, to pave the way for the development of human civilization.

4. The exclusive control by any one country of resources, trade and international communications shall be done away with, in order to secure mutual co-operation of nations and thereby to rectify the economic disproportion of the world, and also to promote the diffusion of economic prosperity concomitant with the originality and the enterprise of the respective peoples.

5. The cultural traditions of the various nations shall be respected reciprocally, and friendship between nations and the prosperity of mankind shall be advanced by means of cultural intercourse.

6. Armaments which may prove a menace to other nations shall be prohibited, in conformity with the principles of nonmenace and non-aggression, while obstacles to international trade shall be removed, in order to prevent any oppression or challenge by economic means, not to speak of those by force.

7. With respect to organization for guarantee of security, arbitrary decision on the part of larger Powers and a uniform design for all the

world shall be avoided. An order shall be established having as its framework a structure for regional security suitable to the actual state of affairs, concurrently with an appropriate world-wide system, while, in the meantime, a way shall be sought to reform the international order peacefully in accordance with the development of the ever-changing state of the world in all spheres.

This resolution, based on my proposal, was adopted with the approval of all participants as the expression of the guiding principles of a world order. At the same time, it represented Japan's war aims as I conceived them.

With regard to Germany's prospects, our Embassy in Berlin had been sending reports on the strength of the Westwall and the high morale of the German forces; but it was evident that for Germany the sands were running out, in the face of the Allied advance from east and west added to the intensification of the air offensive. The downfall of the Nazi regime, toward the end of April, was therefore no surprise. In the beginning of May Doenitz was forced to surrender Germany unconditionally. Ambassador Stahmer in Tokyo explained to me the circumstances of the German surrender; but I reminded him that it constituted a violation of Germany's treaty obligations. I had already decided to abrogate all existing treaties with Germany, including the Anti-Comintern Pact, and hereupon took the necessary steps to do so.

With the collapse of Germany, not only would the American and British offensive be concentrated on Japan, but the probability of a Russian move toward the east must be regarded as increased. It was accordingly necessary to make a comprehensive survey of international relations. Our own war, however, had become hopeless—with the fact of defeat in Okinawa now beyond debate, the position had become irretrievable. I therefore used

275

the occasion of the defeat of Germany to try to get agreement to making peace while our military strength was not yet wholly exhausted; the results of my efforts will be detailed in the next chapter. Even before Germany's surrender, when after the middle of April her war had taken a marked turn for the worse, I had submitted these considerations to the Emperor, emphasizing that as a result of the collapse of our ally, and with the air attacks on our country steadily growing in weight, we should put an end to the war. The Emperor replied that it was his wish that we do so as early as possible.

In the time of the Koiso Cabinet the Liaison Conference had undergone a slight reorganization, and when I became Foreign Minister in 1945 it was the Supreme Council for Direction of the War which effected the necessary co-ordination between high command and government. During the Tōjō Cabinet's days, as I have mentioned, all important decisions at the Liaison Conference were reported to the Throne for the Cabinet by the Premier only, and it had seemed to me in the result that the Emperor had not been fully or accurately informed. For this reason—and because both the Premier and the Lord Keeper of the Privy Seal so desired—during my second ministership I reported to the Emperor directly, and as thoroughly and extensively as possible, on concerns within my province.

Before turning to my fight to end the war, I must tell of an incident which occurred soon after my becoming Foreign Minister. On 11 April, two days after I took office, Sakaya Tadashi, former Minister to Finland, called on me, and related the following facts. Minister Bagge of Sweden—whom Sakaya had known for a long time, and who was to leave Japan for home the following day—had told him toward the end of March that although the Allied Powers had publicly demanded the unconditional surrender of Japan, they did not in his opinion attach much importance to the question of preservation of the Imperial system, which seemed to be of transcendent moment to Japan. Bagge said that he thought there could be no harm in Sweden's sounding out the intention of the United States, and he wanted to know the opinion of then Foreign Minister Shigemitsu concerning the idea. Sakaya reported that he had thereupon communicated Bagge's message confidentially to Shigemitsu, and that subsequently there was a meeting at which—as Sakaya learned from them—Shigemitsu told the Swedish Minister that he would appreciate it if the Swedish government should on its own initiative explore the feeling of the United States about peace terms. Sakaya asked my opinion regarding this.

The story was quite new to me—I had heard nothing of it from my predecessor Shigemitsu, or anyone else—and I was much interested; I thought that it would be very convenient for Japan if the Swedish government should ascertain the intentions of the United States, because I was ardently desirous of ending the war with all dispatch, and this seemed a promising gambit. I therefore replied that I should like if possible to see the Swedish Minister before his departure, and I asked Sakaya to convey this message to him. Sakaya later reported that when he called on Bagge and told him that the view of Foreign Minister Tōgō was in harmony with that of the former Foreign Minister, Bagge was much pleased, and promised to carry out the plan without delay upon his return home. As to a meeting with me, he said, according to Sakaya, that he could not postpone his departure, as in the circumstances it was impossible to know when he would be able to make another reservation if he should miss the plane scheduled for the following day, but that he would by all means call on me if the flight should be delayed. As it turned out, the plane took off the following morning, and I had no opportunity to talk with the Minister.

The next that I heard of the scheme was when—in the latter part of May, I believe—our Minister in Sweden, Okamoto, cabled me that he had met Minister Bagge, who inquired of him whether the Japanese government was interested in requesting the Swedish government to canvass the intention of the United States. Whereas the story conveyed by Sakaya had been that the Swedish government was to take the initiative, Okamoto's report seemed to imply that we should ask the Swedish government to take the action. For a number of reasons, any such procedure was unacceptable. Before Japan could request the Swedish government to act, preparations would still have to be made within Japan. In response to any sort of formal inquiry, moreover, it was highly probable that the United States would merely reiterate the demand for unconditional surrender—in fact, there had already been reported through Count Bernadotte in Stockholm the rumor that, in connection with the recent capitulation of Germany, there would be a proposal of unconditional surrender from Japan too. I was at this time in the midst of efforts, making use of the desire of the military and other circles for an approach to the U.S.S.R., to prepare for peace. For all these reasons, the Swedish suggestion in the guise in which it was now presented had to be declined, and I instructed Okamoto to take no action on Bagge's proposal for the time being.

On the last day of the life of the Koiso Cabinet—5 April—notification had been given by the U.S.S.R. that it would not be able to renew the Russo-Japanese Neutrality Pact. The pact had another year of validity, and we had been assured, in response to a previous inquiry (made in February by Foreign Minister Shigemitsu through Ambassador Satō), that there had been no consultation concerning Japan at the Yalta Conference of Stalin, Roosevelt and Churchill. Suspicion of the U.S.S.R. was, however, irrepressible in view of Stalin's having referred to Japan in November 1944 as an aggressor, and especially of the statement, in the communication refusing to renew the Neutrality Pact, that the reason for that step was that Japan had been assisting Germany, the enemy of the U.S.S.R., and fighting America and Britain, its allies.

I felt impelled to do what I could about Russian relations. As an initial step, on the occasion of my first reception of the Diplomatic Corps soon after becoming Foreign Minister, I pointed out to the Soviet Ambassador that the U.S.S.R.'s obligation of neutrality remained effective. I also instructed Ambassador Satō in Moscow to obtain an assurance from the U.S.S.R. concerning her intentions, and the Ambassador subsequently reported that, on 27 April, Foreign Commissar Molotov had given him the assurance that the attitude of the U.S.S.R. in connection with maintenance of neutrality had not altered. Nevertheless, after late March it was being observed that the eastward movement of Soviet forces was on the increase. Early in my tenure of office the Vice-Chief of the Army General Staff, General Kawabe, called on me with some of his subordinates and, explaining in detail the concentration of the Red Army in Siberia, requested me to do all possible to prevent Russian participation in the war. The Vice-Chief of the Naval General Staff, Admiral Ozawa, made a similar request, as did also the Army Chief of Staff, General Umezu.[2]

---

[2] General Umezu Yoshijirō (1882–1949) had a distinguished military career commencing with citation for gallantry at Port Arthur, in 1905, and running through the positions of Vice-Minister of War (designated to clean out the Army after the 26 February 1936 Incident) and long-time (1939–44) Commander in Chief of the Kwantung Army in Manchuria. He was noted as the Army's outstanding moderate, a circumspect, efficient, civil-servant type of soldier. Succeeding Tōjō as Chief of the General Staff, he held the position to the end of the war. He was convicted by the IMTFE of "crimes against peace," was sentenced to life imprisonment, and died in prison

I became aware also of some criticism of Ambassador Satō, but I could not consider replacing him, both because it would be difficult to find a superior to the incumbent and because it would have been highly disadvantageous to us to leave the post vacant even for a month at that critical moment.

Our opportunity to perform Russo-German mediation, between the autumn of 1942 and the summer of 1943, had long since been lost. Subsequent attempts to improve relations between Japan and the U.S.S.R. had (as I have mentioned earlier) borne no fruit by reason of the government's shilly-shallying over coming to a decision on the compensation to be paid to the Russians; and meanwhile the United States had been unremittingly wooing them, and meetings of the three chiefs of the enemy states had been held at Teheran and Yalta. The time for employment by us of artifices designed to win the U.S.S.R. to our side patently had passed. Nevertheless, it would be fatal for Japan if the Soviet Union threw herself unreservedly into the enemy's camp, and it was imperative to prevent her from entering the war against us; even more, now that the further prosecution of the war had become so awkward, the Russian problem had to be attacked from the point of view of ending the war rather than of merely achieving maintenance of the Soviet status of nonbelligerent. I was intending to move for an early peace, and I determined for that purpose to make use of the desires of the military services. Many, who did not comprehend that our opportunity to take positive Russian measures had been lost, demanded that we approach the U.S.S.R. with the object of obtaining aid in coping with the United States and Great Britain; the Navy, for example, expressed the desire to offer to purchase petroleum and aircraft, in return for which it was ready to transfer some of its cruisers. I silenced the Navy's request, convincing them that for the Russians to supply Japan with munitions would constitute a breach of neutrality such as could not be committed by the U.S.S.R. without the determination to fight on Japan's side, which was out of the question in the current international climate.

The Russian victory over Germany was owed in no small measure to Japan's maintenance of neutral relations with the U.S.S.R., whose hands were thereby freed in the East. Despite this, the attitude of Japan—and especially of the Japanese Army —had caused the Russians over a long course of years to be extremely suspicious of Japan and firmly determined to neutralize her. Not only, therefore, could Japan not realistically expect any benevolence to be shown her by the U.S.S.R.; we had to realize that when it should have become apparent in the course of the war that Japanese national strength had been exhausted, the U.S.S.R. might, instead of negotiating with Japan, make common cause with the United States and Great Britain to the end of sharing in the fruits of victory. Now that the U.S.S.R. was bound by strong ties to America and Britain, it was too late for us to be making plans in the endeavor to induce her to act to our advantage; efforts even to persuade her to maintain neutrality could be expected to meet with reward only if made while Japan retained some quantum of power, and only if with the determination to offer a generous *quid pro quo* in return for any favors. What was essential now was to unify opinion within the country on these aspects of the problem.

CHAPTER 5

Toward Ending the War

FROM the moment of the outbreak of the war I had had in mind the ending of it, and that had been the almost exclusive purpose of my taking the Foreign portfolio in the Suzuki Cabinet. The proposals which the Army and the Navy had made to me, that I act to prevent Russian entry into the war, appeared to me to offer a God-sent opportunity to lead the entire nation in the direction I had in mind—the direction of peace.

As it was the function of the Supreme Council for Direction of the War to decide the fundamental policies concerning the war, I thought it most convenient to work through that body. However, my experience with the predecessor Liaison Conference had taught me that not only was it difficult for the members to talk openly and without reserve among themselves at the official meetings, which were attended by secretaries in addition to the actual members, but also there was always a tendency for those meetings to assume a very formal character, and to indorse the more pugnacious opinions and utter the firm pronouncements expected of them. My conclusion was that we could avoid these futilities only if we held more informal conferences, of the actual members of the council solely, to promote frank interchange of views. I proposed this to General Umezu when for the second time he called on me to discuss keeping the U.S.S.R. from coming into the war; he agreed with me, and it was arranged that he should obtain War Minister Anami's [1] concurrence, while I would present the plan to the Premier and Navy Minister Yonai.[2] All of them fell in with my suggestion, and as a result, from about 10 May we held "members' meetings" of the Premier, War and Navy Ministers, Army and Navy Chiefs of Staff, and Foreign Minister, only.

During the days of the Suzuki Cabinet, meetings of the Supreme Council as such were almost never held except in the presence of the Emperor, but the "members' meetings" became frequent, and all important questions relating to the ending of the war were considered at them. The members' meetings must be allowed much credit for the harmony which to the last, despite irreconcilable conflicts of opinions, attended and made for the eventual success of our discussions of these questions. When in the course of those discussions we reached the stage of examining the necessity of working for peace, about the middle of May, one of the military members proposed that our deliberations be kept a close secret, as the morale of the armed forces, it was feared, would be seriously shaken if the nature of them should become known. To this all agreed, and not even the vice-ministers and vice-chiefs of staff, not to mention other subordinates, were to be

[1] General Anami Korechika (1887–1945) had been Vice-Minister of War, commander of units in China and Indonesia, and Inspector of Aviation, before becoming Minister of War in April 1945. He committed suicide upon Japan's surrender, on 15 August 1945.

[2] Admiral Yonai Mitsumasa (1880–1948), during a long career in the Navy, held most of the top offices, including those of Commander in Chief of the Combined Fleet, 1936–37, and Minister of the Navy, 1937–39. Being retired, he was Premier for one of the shortest terms on record (January–July 1940), his cabinet falling when his opposition to the German alliance lost him the support of the Army. In Koiso's cabinet he became not only Navy Minister, which position he retained until the final demise of the Japanese Navy, but also "Co-Premier"—a newly created post devised chiefly to give the Navy an equal share with the Army in the government.

made privy to them. Even in the Foreign Ministry, this extraordinary secrecy was maintained throughout June, no one being informed; and in general the plan worked out well, the subject of our discussions being known to none but the council members for a considerable time—until the middle of July, when the question (to which I refer later) of the dispatch of Prince Konoe as special envoy arose. This guarding of secrecy was vital, because it was certain that should the discussions at the meetings become known at the lower levels, fanatical opposition would be raised by some of the military officers, and the effort to make peace would be seriously hampered or even frustrated. Moreover—a most important consideration—as the result of frank talk at these meetings, the council members, including the soldiers, became prepared psychologically for termination of the war; without such a unity of feeling it might well have proved that in the great unrest immediately preceding the surrender the military leaders would have turned obstinate and, their subordinates inciting them on, would have been impossible to control. The war ultimately was stopped by the Imperial decision; but there is no doubt that the difficulties of achieving this were greatly lessened by this psychological preparation of the military leaders. Premier Suzuki, immediately before his resignation, highly praised the role played by the council members' meetings in attaining peace.

At meetings of the council members from 11 to 14 May the Russian problem was discussed. As I have mentioned, while the Army viewed the task as being the keeping of the U.S.S.R. out of the war, the Navy went beyond this, and expressed the desire to induce her to adopt a friendly attitude, in order that we could purchase from her petroleum and other supplies. I contended that there was no longer any room for utilizing the U.S.S.R. militarily or economically, that it was too late for Japan to obtain any significant supply of munitions from her or persuade her to play the friend to us. Had Japan really desired to try to induce the Soviet Union to act to her advantage, the effort should have been made (as I had pointed out at the time to members of the government) before the American, British and Soviet chiefs of state met for conferences. Japan should have realized that the adjustment of Russo-Japanese relations or mediation for Russo-German peace would no longer be possible after such conferences; yet the Cairo Declaration was promulgated, the three met at Teheran and again at Yalta, while Japan idly looked on, doing nothing. Despite these facts, Navy Minister Yonai maintained that there was still time—and he quoted a former Foreign Minister as being of the same opinion. I retorted that the holder of such an opinion could only be one who had no understanding of the U.S.S.R.; this was the only occasion on which I had a dispute with Yonai which approached the rancorous.

Of course, it was desirable that we prevent Russia from attacking us, and I was entirely agreed that we should try to do this. I warned, however, that to achieve this purpose we must be prepared to pay a price, now that our power to fight had diminished—and, naturally, to pay all the more if we had any hope of persuading the U.S.S.R. to act to our advantage. But it was now too late; we could not waste the precious time left to us in endeavors to obtain assistance from the U.S.S.R.; it was no longer realistic to think in such terms, and mediation at most could now be hoped for as possible. I therefore proposed that we should first of all examine the whole field of international relations, including those with the U.S.S.R., from that point of view. The Premier, however, stated that he could see no reason that we should not feel out whether there was a friendly attitude on the part of the Russians. It was then settled that the points to be considered at the moment should be (1) the prevention of Russian entry into the war; (2) inducing the U.S.S.R. so far as might be possible to adopt an attitude favorable for us; and (3) opening a way to peace.

As possible means for attainment of Point 3, mediation by China, Switzerland, Sweden or the Vatican was studied, but all members of the Supreme Council agreed that such efforts would but end in the Allies' demanding Japan's unconditional surrender. General Umezu thereupon voiced the conclusion, that it was the U.S.S.R. only which would be able to mediate for a peace with the United States and Great Britain on terms at all favorable to us. War Minister Anami added that, as the U.S.S.R. would find itself in confrontation with the United States after the war, and therefore would not desire to see Japan too much weakened, the Soviet attitude toward us need not be severe.

My response to this was that we could not be optimistic about the U.S.S.R., as she acted always realistically and ruthlessly. Premier Suzuki remarked that there seemed to be something in Premier Stalin's personality like that of Saigō Nanshū [3]—the Admiral apparently had in mind the transfer of Edo Castle at the time of the Meiji Restoration—and that he felt that Stalin would act fairly and that we should request the rendition of good offices by the U.S.S.R. I pointed out the danger of setting a course on the basis merely of the Japanese way of thinking; nevertheless, I too was of the opinion that if there was any country which could promote a peace more acceptable than unconditional surrender,

[3] Saigō Takamori ("Nanshū") (1827–1877) was the chief military hero of the Restoration days. After the last Tokugawa Shōgun had resigned his administrative power into the hands of the Emperor, in 1867, some of his great vassals refused to obey his command to turn over the city of Edo (the Tokyo of today) to the Imperial forces. Saigō, commanding the Imperial troops, succeeded in arranging by a personal meeting with the Shogunate's commander the peaceable transfer of the city. The story is a Japanese textbook illustration of the power of sincerity and personal trust to draw out those qualities from the opponent.

it was the U.S.S.R. Moreover, the Army's desire for peace had originated in the idea of acting through the U.S.S.R., a fact which would facilitate utilization of it as the intermediary. I therefore repeated that while I was in accord with the Premier's suggestion of initiating negotiations with the U.S.S.R. aimed at the three points agreed upon, we would certainly have to pay a high price for the achieving of any one of these three objectives, and this problem had to be considered from the viewpoint of postwar Far Eastern policy as well. We thereupon went to consideration of the question of payment. This, it was tentatively agreed, might include abrogation of the Treaty of Portsmouth and the Russo-Japanese Basic Treaty, and the restoration in general of the status prior to the Russo-Japanese War; provided, that autonomy for Korea should not be included—that question being reserved to Japan's arbitrament—and that South Manchuria should be neutralized. This decision being a momentous one, the gist of it was put into writing at the time, and signed by the participants; the document was lost when the Foreign Minister's Official Residence was burned down in the air raid of 25 May, but I had another copy made and signed by the Premier and myself.

Our measures vis-à-vis the U.S.S.R. being settled upon, I informed the Supreme Council that it was my intention to entrust to former Premier Hirota the conduct of preliminary negotiations with the Soviet Ambassador, and we turned thence to discussion of terms for peace with the Allies. Here controversy at once developed among the council members. When the topic came up, on 14 May, War Minister Anami reminded us that Japan currently still held extensive enemy territories, with the enemy's occupation of our territories negligible, and he asserted that the peace terms should be such as to reflect those facts. Umezu supported Anami, to the extent of saying that the latter's opinion should be given full consideration; although, he said, he had no objection to our declaring that we had no territorial ambitions. I opposed this argument, saying that the reasonable method of approach was to draft peace terms on the basis not of the relative extent of territory occupied but of the general trend of the entire war, giving effect especially to the future prospects. Navy Minister Yonai seconded me; the Army's spokesmen, however, insisted stubbornly on their point, arguing that Japan had by no means been defeated. The atmosphere of the meeting having become threatening, Yonai suggested that effectuation of Point 3 be deferred for the time being. Since, however, any move toward securing mediation for peace must be nugatory in the absence of prior settlement of the terms, I contended that it was essential at this moment to discuss them at least in general outline. The Premier intervened, saying that even if we did not now come to agreement on terms, it would still be possible to proceed with exploring the Soviet attitude; and the realization of Point 3 was accordingly dropped temporarily. The report to the Emperor on these decisions was left to the Premier.

I called at once on Mr. Hirota to ask him to carry on the negotiations with the Russians. As is well known, Hirota was one of our top-ranking Russian experts of the time. I had previously sounded him out when there was a question of replacing our ambassador to the U.S.S.R., but his position then had been that while he had no objection to rendering services at home in connection with Russian affairs, he did not wish to go abroad. Now, after explaining how things stood—that, considering prevailing world conditions, Japan should endeavor promptly to make peace —I said to Hirota that in furtherance of the idea of requesting mediation by the U.S.S.R. it was necessary to ascertain the extent to which we could make use of her, and that we were asking him to hold conversations with Soviet Ambassador Malik.[4] In view of the disastrous state of the war, the cost of inducing the Russians to work in favor of Japan would, I told Hirota, be high, but he could if necessary offer a substantial consideration; I wanted him, bearing these things in mind, to work to prevent the Soviet weight from being thrown into the war against us, and if possible to persuade the U.S.S.R. to act to our advantage.

Hirota assented to my appeal, and it was arranged that the discussions with Malik should be held confidentially at the resort of Gōra, in Hakone, which was most convenient for both parties. The preparations for the meetings were delayed, the 25 May air raid intervened, and it was only on 3 June that the conversations got under way at Gōra; a second meeting followed, the next day. Hirota reported to me that opinions were exchanged on the fundamental problems involved in relations between the two countries; he said that the atmosphere of the talks was friendly, that the Russian side responded satisfactorily and the conversations looked hopeful, and that arrangements had been made for subsequent meetings. I urged him to do everything possible to expedite his negotiations.

The outlook for the war had already appeared sufficiently gloomy at the time the Suzuki Cabinet took office, despite our concentration since spring on defense of Okinawa. When the high command approached me with the request that I try to restrain the U.S.S.R. from becoming a belligerent, I asked for their forecast of future operations, pointing out to them that if we could destroy the enemy at Okinawa, we could perhaps re-establish a basis for diplomatic activities, which had then arrived at a dead end. If we could win this battle, the U.S.S.R. and other

---

[4] Jacob G. Malik, lately Soviet delegate to the Security Council of the United Nations and at present Ambassador to Great Britain, was Ambassador in Tokyo from 1942 to 1945.

countries would have to recognize that Japan had still a considerable reserve of strength; moreover, the enemy would be faced with the necessity of devoting some amount of time to mounting a new offensive. If, on the other hand, we suffered another defeat in Okinawa, Japan would have no basis for diplomacy. Wartime diplomacy being thus dependent on the development of military operations, it was vital that our forces do all within their power to expel the enemy from Okinawa, and I urged the high command to strive resolutely to do so, and stressed the point at every opportunity—I spoke to this effect to the War and Navy Ministers, the Army Chief of Staff and the Navy Vice-Chief of Staff, individually, also repeatedly at meetings of the members of the Supreme Council for Direction of the War, and at an Imperial Conference in early June. Nevertheless, the high command, who at first were talking in confident terms of the Okinawa campaign, gradually became less dogmatic; they admitted the existence of discrepancies between the operational policies of Army and Navy; they were evidently losing confidence in the campaign, and the fear was general that the loss of the island was but a question of time. Meanwhile, the air raid on Tokyo of 25 May was a blow no less devastating than that of 10 March. Air attacks on central and southern Japan became more severe.

I must here refer to the incident of adoption of an Imperial Conference decision, on 8 June, seemingly incompatible with the move for peace. In view of the conditions which I have mentioned, the Cabinet decided on taking various emergency measures, including the calling of an extraordinary session of the Diet. Opinions on the advisability of convening the Diet varied, the Navy opposing and the Army earnestly supporting the idea; but the Premier wanted to hold a session in order to raise the morale of the people—the government in general, at any rate, felt the need of taking such steps as were available to reinvigorate the enfeebled war effort. It was in these circumstances that I received, on 6 June—just preceding the scheduled opening of the Diet on the 9th—and without previous intimation, a notice of an immediate meeting of the Supreme Council for Direction of the War. Upon attending the meeting, I was astounded to find that its purpose was to determine on the fundamental policy for carrying on the war. What was particularly regrettable, without any advance consultation with me, a secretary of the council undertook a review of international conditions (for this I subsequently reprimanded him severely).

At this meeting of the Supreme Council, the secretaries (Director of the General Planning Bureau Akinaga, and Chief Cabinet Secretary Sakomizu) first explained the state of the national strength, and international affairs, after which the high command (Chief of the Naval General Staff Toyoda,[5] and Vice-Chief of the Army General Staff Kawabe speaking for Chief of Staff Umezu, who was absent from Tokyo) made statements on the military position. I then took the floor, and commented somewhat as follows. The ebb of our national strength, as explained by the secretary, had made apparent the difficulties in the way of going on with the war. With the increase in air attacks, there was already a drastic curtailment of production, and this could be expected to be progressive as they should be still further intensified. The high command's theory was that the nearer the battlefield to Japan the more advantageous for us; but this could not be conceded, when we had no supremacy in the air. As for the suggestion, made by the secretary in his discussion of international affairs, that our perilous position might be

---

[5] Admiral Toyoda Soemu (see Note, p. 55) had become Chief of the General Staff on 29 May.

retrieved through diplomatic activities, this was mere daydreaming, which we could not afford to indulge in; Japan's diplomacy had already come head-on against a blank wall, and no external help could be anticipated now that the war had become so desperate.

Munitions Minister Toyoda [6]—who attended the meeting specially—voiced the opinion that the enemy seemed to expect that after paralyzing our industry through the air offensive it would be able to effect landings successfully on Japan proper, but that increase in production need not be regarded as impossible if certain conditions, which he outlined, were accepted by the Army and the others concerned. The general opinion of the meeting seemed to favor approving a policy for continuation of resistance, though I maintained that since the conditions proposed by the Munitions Minister could assuredly not be complied with, such a commitment at this moment would be meaningless. The Army's rejoinder was that the resolution to carry on the fight was a matter of course, and to my renewed objection the Premier only said, "Oh! I think that much will be all right." The Navy Minister remained silent. A decision, based on the opinion of the Munitions Minister with some modifications, was thus adopted. This in substance was that the war should go on, provided production could be increased; but the impossibility of satisfying the proviso was beyond any doubt. After the meeting adjourned, I chided Admiral Yonai, saying, "I expected help from the Navy Minister today, but I got none." "Well, at this point a thing like that can't be helped, can it?" was Yonai's only elucidation of his attitude.

The decision so arrived at was submitted to and approved by the Imperial Conference of 8 June. The state of mind of the

[6] Admiral Toyoda Teijirō, who had been Foreign Minister in the Third Konoe Cabinet. See Note, p. 51.

Premier and the Navy Minister at that time evidently was that it was unavoidable to go this far on the course marked out by the Army; even more, I think, they felt that such a decision would be of assistance in heightening public morale through the Diet. I heard from friends of the Premier that he was saying that a war must be fought to the very end; but I thought that it would not be mistaken to assume that he had in his mind the desire for peace in a not-distant future. This was evidenced, for example, by the fact that, overriding expressed opposition of some of the Cabinet ministers, he inserted into his speech before the Diet some stories of his experiences at San Francisco when Commander in Chief of the Training Fleet, and recalled that he had said then that if Japan and the United States should become involved in war, they would "incur the wrath of the gods."

I was therefore not especially disturbed by the action of the Imperial Conference—as for myself, in particular, I had of course had an understanding with the Premier when I joined his Cabinet. When, however, on one occasion shortly after the Imperial Conference, Lord Keeper Kido told me that the Emperor wished to receive the members, only, of the Supreme Council for Direction of the War, I immediately thought of the Imperial Conference, and said to Kido, "We're not in good condition if the decision of 8 June is left as it is." Kido only said, "Oh! That! It's all right."

In any event, this Imperial Conference decision was contradictory of the agreement of the members of the Supreme Council of 14 May, and in that sense was most unfortunate. I surmised that it might have been composed by the secretaries of the council, who had no knowledge of the agreement of the members at their own meetings. The Premier acquiesced in it, I suppose, out of the considerations above mentioned—he did not, in general, attach much importance to documents as such. Curiously, never thereafter did the Army make a point of continuance of the war on the ground of this decision; and it remained a complete mystery to me why it had been taken at all.

The Diet convened, and adopted sundry wartime enactments, but the raising of the people's morale was scarcely to be hoped for. Immediately after the session adjourned on the 12th, therefore, I said to Navy Minister Yonai that our position had daily become weaker, until it was now necessary to implement Point 3 of the council members' agreement, hitherto uninvoked, and open a way to peace. Yonai agreed, and promised to talk with the Premier and the War Minister.

I had had occasion earlier to discuss with Lord Keeper Kido the problem of Russian relations and the hastening of the ending of the war. On 15 June, Kido said to me that since, as reported at the Imperial Conference of the 8th, the decline in our national strength was marked and would continue, it would be most appropriate (though no doubt difficult in the circumstances) to get the military leaders to admit that the war could not go on. The Emperor, he said, having recognized after the Imperial Conference that the condition was more serious than had been thought from the reports to him of the Army Chief of Staff and others, and that the recent statements of the Army Vice-Chief and the Navy Chief of Staff were not in accord with the actualities, was of opinion that we should endeavor to make peace now. Kido therefore thought that while it was necessary that we take this momentous step, in accordance with the words of the Emperor, the only way to go about it was to request mediation by the U.S.S.R., making sufficient concessions for the sake of peace with honor and thereby bringing the hostilities to an end.

I told Kido that I regretted the Imperial Conference decision, made over my opposition to the original hasty proposal at the Supreme Council on 6 June, and said that it would be extremely gratifying to me if the Emperor should say now that we were to work to end the war without delay, for there could be no greater aid to the attainment of my purpose than such words from the Throne. I went on to explain to Kido the three-point agreement of the members of the Supreme Council made in mid-May, and told him that the agreement had been implemented by having former Premier Hirota sound out the U.S.S.R. with the ultimate objective of ending the war—this, I added, should have been reported to the Throne by the Premier. I mentioned also my discussion with Yonai, the previous day, of hastening the taking of decisive action, and said that I would suggest to the Premier the calling of a meeting of the members of the Supreme Council to forward an accord between the leaders of government and high command. Kido answered, however, that he had never learned of the agreement of the council members or of the negotiations being conducted by Hirota, and that he thought that the Emperor also had not been informed of those things.

After the Cabinet meeting of that day, 15 June, Navy Minister Yonai told me that he had mentioned to the Premier our conversation of the 12th; the Premier, he said, had no objection to proceeding with our attempt to obtain Russian mediation, but thought it best that the Foreign Minister himself should go to Moscow to conduct the negotiations. I pointed out that I could not go abroad at the moment, as I had to remain in Tokyo to work on preparations at home for peace; moreover, it was necessary first of all that a unity of opinion be reached with the Army, as the peace negotiations, once commenced, must be carried on without interruption. We therefore arranged that the Navy Minister should talk with the War Minister upon the latter's return from the inspection tour in which he was then engaged. I heard nothing, however, of such a conversation's occurring.

At a meeting of members of the Supreme Council on 18 June, I reported on the wish of Court circles for an end to the war, and proposed the carrying out at once of the May decision, still unexecuted. There was general agreement that we must inevitably continue resistance so long as the United States and Great Britain persisted in exacting from us an unconditional surrender. It was also agreed that nevertheless, while we still retained a modicum of fighting strength we should enter into peace negotiations through the mediation of a third Power, the U.S.S.R. preferably, to try to conclude with the enemy nations a peace which would include at least the preservation of our national polity. The conclusion was that it would be very satisfactory if the war could be stopped by late September, and that the U.S.S.R. should accordingly be sounded out by early July and steps taken to that end as soon as possible. On this occasion also I learned that the Premier had in fact failed to report to the Emperor the council members' agreement of mid-May; when I inquired, he confessed, "I have not reported it yet. Please do it."

The day after the council members' meeting, the 19th, I called on Hirota in Kugenuma. After bringing him up to date on developments, I pointed out the necessity that any Russian mediation materialize in advance of the recently rumored meeting of the chiefs of state of the United States, Britain and the U.S.S.R. It was planned that Hirota should do all possible to speed up his conversations with Malik.

On the 20th I was received in audience and reported to the Emperor—in accordance with the arrangement made with Premier Suzuki—on the purpose of initiating the negotiations with the U.S.S.R., why we had considered the U.S.S.R. the proper mediator, and our recognition that Japan would have to be ready to pay liberally to the Russians for any services rendered. I explained also how it had come about that Hirota had been entrusted with the negotiations, and the development of the Hirota-Malik conversations. The Emperor approved the steps taken as entirely satisfactory. He said also that from recent reports of the Army and Navy Chiefs of Staff it had come to light that operational preparations in China and even in Japan were deficient, which made it imperative that the war stop as soon as possible, and that he desired that, difficult though it might be to end it, every effort be devoted to that purpose. I replied that since, needless to say, wartime diplomacy depended predominantly on the course of the war, it would be impossible to make peace on terms favorable to us, but that I would do my utmost to comply with his wishes.

On the 22d, the members of the Supreme Council for Direction of the War were called into audience. Evidently, I thought, this audience had resulted from my conversation with Kido, on the 15th, concerning the necessity of the Emperor's making his wishes clearly known, and the Emperor's purpose was, I assumed, the assembling of the independent leaders of government and high command for doing so. This surmise proved to be correct. The Emperor stated to the council members that both domestically and internationally a critical stage had been reached, the war was extremely ominous, and our difficulties would become all the greater with increased air attacks. It was therefore his desire that, even though the recent decision of the Imperial Conference might be left unchanged, the members exert every effort to make an end to the war with the greatest expedition. The Navy Minister replied that the six council members had been carrying on consultations with objects which would conform to the Emperor's wishes, and that the Foreign Minister should relate the results of them.

Notwithstanding I had reported to the Emperor in detail, just two days before, on the consultations and understandings among the council members, I now repeated the same explanation in a general way, thinking it well that the report be made in the presence of all the other members. Following my explanation, the Chief of the Army General Staff said that the proposal to make peace, being one which would have a profound impact at home and abroad, should be advanced only after thorough deliberation, and should be treated with the utmost caution. The Emperor inquired of him if "treating the proposal with the utmost caution" did not imply acting only after having struck another blow at the enemy, but the Chief of Staff denied this. No further discussion occurred, the Emperor retiring after confirming that no one else desired to voice an opinion.

Meanwhile, Hirota was keeping contact, either directly or through friends, with Malik, but the conversations had to be speeded up. In response to my urging to Hirota to do this, he reported that the Soviet Ambassador wanted to know Japan's intentions in concrete terms. I accordingly arranged with him that he should communicate to Malik that Japan's basic desire was to enter into an agreement of mutual assistance and non-aggression aimed at maintenance of peace in the Far East; that in this connection Japan stood ready to neutralize Manchuria and to surrender its fishery rights in Soviet waters, and moreover left the door open for discussion of any other issue which the U.S.S.R. might wish to bring up. Hirota met with Malik on 29 June, and reported to me that the Ambassador had promised to convey our proposal to his government and to resume the conversations upon receipt of instructions. In order to promote a solution, I informed Ambassador Satō of the Gōra conversations, and instructed him to endeavor in Moscow also to expedite them. Satō reported to me that he made requests to that effect in interviews with Foreign Commissar Molotov and his deputy Lozovsky.

Already, from before this time, the United States had frequently broadcast reports that Japan would sue for unconditional surrender. Japan, however, was in no state to surrender unconditionally—indeed, Japan maintained to the end, up to the ultimate acceptance of the Potsdam Declaration, the position that she accepted the declaration unconditionally, but that that was not to surrender unconditionally. The unconditional surrender applied to the armed forces only (as was clearly stated in the declaration itself), not to the nation. This American propaganda and insistence on "unconditional surrender," therefore, hampered to no small extent the progress of the movement in Japan for peace.

At one time another possible avenue of approach to peace seemed to be opening up. One day shortly after the events just mentioned, Navy Minister Yonai told me that one Dulles,[7] an American official stationed in Switzerland, had suggested to the Japanese naval attaché in Bern through Kitamura, our representative in the Bank for International Settlements, that Japan had better surrender unconditionally. Yonai asked me who this Dulles was, and what to tell the naval attaché to answer him. At that time Kase Shun-ichi, the Japanese Minister to Switzerland, was —like our Minister to Sweden—not on good terms with the military and naval attachés assigned to his legation, and in Switzerland and Sweden alike the Minister and the attachés could not work together. I had therefore previously asked the War and

[7] Allen W. Dulles, now director of the Central Intelligence Agency, was then in the Office of Strategic Services.

Navy Ministers and the two Chiefs of Staff to cable to their representatives warnings about recent developments. The report now in question, Yonai told me, had been kept secret from Minister Kase and the military attaché as well. I thought the present a good opportunity to plumb the intentions of the United States, and I suggested to Yonai that the Navy instruct its attaché in Bern to have Kitamura reply to Dulles that Japan could not consider acceptance of an unconditional surrender and any surrender must be on terms, and to see what the response would be. It was arranged that the Navy should so instruct its attaché; two or three weeks later, however, Yonai told me that the instruction had not yet been sent, and as it was by then too late for such an attempt, the plan was dropped.

By late June the war in every aspect had become critical. Production decreased drastically, on account of the air attacks and the breakdown of transportation facilities—not only did the production of aircraft dwindle, but even (for example) salt, essential to the manufacture of explosives, became scarce. The food shortage grew acute, and serious unrest of the populace by winter could be predicted. It seemed that informed quarters everywhere, official and private alike, were realizing the impossibility of going on with the struggle, and from every side the pressure to make peace mounted. Agriculture and Forestry Minister Ishiguro and Minister without Portfolio Sakonji called on me specially to confide their fears, as did other ministers. The feeling of nonofficial circles was expressed by Professors Nambara and Takagi of Tokyo Imperial University, who came to urge upon me the speedy achieving of peace—I told them that the moves which I was making were in exact conformity with their object, and added that I would appreciate it if Professor Takagi, an expert on American affairs, could suggest any plan by which to make direct contact with some quarter in the United States in order to try to bring about a negotiated peace. The politicians joined in, including even a Socialist Diet member who wanted me, despite the traditional bad relations between the Second and Third Internationals, to arrange for him to go to Moscow to get in touch with the United States. I found it strange that from former officials of the Foreign Ministry only had I no communications concerning the necessity of ending the war.

The ties among the Allies, on the other hand, were meanwhile drawing closer—T. V. Soong was in Moscow conferring with the Russians, and another meeting, at Potsdam, of the chiefs of American, British and Soviet governments was being talked of. It was plain that Japan's position would become increasingly untenable, and I wanted to place a steppingstone on the path to peace before the tripartite meeting. However, the Hirota-Malik conversations, despite all efforts, did not progress; and when I invited Ambassador Malik to call on me, that I might directly ascertain his feelings, he did not do so, declining on the plea of illness. When the report came to me that the Soviet Embassy staff had told our officials in charge that our proposal of terms had been sent to Moscow by courier, instead of by telegram, I recognized that there was no further hope of those negotiations. I therefore discussed with the Premier, as we entered July, the dispatching to Moscow immediately of a special envoy to take steps toward peace. I had in mind for the mission Prince Konoe. Normally the envoy-designate would be informed of the appointment by the Emperor himself, and he would of course feel honored by being so informed; in view, however, of the vicissitudes which this mission might undergo, it appeared appropriate to notify Prince Konoe informally beforehand. After having conferred with the Premier, therefore, I broached the question with the Prince at Karuizawa, on the 8th. He consented to go if designated, but pointed out that he would be embarrassed if he was to be bound by too rigid instructions laid down before he went.

On the 9th I returned to Tokyo and promptly reported to the Premier the result of my talk with Prince Konoe. The Premier told me that the Emperor had inquired of him on the 7th whether a special envoy should not be sent to Moscow to hasten a solution; he had replied, he said, that the Foreign Minister had gone to Karuizawa to consult with Prince Konoe, and the plan would be put under way upon his return. The Emperor's wish was disclosed to the Supreme Council for Direction of the War, and my consultations with the Premier of the preceding days were reported, at a meeting on 10 July. My report was that we had not been able to ascertain the attitude of the U.S.S.R., the Hirota-Malik conversations having failed to develop, but that with the war in the condition that it was and with an American-British-Russian conference apparently approaching, we might lose our opportunity unless the wish of the Emperor regarding peace was communicated to the U.S.S.R. at once. I explained that therefore the Premier and I had agreed, after deliberation, that we should do this, and after learning the Soviet response should dispatch a special envoy to conduct negotiations.

I shall return presently to the later development of this project. While we had been planning it, enemy task forces were operating close off our shores, and air raids were destroying not only the large cities, but medium and small towns throughout Kantō, Tōhoku, Hokkaidō, Kyūshū and Chūgoku—almost the whole of Japan proper. To this there was no appreciable defense from land or sea; rather, it was almost as if we sat with arms folded while attacked. I said to the high command that there could hardly be any thought of diplomatic activities with the war at such a pass; in particular, if the enemy and the U.S.S.R. entertained the view, on the eve of the tripartite conference, that Japan's fighting power had been exhausted, they would assuredly establish their policy toward us on the basis of that estimate. Even if we should then, after the conference, achieve substantial victories, they would come too late to serve our purposes in the diplomatic aspect. I accordingly urged the high command to grapple with the American task forces and deliver a heavy blow to them prior to the conference. I explained this necessity also to the Emperor; and I asked the War and Navy Ministers to convince the high command. War Minister Anami agreed with me fully, and told me confidentially that he had spoken earnestly to the high command in this sense.

It may be of interest if I sketch here my relations with the War Minister. After the collapse of Germany at the end of April I had opportunities for frequent exchanges of views with him on the China problem and the prospects of the Greater East Asia War. He had not entirely given up the hope of being able to settle the China Affair by concluding a separate peace with the Chiang regime, and it was his desire to enter into an agreement for cessation of hostilities on the occasion of a withdrawal, then being considered, of our troops from southern China, and by this paving the way to a general peace with Chungking. He agreed with me that it was impossible to bring about an over-all peace by the agency of the Nanking regime, though he was not entirely persuaded of the correctness of my opinion that we would not be able to make peace with Chungking separately from the United States. It was in the end left at the understanding that an attempt should be made by the Army, at the time of the withdrawal of troops mentioned by the Minister, to enter into local agreements for cessation of hostilities.

So far as concerned the prospects of the Greater East Asia War, General Anami concurred in my opinion that from the time of the establishment by the Americans of a beachhead on our mainland, there would remain for Japan only to carry on guerrilla activities, and defeat would be but a question of time. We discussed this often. The strategy of the War Minister was, on the supposition that the enemy would make landings first in July and thereafter during August, to deal the landing forces the heaviest blow possible, then to make peace.

There were some other subjects on which it was interesting to find General Anami in accord with my views. Thus, I repeatedly made representations to him—in connection with such questions as the freeing of former Ambassador Yoshida [8] and the treatment of aliens—concerning the harmful effects of the intervention into politics of the armed services, especially of the Kempei, and the impropriety, even for the end of conducting a war, of a Cabinet of military men; General Anami expressed full agreement with me, and on occasion even acted upon his expressions. It was, I assume, by reason of that basic outlook of his that on the night of the war's ending, when a *coup d'état* was attempted by younger officers, he ultimately withheld his approval from it.

Although the selection of the special envoy to the U.S.S.R. was within the authority of the Premier and the Foreign Minister, I had recommended to the Premier that the envoy should be informed of the appointment by the Emperor directly. Prince Konoe was accordingly received in audience on 12 July, when he came to Tokyo to attend the opening meeting of the Japan-China Association. As he told me later, the Emperor had asked

[8] Yoshida Shigeru (1878–   ), a diplomat, was Ambassador to England, 1936–38. After the war he became Foreign Minister in 1945, then was Premier intermittently from 1946 to 1954. Toward the end of the war he had been imprisoned by the Kempei on suspicion of dangerous thought, and was released by the exertions of Foreign Minister Tōgō.

him on this occasion if in view of the necessity of ending the war quickly a special mission should not be sent to the U.S.S.R., and upon his replying that he thought it desirable, the Emperor had asked him to go to Moscow. The Prince and I went from the meeting of the Japan-China Association to the Premier's Official Residence, where with the Premier we talked over the plan.

I have heard a variety of absurd rumors concerning the proposed Konoe mission. It is said that the Emperor told Prince Konoe at the audience that he should cable direct to the Emperor whatever terms might be offered in Moscow. Neither then nor thereafter did I hear such a thing from anyone who should have had knowledge of it, had it happened—especially, I asked Marquis Kido, who should have been most *au courant* with such affairs, about the rumor, and he said that he had never heard of it, nor could it have happened. Some say also, I hear, that the Emperor was profoundly influenced shortly thereafter by a cablegram from Ambassador Satō recommending Japan's unconditional surrender. Not only did Kido deny that story also, but it did not even fit logically, for all informed quarters in Japan were at that time aware that the war must end in something which might be very near to unconditional surrender, but should still be peace with terms. Certainly, the U.S.S.R. never intimated to us that she would transmit nothing other than an offer of our unconditional surrender.

At the conversation which I have mentioned, Prince Konoe, the Premier and I agreed that as things were moving rapidly and our intentions had to be communicated to the other party as soon as possible, not only the Emperor's wish for peace but as well the plan for dispatch of the envoy should be made known to the U.S.S.R. forthwith. Instructions were sent to Ambassador Satō that very evening that he should say to Commissar Molotov that the Emperor, being grieved at the increasing havoc and sacrifices being inflicted on the peoples of the belligerents of this war, was earnestly desirous of seeing the war ended early, for which purpose he intended to send Prince Konoe to Moscow as his special representative. Ambassador Satō was further instructed to obtain the *agrément* of the U.S.S.R. for the Prince's visit.

Satō reported from Moscow that although on the 13th he had requested an interview with Molotov, he had been unable to obtain an appointment by reason of Molotov's being busy preparing for his departure for Berlin, and that he had therefore asked to see Deputy Commissar Lozovsky at 5:00 P.M. of that day. Later in the day, there was another report from Satō; he had conveyed our request to Lozovsky, but later the Chief of the Japanese Section, he said, had informed him that the reply would be delayed, inasmuch as Stalin and Molotov were busy on the eve of their trip to Berlin. I thought it very strange that, on the ground of being occupied with preparations for a trip, the high Russian authorities should refuse to receive our Ambassador and should delay their reply to an address so portentous. Stupidly, I failed to imagine the truth: now that three months had elapsed since the defeat of Germany, the Russians were due, in accordance with their promise given at Yalta, to attack Japan; hence, they had no intention of seeing our Ambassador or of receiving Prince Konoe in their country.

The members of the Supreme Council for Direction of the War met on 14 July. The Premier reported on Prince Konoe's audience with the Emperor, and I on the communication to the U.S.S.R. Arrangements for the entourage of the Konoe mission were agreed upon. When it came to discussion of the terms for making peace, however, the War Minister and some others asserted determinedly that they must be settled with due regard to the fact that Japan had not yet been defeated. The Navy Minister and I argued that in considering terms we must take into consideration the possibility of the war's taking the worst turn, and that it might be necessary to draw back once in order the better to leap. There was much discussion, but the members came to no agreement.

Truman, Churchill and Stalin commenced their Potsdam Conference on 17 July. I was received in audience on the 18th, and reported to the Emperor in detail the views of the government concerning this tripartite conference and our measures vis-à-vis the U.S.S.R. In response to the Emperor's inquiry whether our communications had reached the Soviet leaders, I told him that since his wishes for peace had been made known by Ambassador Satō at 5:00 P.M. on the 13th, while Stalin and Molotov had left Moscow only in the afternoon of the 14th, it seemed certain that our requests had reached them. The Emperor said simply that the fate of our proposal was now beyond our control; it depended on the response of the other party not only, but on the destiny itself of Japan; and he expressed himself as satisfied that we had been able to get it delivered to the Soviet leaders in time. From American sources which became available after the war I learned that the United States Department of State had sent to Potsdam a draft of a declaration, worked out by former Ambassador Grew and others, in preparation for peace with Japan; and that, upon learning there from the Russians that Japan wished peace, they promulgated the draft—which turned out to be the Potsdam Declaration. If those are indeed the facts, the Emperor's wishes reached not only the Russian but the other Allied leaders as well, thereby inducing a peace on terms—the terms of the Potsdam Declaration. Considering the outcome, therefore, it can be said that our proposal did in general serve our purpose.

On the 19th I had a telegram from Ambassador Satō reporting that the Soviet authorities had informed him that they could give no definite reply to our request, because it made no concrete proposal and left the purpose of the Konoe mission obscure. (Although cables from Moscow had theretofore come through in good time, from this point on important communications between Moscow and Tokyo were noticeably delayed.) Shortly afterward, another telegram arrived from Ambassador Satō recommending that, there seeming to be no prospect for a negotiated peace, Japan should without delay surrender unconditionally. The government, however, could not decide on unconditional surrender, for it had to consider the state of mind of the armed forces as well as of the people, who had endured much hardship, and of course had to take into account the prior developments. In any event, there was no need of asking Soviet mediation if Japan was to surrender unconditionally. I therefore instructed Ambassador Satō on the 21st to give the Russians to understand that the purpose of our communication was to request the good offices of the Soviet government to bring the war promptly to an end, and that Prince Konoe was to be sent to conduct negotiations for adjustment of Russo-Japanese relations and simultaneously to convey Japan's concrete offer of terms for peace.

The delivery of this telegram of the 21st being delayed, Ambassador Satō carried out my instructions on the 25th. He reported that Lozovsky heard him attentively and politely, and promised to transmit the explanation to his government and give a reply as soon as possible.

CHAPTER 6

The Potsdam Declaration

DURING the early morning of 26 July, the day after Prime Minister Churchill's return to London for announcement of the result of the British general election, a joint declaration in the names of President Truman, Churchill and Generalissimo Chiang Kai-shek was issued at Potsdam. The text of this "Potsdam Declaration" is as follows.

1. We—the President of the United States, the President of the National Government of the Republic of China, and the Prime Minister of Great Britain, representing the hundreds of millions of our countrymen, have conferred and agree that Japan shall be given an opportunity to end this war.

2. The prodigious land, sea and air forces of the United States, the British Empire and of China, many times reinforced by their armies and air fleets from the west, are poised to strike the final blows upon Japan. This military power is sustained and inspired by the determination of all the Allied Nations to prosecute the war against Japan until she ceases to resist.

3. The result of the futile and senseless German resistance to the might of the aroused free peoples of the world stands forth in awful clarity as an example to the people of Japan. The might that now converges on Japan is immeasurably greater than that which, when applied to the resisting Nazis, necessarily laid waste to the lands, the industry and the method of life of the whole German people. The full application of our military

power, backed by our resolve, will mean the inevitable and complete destruction of the Japanese armed forces and just as inevitably the utter devastation of the Japanese homeland.

4. The time has come for Japan to decide whether she will continue to be controlled by those self-willed militaristic advisers whose unintelligent calculations have brought the Empire of Japan to the threshold of annihilation, or whether she will follow the path of reason.

5. Following are our terms. We will not deviate from them. There are no alternatives. We shall brook no delay.

6. There must be eliminated for all time the authority and influence of those who have deceived and misled the people of Japan into embarking on world conquest, for we insist that a new order of peace, security and justice will be impossible until irresponsible militarism is driven from the world.

7. Until such a new order is established and until there is convincing proof that Japan's war-making power is destroyed, points in Japanese territory to be designated by the Allies shall be occupied to secure the achievement of the basic objectives we are here setting forth.

8. The terms of the Cairo Declaration shall be carried out and Japanese sovereignty shall be limited to the islands of Honshu, Hokkaido, Kyushu, Shikoku and such minor islands as we determine.

9. The Japanese military forces, after being completely disarmed, shall be permitted to return to their homes with the opportunity to lead peaceful and productive lives.

10. We do not intend that the Japanese shall be enslaved as a race or destroyed as a nation, but stern justice shall be meted out to all war criminals, including those who have visited cruelties upon our prisoners. The Japanese Government shall remove all obstacles to the revival and strengthening of democratic tendencies among the Japanese people. Freedom of speech, of religion, and of thought, as well as respect for the fundamental human rights, shall be established.

11. Japan shall be permitted to maintain such industries as will sustain her economy and permit the exaction of just reparations in kind, but not those which would enable her to re-arm for war. To this end, access to, as distinguished from control of, raw materials shall be permitted. Eventual Japanese participation in world trade relations shall be permitted.

12. The occupying forces of the Allies shall be withdrawn from Japan as soon as these objectives have been accomplished and there has been established in accordance with the freely expressed will of the Japanese people a peacefully inclined and responsible government.

13. We call upon the government of Japan to proclaim now the unconditional surrender of all Japanese armed forces, and to provide proper and adequate assurances of their good faith in such action. The alternative for Japan is prompt and utter destruction.

My first reaction to the declaration upon reading through the text as broadcast by the American radio was that, in view of the language, "Following are our terms," it was evidently not a dictate of unconditional surrender. I got the impression that the Emperor's wishes had reached the United States and Great Britain, and had had the result of this moderation of their attitude. It appeared also that a measure of consideration had been given to Japan's economic position; at a time when such Draconian retribution upon Germany as the "Morgenthau Plan" for her reduction to a "pastoral state" was being proposed, I felt special relief upon seeing the economic provisions of the declaration—the gist of them being that the function of Japan as a processing nation, as contemplated by Secretary Hull during the Japanese-American negotiations, would be recognized, and that to this end severe reparations would not be imposed.

The territorial provisions of the declaration I did not deem in the light of the Atlantic Charter to be fitting, for—putting aside the question of the independence of Korea—Formosa and our other territories would have to be surrendered in conformity with the edict of the Cairo Declaration, and our sovereignty would in effect be limited to the four main islands of Japan. As to the occupation, also, there were some doubts. The occupation seemed, it is true, to have applicability to designated points in our country, and it apparently was to be—unlike the treatment

311

of Germany after her surrender—a guarantee occupation not involving extensive administration; there was a question, however, whether Tokyo and the other large cities would be included among the points designated. I considered, further, that there were some ambiguities concerning the eventual form of the Japanese government, and also that complications might result from the language relating to disarmament and war criminals. I therefore instructed Foreign Vice-Minister Matsumoto [1] to make a careful study of the legal aspects of the declaration.

Simultaneously, I thought it desirable to enter into negotiation with the Allied Powers to obtain some clarification, and revision —even if it should be slight—of disadvantageous points in the declaration.

I was received in audience on the morning of the 27th, and reported to the Emperor on recent happenings, including the negotiations with Moscow, the British general election and the Potsdam Declaration. I stressed that the declaration must be treated with the utmost circumspection, both domestically and internationally; in particular, I feared the consequences if Japan should manifest an intention to reject it. I pointed out further that the efforts to obtain Soviet mediation to bring about the ending of the war had not yet borne fruit, and that our attitude toward the declaration should be decided in accordance with their outcome.

At a meeting of the members of the Supreme Council for Direction of the War, held on the same day, I spoke to the same effect. On this occasion, Chief of Staff Toyoda said that news of the declaration would, sooner or later, transpire, and if we did

---

[1] Matsumoto Shun-ichi (1897–   ), a career diplomat, was Ambassador to Indochina, 1944–45, and Vice-Minister from May to September 1945. He was Ambassador to Great Britain, 1952–55, and since 1955 has been special envoy to negotiate, in London, a treaty of peace with the U.S.S.R.

nothing it would lead to a serious impairment of morale; hence, he suggested, it would be best at this time to issue a statement that the government regarded the declaration as absurd and could not consider it. Premier Suzuki and I objected to this, and as a result it was agreed that for the time being we should wait to see what the response of the U.S.S.R. would be to our approach to her, planning to decide our course thereafter. On the same afternoon there was a Cabinet meeting, at which I reported on the negotiations with the U.S.S.R. which Mr. Hirota had been conducting, and on recent international developments in general. I went into detail concerning the Potsdam Declaration, and recommended that we should act on it after having ascertained the attitude of the Soviet Union. No dissent from this treatment of the declaration was expressed, though there was considerable discussion of the way and the extent of making it public. In the end it was agreed that it should be passed without comment by the government, the competent authorities releasing it in summary, while the Board of Information should lead the press to minimize publicity.

To my amazement, the newspapers of the following morning reported that the government had decided to ignore the Potsdam Declaration. I protested without delay to the Cabinet when it met, pointing out that the report was at variance with our decision of the preceding day. What had happened, I learned, was this. There had been held in the Imperial Palace, after adjournment of the Cabinet the day before, a conference for exchange of information between government and high command. This was a routine weekly meeting without special significance, and I had been absent because of more important business. One of the military participants in that meeting, as I heard it, had proposed the rejection of the Potsdam Declaration; the Premier, the

War and Navy Ministers and the two Chiefs of Staff had hastily assembled for consultation in a separate room, and the Premier had been persuaded by the more militant elements to that course. He then stated at a subsequent press conference that the government had decided to ignore the declaration, and this announcement it was which the press had played up so sensationally. It was only after the affair had developed to this point that I first knew of it; despite my thorough dissatisfaction with the position, there was of course no way of withdrawing the statement released by the Premier, and things had to be left as they stood. In the result, the American press reported that Japan had rejected the declaration, and President Truman in deciding for use of the atomic bomb, and the U.S.S.R. in attacking Japan, referred to the rejection of it as justification for their respective actions. The incident was thus a deplorable one in its embarrassment of our move for peace, and was most disadvantageous for Japan.

Meanwhile, despite my repeated instructions to Ambassador Satō in Moscow to press the U.S.S.R. to act quickly on our request for mediation, he did not succeed in obtaining access to any of the Russian officials save Vice-Commissar Lozovsky, until finally he reported that Molotov was back in Moscow from Potsdam on 5 August, and would receive him at 5:00 P.M. (11:00 P.M., Japan time) on the 8th. That interview proved, however— as we learned only after the war—to have no relation to our request, but to be for the quite different purpose of notifying the Ambassador of the U.S.S.R.'s commencement of war against Japan.

At 8:15 A.M. on 6 August the United States Air Force released over Hiroshima the atomic bomb the detonation of which was to reverberate down through the history of the world. I was informed that the damage was vast. I immediately demanded of the Army the particulars; the American radio had announced that the bomb was one employing atomic fission, and if such a singular explosive had in fact been used, in violation of the international law of warfare, it would be necessary to lodge a protest with the United States. The Army replied to my inquiry that it could as yet say only that the bomb dropped on Hiroshima was one of high effectiveness, and that the details were under investigation. The United States and Great Britain launched large-scale propaganda on the atomic bomb, declaring that its use would alter utterly the character of war and would work a revolution in the life of the human race, and that if Japan did not accept the declaration of the three Powers the bomb would continue to be used until the nation was annihilated.

At a meeting of the Cabinet on the afternoon of 7 August the War and Home Ministers made reports on the Hiroshima bombing. The Army, pleading the necessity of awaiting the results of the investigation which had been ordered, obviously intended not to admit the nature of the atomic attack, but to minimize the effect of the bombing. On the 8th I had an audience, in the underground shelter of the Imperial Palace, with the Emperor, whom I informed of the enemy's announcement of the use of an atomic bomb, and related matters, and I said that it was now all the more imperative that we end the war, which we could seize this opportunity to do. The Emperor approved of my view, and warned that since we could no longer continue the struggle, now that a weapon of this devastating power was used against us, we should not let slip the opportunity by engaging in attempts to gain more favorable conditions. Since bargaining for terms had little prospect of success at this stage, he said, measures should be concerted to insure a prompt ending of hostilities. He further added that I should communicate his wishes to the Pre-

315

mier. Withdrawing, I spoke to Lord Keeper Kido of what had passed at my audience, and I then proceeded to inform the Premier at once of the Emperor's wishes and to request him to call a meeting of the members of the Supreme Council for Direction of the War.

In the early hours of the 9th the radio room of the Foreign Ministry telephoned to inform me of the U.S.S.R.'s broadcast of her declaration of war on us and the large-scale invasion of Manchuria by her forces. (Ambassador Satō, when he met with Commissar Molotov at 11:00 P.M., our time, on the 8th, had been notified of the declaration of war; but the cable report of the interview—and consequently of the declaration—which the Russians had assured him would be cleared for dispatch never reached Tokyo.) I visited the Premier early in the morning and told him of the Russian attack. Again I pointed out that the war must stop immediately, and Admiral Suzuki agreed. It was arranged that Chief Cabinet Secretary Sakomizu, who was present, should summon the members of the Supreme Council to an urgent conference. On the way to the Foreign Ministry I called at the Navy Ministry, and reported to Admiral Yonai as I had done to the Premier. While at the Navy Ministry I encountered Prince Takamatsu,[2] to whom also I explained why we must accept the Potsdam Declaration without further procrastination.

The members of the Supreme Council met at 11:00 A.M. I opened the discussion by saying that the war had become more and more hopeless, and now that it had no future, it was necessary to make peace without the slightest delay. Therefore, I said, the Potsdam Declaration must be complied with, and the conditions for its acceptance should be limited to those only which

[2] Prince Takamatsu (1905–   ), the Emperor's second brother, was a rear admiral then on duty with the Naval General Staff.

were absolutely essential for Japan. All members of the Supreme Council already recognized the difficulties in going on with the war; and now, after the employment of the atomic bomb and Russian entry into the war against us, none opposed in principle our acceptance of the declaration. None disagreed, either, that we must insist upon preservation of the national polity as the indispensable condition of acceptance.

The military representatives, however, held out for proposing additional terms—specifically, that occupation of Japan should if possible be avoided or, if inescapable, should be on a small scale and should not include such points as Tokyo; that disarmament should be carried out on our responsibility; and that war criminals should be dealt with by Japan. I objected that in view of the recent attitude of Britain, America, Russia and China it was greatly to be feared that any proposal by us of a number of terms would be rejected, and that the entire effort for peace would be in danger of failing. Unless, therefore, the military services saw a prospect of winning the war, any terms proposed by us should be limited to the minimum of those truly vital; thus, while it was in order to propose other points as our desire, the only condition as such which we should hold out for was that of inviolability of the Imperial house. I asked, then, whether the armed services could offer any hope of victory in case negotiations on terms should be undertaken and should fail.

The War Minister replied that although he could give no assurance of ultimate victory, Japan could still fight another battle. I pressed them to say whether they could be certain of preventing the enemy from landing on our mainland. The Army Chief of Staff answered that we might drive the enemy into the sea if all went very well—though, in war, we could not be confident that things would go well—but that even conceding that a certain percentage of the enemy's troops might succeed in establishing beachheads, he was confident that we could inflict heavy losses on them. I argued that this would be of no avail: according to the explanation given us by the Army, some part at least of the attackers might still land even after sustaining serious losses; but while it was obvious that the enemy would follow up with a second assault though the first was inadequately rewarded, we should have sacrificed most of our remaining aircraft and other important munitions in our efforts to destroy the first wave. There being no possibility of replenishing our supply of armaments in a short period, our position after the first enemy landing operations would be one of defenselessness, even leaving the atomic bomb out of account. My conclusion was that we had no alternative to stopping the war at this very moment, and we must therefore attempt to attain peace by limiting our counterdemands to the irreducible minimum.

The discussion became rather impassioned, but remained inconclusive, and it neared one o'clock, with a Cabinet meeting scheduled for the afternoon. The Premier stated that the question had to be submitted to the Cabinet also, and the Supreme Council adjourned without having come to any agreement how we should proceed.

The Cabinet met at two. Prior to the meeting, I said to Premier Suzuki that the Cabinet also was unlikely to arrive at a unanimous conclusion, in which event the only possible solution would be to request an Imperial decision; but it was necessary that the Premier take care lest the Cabinet be disabled, before that could be done—by the resignation of the War Minister, for instance. Also before the Cabinet meeting Vice-Minister Matsumoto came to me and said that the prevailing opinion of the Foreign Ministry likewise was that we should not present numerous conditions.

At the Cabinet, I again detailed the course of the negotiations with the U.S.S.R., the use of the atomic bomb and the Soviet attack on us. There was the same controversy—whether we should accept the Potsdam Declaration with the one indispensable condition only, or should add the others, as proposed by the War Minister, relating to occupation, disarmament and war criminals. The Navy Minister sided with me, saying that there were no expectations to be indulged if we went on with the war; the War Minister opposed on the ground that if it came to a final battle on Japanese soil we could at least for a time repulse the enemy, and might thereafter somehow "find life out of death," even though there was no certainty of victory. In rebuttal I observed that according to the opinion of the high command as made known at the meeting of the council members, the prospects of driving the enemy into the sea were by no means bright, while even if we managed to punish them severely during their landings, our relative position would be far worse in the sequel. Discussion reached no issue. The meeting had gone on for hours, and it was now late at night. The Premier asked the Cabinet members to state their conclusions; some equivocated, some agreed with the Army's view, but most supported me.

At that point the Premier stated that he wished to report to the Emperor with me alone. Leaving the Cabinet in session, we went together to the Palace. Upon our being received, the Premier requested that I outline to the Emperor the disagreement in the Supreme Council and the Cabinet, which I did fully. The Premier then asked the Emperor's sanction for calling at once, that night, a meeting in his presence of the Supreme Council for Direction of the War. The Emperor approved, and the Imperial Conference convened shortly before midnight of the 9th. It was a full meeting; in addition to the Premier, the service ministers,

319

the two Chiefs of Staff and myself, Baron Hiranuma, President of the Privy Council, attended as a participant, and as secretaries there were the Chief Cabinet Secretary, the Director of the Combined Planning Bureau, General Ikeda, Director Yoshizumi of the War Ministry Military Affairs Bureau and Director Hoshina of the Navy Ministry Naval Affairs Bureau.

The Premier opened the conference by saying that, the deliberations at that morning's Supreme Council having failed to result in agreement on the accepting of the Potsdam Declaration, he wished to ask the Emperor to hear personally the opposing views. Thereupon two alternatives were submitted for consideration: one, to accept the Potsdam Declaration with the understanding that it comprised no demand which would prejudice the traditionally established status of the Emperor; the other, to attach in addition the three conditions before mentioned as insisted upon by the Army. I dilated upon the same points which I had argued at the Supreme Council members' meeting and that of the Cabinet, and contended that we must now end the war by accepting the Potsdam Declaration in accordance with the first alternative. The Navy Minister said simply that he fully concurred in the opinion of the Foreign Minister. But War Minister Anami reiterated his argument that we should propose the additional conditions, and the Army Chief of Staff announced a similar conviction. Baron Hiranuma, after having asked a number of questions, called for amendment of the reservation in the first alternative to provide that the declaration "comprised no demand which would prejudice the prerogatives of the Emperor as a sovereign ruler"; this amendment being approved by all, Hiranuma agreed to that alternative.

There being still a division of opinion, the Premier said that he regretted that he must humbly beg the Emperor's decision.

The Emperor quietly said that he approved the opinion of the
Foreign Minister; the confidence of the services in ultimate victory, he said, could not be relied upon, their earlier forecasts
having often been at variance with the realities. As to the prospects of resisting invasion, even yet, he pointed out, the defenses
of Kujūkurihama [3]—for example—were far from completion.
Now, bearing the unbearable, he would submit to the terms of
the Potsdam Declaration, thereby to preserve the national polity.

The Imperial Conference thereupon ended, at about half-past
two. The Cabinet met at 3:00 A.M., and unanimously adopted
a decision in conformity with the Emperor's words.

I hastened to the Foreign Ministry and drafted the telegram of
notification to the Allies on the basis of the Imperial Conference
decision. Communication to the United States having to go
through the government of Switzerland, the Power protecting our
interests, the message which follows was dispatched to Minister
Kase in Bern at 7:00 A.M. of the 10th. An identical note went
to Minister Okamoto in Stockholm for communication through
the Swedish government to Great Britain and the U.S.S.R., and
steps were taken to have our decision conveyed to the Chinese
government also, through Switzerland.

In obedience to the gracious command of His Majesty the Emperor
who, ever anxious to enhance the cause of world peace, desires earnestly
to bring about a speedy termination of hostilities with a view to saving
mankind from the calamities to be imposed upon them by further continuation of the war, the Japanese Government several weeks ago asked
the Soviet Government, with which neutral relations then prevailed, to
render good offices in restoring peace vis-à-vis the enemy powers. Unfor-
tunately, these efforts in the interest of peace having failed, the Japanese

[3] "Ninety-Nine-League Beach," on the Pacific seventy miles east of Tokyo. The Army
had promised and had reported to the Emperor that the beach, expected to be a
point of invasion, would be newly fortified and garrisoned by June.

Government in conformity with the august wish of His Majesty to restore the general peace and desiring to put an end to the untold sufferings entailed by war as quickly as possible, have decided upon the following.

The Japanese Government are ready to accept the terms enumerated in the joint declaration which was issued at Potsdam on July 26th, 1945, by the heads of the Governments of the United States, Great Britain, and China, and later subscribed by the Soviet Government, with the understanding that the said declaration does not comprise any demand which prejudices the prerogatives of His Majesty as a Sovereign Ruler.

The Japanese Government sincerely hope that this understanding is warranted and desire keenly that an explicit indication to that effect will be speedily forthcoming.

August 10th, the 20th year of Shōwa.

On 9 August, meanwhile, Soviet Ambassador Malik had requested an interview with me. I instructed my subordinates to tell him that I could not receive him on that day—which was taken up, as explained above, with conferences of first importance—and that if his business was pressing he should see the Vice-Minister. The Ambassador replied, however, that the following day would do, and I therefore received him on the 10th. Malik stated that at the instruction of his government he was now to serve the declaration of war. After hearing him out, I reminded him that his country had attacked us while the treaty of neutrality between the U.S.S.R. and Japan was in full effect, and also adverted to its conduct in commencing a war on us before having given any answer to our request for rendition of good offices for the making of peace; moreover, while the ostensible reason for the Soviet declaration of war was that Japan had rejected the Potsdam Declaration, the U.S.S.R. had made no effort to ascertain the actual position of the Japanese government. The U.S.S.R.'s act, I said, would incur the condemnation of history. Ambassador Malik said nothing to the point, merely answering in general terms that there was nothing censurable in the actions of the U.S.S.R. I proceeded to tell him of the notification of the Japanese government of acceptance of the Potsdam Declaration, requesting him to transmit it to his government.

At three o'clock that afternoon there was an audience for the Senior Statesmen. I met with them beforehand at the Premier's Official Residence and explained the recent negotiations. General Koiso asked what was the relation between the Potsdam Declaration and Japan's armament; my answer was that we must expect the imposition of strict limitations, for although the declaration did not specifically prescribe disarmament, it did mention "driving militarism from the world" and the prohibition of "rearming for war." Koiso objected that by divine edict the maintenance of adequate armament was prescribed; General Tōjō joined in, announcing that, while he was in agreement with Koiso's opinion, now that the Imperial decision had been given he had nothing to say.

On the following day, the 11th, Princes Takamatsu, Mikasa, Kan-in, Asaka, Higashi-Kuni, Kaya and Takeda [4] assembled at Prince Takamatsu's palace, and for about two hours I discussed with them recent events and our activities in connection with them. I felt that the Princes fully understood the situation when I left them.

At 12:45 A.M. of the 12th the Foreign Ministry notified me by telephone of a broadcast announcement of the reply to Japan from America, Britain, Russia and China. There were some unclear points in the reply as we monitored it, and I instructed the Ministry officials in charge to study it; this was done by Vice-Minister Matsumoto and the Directors of the Political Affairs and

---

[4] Princes Takamatsu and Mikasa are the second and third brothers of the Emperor; the others, heads of separate Imperial princely houses, now abolished.

Treaty Bureaus, who foregathered at my house in Azabu at five-thirty in the morning. They reported to me as the result of their study that the Allies had in general confirmed the understanding which we had stated in our communication to them. The Allied reply—the official form of which, sent by Secretary of State Byrnes through the Swiss government, arrived only in the early hours of the 13th—was as follows:

With regard to the Japanese Government's message accepting the terms of the Potsdam proclamation but containing the statement, "with the understanding that the said declaration does not comprise any demand which prejudices the prerogatives of His Majesty as a sovereign ruler," our position is as follows:

From the moment of surrender, the authority of the Emperor and the Japanese Government to rule the state shall be subject to the Supreme Commander of the Allied powers, who will take such steps as he deems proper to effectuate the surrender terms.

The Emperor will be required to authorize and ensure the signature by the Government of Japan and the Japanese Imperial General Headquarters of the surrender terms necessary to carry out the provisions of the Potsdam Declaration, and shall issue his commands to all the Japanese military, naval and air authorities and to all the forces under their control wherever located to cease active operations and to surrender their arms, and to issue such other orders as the Supreme Commander may require to give effect to the surrender terms.

Immediately upon the surrender the Japanese Government shall transport prisoners of war and civilian internees to places of safety, as directed, where they can quickly be placed aboard Allied transports.

The ultimate form of government of Japan shall, in accordance with the Potsdam Declaration, be established by the freely exprexed will of the Japanese people.

The armed forces of the Allied Powers will remain in Japan until the purposes set forth in the Potsdam Declaration are achieved.

After the Foreign Ministry officials had left me on the morning of the 12th, I called on Premier Suzuki to inform him of the

Allies' response, and thence proceeded to the Imperial Palace at eleven to report it to the Emperor, who said that he considered that, the reply being satisfactory, we should accept it as it stood. The Emperor instructed me to communicate his wishes to the Premier, and I immediately returned to the Premier's Official Residence and did this.

While I was talking with the Premier, Baron Hiranuma came in. He said that he was not content with paragraphs 2 and 5 of the American note; I told him in brief the nature of the statement which I proposed making to the Cabinet—to which I shall come presently—and left the conference. I had got the impression, however, that the Premier had already had an intimation from the War Minister of some dissatisfaction with Byrnes' reply, the handling of which as a result promised to be far from easy. This question of the national polity was a very delicate one; it was self-evident that there were potent opinions in the U.S.S.R. and China against our Imperial system, nor could the United States be expected to show sympathetic understanding for it, either, as the events at the time of ratification of the Kellogg-Briand Pact had demonstrated.[5]

The Cabinet was called into special session again at 3:00 P.M. to consider the American reply. I commenced with a statement which, as it expressed the view which finally prevailed, I here record in some detail. The United States' response to our inquiry could not be said to be entirely reassuring. We had raised the question of the sovereignty of the Emperor, and the answer was that Japan's sovereignty would not be unlimited during occupa-

---

[5] The Pact of Paris—the "Kellogg-Briand Pact"—of 1928 recited that it was entered into by the signatories "in the names of their respective peoples." This phraseology aroused in Japan a storm of objection that it was *lèse-majesté* to speak of the Emperor as acting "in the name of the people," and prompted efforts, which however were fruitless, to obtain from the other signatories revision of the language of the pact.

tion, but that the authority of the Supreme Commander for the Allied Powers would be paramount, in order that the provisions of the Potsdam Declaration might be effectuated. This was not unforeseen; it is inevitable that under a guarantee occupation the sovereignty of the state will be limited to the extent requisite to implement the surrender terms. The position of the Emperor nevertheless remained, in principle, unimpaired; paragraph 2 of the reply was accordingly not unacceptable. Paragraph 3 provided that the Emperor was under obligation to carry out the terms of surrender, which was natural. Paragraphs 4 and 6, on the delivery of prisoners of war and the duration of the occupation, respectively, were self-explanatory and offered no difficulty. The problem was paragraph 5.

I reminded my listeners that the idea of establishing the form of government by the freely expressed will of the people appeared in the Atlantic Charter, which the Potsdam Declaration in this particular echoed; but this very provision, that the national polity of Japan was to be determined by the Japanese themselves, negatived any suggestion that there should be interference from without. At all events, even if the Allies had any intention of submitting the question to a referendum, it was impossible to conceive that the overwhelming loyal majority of our people would not wish to preserve our traditional system. On the other hand, there were reasons to believe that much antagonism existed among the Allies to the Imperial system of Japan, but that the Anglo-American leaders had managed to restrain it to the extent that Byrnes' reply evidenced. If we should now demand revisions in its phraseology, it was most probable that we should fail—just as we had failed in the case of the Kellogg-Briand Pact—to obtain them, and if we persisted in debating the point, it was quite likely that the harsher opinions among the Allies would then be given free rein, and demand for abolition of the Imperial house would be the upshot. In such an event, we should have to be resigned to the complete breaking off of the negotiations. But—I concluded —inasmuch as the Imperial Conference decision of the 9th constituted a recognition that continuation of the war was intolerable even if not impossible, the negotiations for surrender should at all hazards be consummated at their present stage.

In answer to my long argument, War Minister Anami expressed disappointment with the Allied reply in two particulars: that the Emperor was to be subject to the authority of the Supreme Commander, and that the ultimate form of government of Japan was to be established by the will of the people. Two or three other Cabinet members followed him with such remarks as that Japan's polity had existed from the time of the gods, and should not be determined by the will of the people, or that there was no alternative to carrying on the fight, because the Empire's soldiers could not bear being forced to disarm. All these suggestions I opposed; the Navy Minister sided with me. Then, suddenly, the Premier came forth with the startling remark that if disarmament was to be enforced upon us, keeping on with the war was inevitable. To obviate the difficulties to which this new argument would patently lead, I thought that the Cabinet meeting had best be adjourned, so I said, "As the official reply of the Allies has not yet arrived, we had better continue our discussion after receipt of it," and the meeting was thereupon recessed to the following day.

I went at once into the Premier's office and expostulated with him that it was no time to be bringing up the question of disarmament, that incessant bandying of words over the enemies' ultimatum was profitless. Unless we were resigned to rupture of the negotiations for peace, I pointed out, there was no alternative

327

to acceptance of their reply as it stood; but, as the Premier himself was well aware, the Emperor did not wish to see the war continue, and not only did it go without saying that the opinion of the Emperor as Commander in Chief should prevail, but the question now at issue involved the very existence of the Imperial house. I warned the Admiral that he should realize that if the opinions of the Premier and the Cabinet should incline to continuation of the war I might be compelled to report individually to the Throne my dissenting view.

I later informed Lord Keeper Kido of the complication which had arisen, but Kido assured me that there was no doubt that it was the intention of the Emperor, even if we did not again report to him, to accept the Allied reply without further parleying. Kido undertook to speak to the Premier himself, and in the evening telephoned me to say that he had done so, and that Admiral Suzuki now understood thoroughly.

On the 13th the members of the Supreme Council met at 8:30 A.M. at the Premier's Official Residence. The military members renewed their insistence that, paragraphs 2 and 5 of Byrnes' communication being unacceptable, we should have them amended, and that we should also advance additional proposals relative to the guarantee occupation and disarmament. I disputed with them, repeating what I had said at the Cabinet of the preceding day, and added that the suggestion of the new demands was absurd, the Emperor having already signified his desire at the last Imperial Conference that those demands be dropped. The Premier and the Navy Minister came to my support, but the discussion dragged on for many hours. When in the course of it the possibility of going on with the war again arose, War Minister Anami and Chief of Staff Umezu said merely that we could wage another battle in case of rupture of the negotiations, but that they could offer no promise of final victory. After the meeting adjourned, I had another audience to report the official receipt of the Allies' reply. I detailed also the deliberations since the day before, and the Emperor said that he approved of my position and that I should so inform the Premier.

The Cabinet resumed at four in the afternoon the session adjourned from the day before. At meetings of both Cabinet and Supreme Council at this period it was War Minister Anami with whom I contended most. Often I felt wearied with fighting; but conditions were too tense to permit any personal feeling to derogate from the utmost sincerity in arguing the issues preoccupying us, and my personal relations with General Anami remained unclouded to the end.

Unrest within the Army seemed to be gathering momentum. Frequent reports had come in from the 12th of plans for *coups d'état*—such as capturing the Emperor and separating the Cabinet ministers from him. The situation was growing very unquiet; the police guard of my house was greatly increased. I sensed that the War Minister was feeling some influence of the activities of the younger officers of the Army which were responsible for these conditions; he continually declaimed at Cabinet meetings and elsewhere the necessity of further bargaining over the surrender terms, since as he maintained we could fight another battle. On each such occasion I argued with equal determination for immediate acceptance of the Potsdam Declaration. The War Minister then endeavored, around the 12th and 13th, to entice Premier Suzuki, Baron Hiranuma and Lord Keeper Kido to his viewpoint; these efforts I forestalled by keeping in contact with the Premier constantly, and with Kido before and after each of my frequent audiences with the Emperor.

Many speculations concerning the sentiments of War Minister

Anami around those days have been offered. From my observation at my divers meetings with him, when he often spoke of "seeking for life out of death," I saw that his mind was possessed by the desire of inflicting one more severe blow on the enemy before making peace. As things turned out, he did not in the end persist in this idea; but there was a danger that if the War Minister and the other Army leaders should be subjected to pressure—from whatever source—for peace before they had been psychologically prepared for it, the Army's internal opposition might prevail, violence break out, and the entire movement for peace be jeopardized. That the War Minister was able at that time to control the growing restiveness of his subordinates, and to bring the Army successfully through its great crisis, was owed of course to the Imperial decision, but also in no small degree to the fact that through earnest discussions, at the meetings of the members of the Supreme Council for Direction of the War and elsewhere, over a long period, each member of the Supreme Council had been able to establish in his own mind a fundamental policy for ending the war.

Now, at the Cabinet meeting of the afternoon of the 13th, the War Minister seemed from time to time to fall into reverie, and —though at that morning's Supreme Council meeting he had borne the burden of disputing with me—to have less zest than theretofore for controversy. Some of the ministers—Home Minister Abe and others—favored trying to secure additional moderation of the Allied terms, with the intention of going on with the war if necessary. I answered that, judging from the Allied Powers' situation, further aproaches to them by us not only would be futile but would lead them to doubt the genuineness of our intention to make peace. Byrnes' reply made to us unquestionably represented the least common denominator of the terms of the several Allies, and it was imperative that we accept them as they now stood, if we were to bring about peace for the sake of the reconstruction of Japan and the welfare of the human race. Navy Minister Yonai, as usual, spoke in agreement with me, but there were still a few dissenting. The Premier then polled the Cabinet. Aside from Munitions Minister Toyoda, who was undecided, and Minister without Portfolio Sakurai, who deferred decision to the Premier, there were Navy Minister Yonai, Finance Minister Hirose, Agriculture and Forestry Minister Ishiguro, Education Minister Ōta, Welfare Minister Okada, Transportation Minister Kobiyama, Ministers without Portfolio Yasui, Sakonji and Shimomura, and myself, favoring acceptance of the Potsdam Declaration. War Minister Anami, Justice Minister Matsuzaka and Home Minister Abe opposed. Faced with a continuing schism, the Premier again adjourned the meeting.

I did not believe that the War Minister would lend himself to any attempt at a *coup d'état*, but I did fear that mutinousness among his officers might compel him to resign, or that disorder might otherwise develop. This danger made it necessary that a decision be arrived at at once, and I pointed this out to Premier Suzuki immediately upon the recessing of the Cabinet meeting, whereupon he said that he would go to the Palace and ask an Imperial decision.

That evening I had a small dinner party, planned from long before, in honor of two senior former ambassadors. Suddenly, during the party, a request for an immediate interview came from the Army and Navy Chiefs of Staff. I said that I would see them at the Premier's Official Residence, and, parting from my guests, there talked with them for two hours from nine o'clock. This discussion made no progress, but was a mere rehashing of the argument at the Supreme Council of that morning. During our conference, Navy Vice-Chief of Staff Ōnishi [6] burst into the room, and with great emotion appealed to the two Chiefs of Staff, saying that whether the American reply was satisfactory was a minor point; the fundamental issue was that the armed services had lost the confidence of the Emperor, their Commander in Chief. Therefore, "it is necessary to submit to the Emperor a plan to gain the victory, and to ask his reconsideration"; and he cried that we would not be defeated if we resolutely risked the lives of twenty million Japanese as a "special-attack corps." As not even the chiefs of staff would comment on this, Ōnishi, turning to me, demanded, "What is the Foreign Minister's opinion?" I replied, "If only we had any real hope of victory, no one would for a moment think of accepting the Potsdam Declaration; but winning one battle will not win the war for us."

I took my leave of them, and dropping in at the Foreign Ministry on the way back went through the telegrams from the overseas offices and the records of foreign broadcasts, which bore in upon me the growing gravity of our peril. I pondered, in the car returning home, that even if we offered the sacrifice of twenty million Japanese lives, they would but fall easy prey to machines and gunfire. We could bear anything, if it promised a return; the arrows and bamboo spears of which the military men were prating promised none. The soldiers' ignorance of the nature of modern warfare was beyond my understanding. In any event, no further delay could be tolerated, and it was, I thought, absolutely necessary that a final decision be reached on the morrow, as planned by the Premier.

---

[6] Vice-Admiral Ōnishi Takijirō (1891–1945), Commander of the 1st Air Fleet in the Philippines, 1944–45, and Vice-Chief of the Naval General Staff from May 1945, was reputed the originator of the idea of "special-attack corps" of suicide planes. At Japan's surrender Ōnishi, himself a pilot, flew out to sea in a fighter plane and disappeared.

I attended at the Premier's Official Residence on the 14th for the extraordinary meeting of the Cabinet. Upon my arrival, the Premier took me aside and told me that he wished to hold immediately, in the presence of the Emperor, a joint meeting of the Cabinet and the high command, and by an Imperial decision to put to rest once for all the question of the surrender. And, he added, the topic had been debated *ad nauseam*, there was nothing new to be said, the Emperor was fully conversant with the whole subject; and he therefore intended to have stated at the Imperial Conference only the arguments in contrariety to my opinion. Being in full accord, I said, "That will be fine." Soon, all the Cabinet members were summoned to the Palace (we were notified that, it being a sudden call to audience, the wearing of formal attire would be dispensed with, and the ministers who in midsummer were without even neckties borrowed them from the secretaries and managed to preserve a decency barely adequate to the occasion). We assembled, the Cabinet ministers, the chiefs of staff and the others who had attended the Imperial Conference of the 9th, in the air-raid shelter.

The Emperor appeared, and the Premier stated that after exhaustive deliberation on the Allies' reply to our communication of the 10th neither the Supreme Council members nor the Cabinet had been able to attain unanimity; and, explaining the position of the Foreign Minister and the opposing views, he asked that the latter be stated in the presence of the Emperor. General Umezu, Admiral Toyoda and General Anami, in that order, were called upon by the Premier. The Army men declared that we should negotiate further with the United States, as acceptance of the Potsdam Declaration on the basis of the American reply would endanger the national polity, and if we could not be sure of maintaining it, there was no alternative to carrying on the struggle even at the cost of a hundred million lives.[7] The Navy Chief of Staff was milder in his opinion, saying only that as we could not bear to swallow the American reply as it stood, it was appropriate once more to put forward our views. The Premier called on no others.

The Emperor then spoke. "It was not lightly, but upon mature consideration of conditions within and without the land, and especially of the development taken by the war, that I previously determined to accept the Potsdam Declaration. My determination is unaltered. I have heard the disputation over the recent reply given by the Allied Powers, but I consider that in general they have confirmed our understanding. As to paragraph 5 of the declaration, I agree with the Foreign Minister that it is not intended to subvert the national polity of Japan; but, unless the war be brought to an end at this moment, I fear that the national polity will be destroyed, and the nation annihilated. It is therefore my wish that we bear the unbearable and accept the Allied reply, thus to preserve the state as a state and spare my subjects further suffering. I wish you all to act in that intention. The War and Navy Ministers have told me that there is opposition within Army and Navy; I desire that the services also be made to comprehend my wishes." All the attendants wept at these reasoned and gracious words, and at conceiving the Emperor's emotions. It was an inexpressibly solemn and moving scene; as we retired down the long corridor, while returning in our cars, and at the resumed Cabinet meeting, each of us in his thoughts wept again.

During the Cabinet meeting which followed the Imperial Conference I called the Foreign Vice-Minister to compose the notification of surrender to the Allies. The Cabinet's deliberation on

[7] "Death in battle of the hundred million"—*"ichioku gyokusai"*—was a favorite slogan of wartime patriotism. The "hundred million" was made up by inclusion of the population of Korea.

the draft of the Imperial Rescript to be issued was not completed until evening, when it was submitted to the Emperor (the rescript was promulgated at 11:00 P.M. of the 14th). While we were still seated around the table after the Cabinet meeting, War Minister Anami came to me and, drawing himself up formally, said, "I have seen the Foreign Ministry's draft of the communication to the Allied Powers regarding the occupation and disarmament, and I am grateful beyond expression. Had I known that the matter would be dealt with in that way, I should not have felt it necessary to speak so zealously at the Imperial Conference." I answered that while I had resisted proposing these points as conditions of acceptance, there was no objection—as I had repeatedly said—to expressing them as our desires. Anami again thanked me formally, saying, "I am much indebted to you for all that you have done." I felt that he was overly polite; but at any rate we all parted with smiles, saying to each other that it was good that it was over.

Late on the night of the 14th, it was communicated to the governments of the United States, Great Britain, the U.S.S.R. and China, through the Swiss and Swedish governments, that the Emperor had promulgated an Imperial Rescript accepting the Potsdam Declaration, and was prepared to take necessary steps in connection therewith. During the night of the 14th–15th, there were some disorders in Tokyo. A segment of the Imperial Guards Division in the Palace grounds, bent upon seizing and suppressing the phonograph record of the rescript ending the war, which the Emperor had made for broadcast on the 15th, rose against the higher officers, and there was some bloodshed. The private residences of the Premier and Baron Hiranuma were attacked. In the early morning, we were told of the suicide of the War Minister; then I understood his attitude of the night before. There were many others who committed suicide, that night and in the following days.

The communication which had so moved General Anami was sent to the United States, through the Swiss government, in the early morning of the 15th. It was as follows.

The Japanese Government would like to be permitted to state to the Governments of America, Britain, China and the Soviet Union what they most earnestly desire with reference to the execution of certain provisions of the Potsdam Proclamation. This may be done possibly at the time of the signature. But fearing that they may not be able to find an appropriate opportunity, they take the liberty of addressing the Governments of the Four Powers through the good offices of the Government of Switzerland.

1. In view of the fact that the purpose of occupation as mentioned in the Potsdam Proclamation is solely to secure the achievement of the basic objectives set forth in the said Proclamation, the Japanese Government sincerely desire that the Four Powers, relying upon the good faith of the Japanese Government, will facilitate discharge by the Japanese Government of their obligations [so] as to forestall any unnecessary complications.

It is earnestly solicited that:

(a) In case of the entry of Allied fleets or troops in Japan Proper, the Japanese Government be notified in advance, so that arrangements can be made for reception.

(b) The number of the points in Japanese territory to be designated by the Allies for occupation be limited to minimum number, selection of the points be made in such a manner as to leave such a city as Tokyo unoccupied and the forces to be stationed at each point be made as small as possible.

2. Disarming of the Japanese forces, being a most delicate task as it involves over three millions of officers and men over-seas and having direct bearing on their honour, the Japanese Government will, of course, take utmost pains. But it is suggested that the best and the most effective method would be that under the command of His Majesty the Emperor, the Japanese forces are allowed to disarm themselves and surrender arms of their own accord.

336

Disarming of the Japanese forces on the Continent be carried out beginning on the front line and in successive stages.

In connection with the disarming it is hoped that Article 35 of the Hague Convention will be applied, and the honour of the soldier will be respected, permitting them, for instance, to wear swords. Further, [that] the Japanese Government be given to understand the Allies have no intention to employ disarmed Japanese soldiers for compulsory labour. It is sincerely hoped that shipment and transportation facilities necessary for the evacuation of the soldiers to their homeland will be speedily provided.

3. Since some forces are located in remote places, difficult to communicate the Imperial Order, it is desired that reasonable time be allowed before the cessation of hostilities.

4. It is hoped that the Allies will be good enough quickly to take necessary steps or extend us facilities for the shipment of indispensable foodstuffs and medical supplies to Japanese forces in distant islands, and for the transport of wounded soldiers from those islands.

In the afternoon of the 15th our Minister in Switzerland reported to me that demand had been made upon him by the United States Minister to transfer to the Allies the properties and archives of the Japanese legations and consulates in neutral countries. I replied that he should not comply with this demand, as it was not contemplated by any of the provisions of the Potsdam Declaration.

A formal conference of the Privy Council had been scheduled for 10:00 A.M. of the 15th, but the disturbance at the Palace during the night had caused it to be delayed, and it was eleven-thirty when the meeting opened in the presence of the Emperor. I reported in detail how the war had been terminated. At that point the meeting went into recess, it being noon, to listen to the Emperor's broadcast of the rescript proclaiming the surrender; as I heard the words, testifying to the ineffable benevolence and unselfishness of the Emperor, I imagined all the nation listening, profoundly moved, as were we all. The conference reconvening, there were a few questions from councilors. General Honjō [8] was apprehensive whether the occupation might be prolonged, but seemed content with my explanation that it would perhaps not continue too long, in view of the nature of a guarantee occupation and also of the recent precedents. Councilor Fukai touched me deeply when he said that while he had been gravely concerned over the outcome of the war and was very thankful that it had now come to an end, and while, needless to say, that result was owed to the glorious virtue of the Emperor, nevertheless he was most grateful for the painstaking efforts of the government, especially the Foreign Minister—so much so that he had come to the meeting in spite of illness, to express his gratitude.

Prior to the meeting of the Privy Council the Premier had consulted with me concerning resignation of the Cabinet, which I told him that I thought entirely appropriate. At a meeting held at two o'clock, following directly on adjournment of the Privy Council, the Premier proposed our resignation en bloc, on the grounds that it was regrettable that the Emperor had twice been troubled to make decisions at the crisis of surrender, and that it was proper that men younger and more capable of carrying out the rebuilding of our country should replace us. All the ministers approved, and the Premier tendered our resignations to the Emperor.

The Imperial command to cease hostilities was issued at noon of the 16th. Owing to the breakdown of communications, it was calculated that it would require two days for the order to reach the troops in Japan proper, six days for Manchuria, China and

---

[8] General Baron Honjō Shigeru (1876–1945) as Commander in Chief of the Kwantung Army in 1931–32 was the successful director of the Manchuria Incident and the establishment of Manchoukuo. He was nominated a Privy Councilor when he retired, in 1936. He committed suicide in November 1945, upon being designated a "war criminal."

the South Seas, and twelve for New Guinea and the Philippines. The Allies were so advised.

The rest was anticlimax. Prince Higashi-Kuni requested me to continue as Foreign Minister of the Cabinet which he was designated to form, but I declined. I felt no misgivings over having carried out the surrender—having only acted in conformity with the desire of the Emperor, I had in no way, as a Japanese, violated his wishes—but the reasons for Premier Suzuki's resignation applied with full force to me. Moreover, though I had worked for a peaceful Japanese-American solution in the days of 1941, now that we were defeated I might be charged as a war criminal, on account of having been Foreign Minister when the war began, and I did not wish to embarrass the new government by my presence. The Higashi-Kuni Cabinet therefore took office with Shigemitsu as Foreign Minister. On 18 August I turned over to Shigemitsu the business of the Foreign and Greater East Asia Ministries, which I had received from him; spoke to the staff members of the two Ministries of how the surrender had come about; and retired forever from public life.

I carried with me, and carry still, the memory ineradicable of those days. As I think today of that time, vividly before my eyes is the scene of the Imperial Conference at which the Emperor decided for surrender, and my feeling of then returns to me: that while the future of Japan is eternal, it is a blessing beyond estimation that this most dreadful of wars has been brought to a close, ending our country's agony and saving millions of lives; with that my life's work has been done, it does not matter what befalls me.

Draft completed 14 March 1950.

Appendixes

APPENDIX "A"

CHIEF FIGURES OF THE
JAPANESE GOVERNMENT AND HIGH COMMAND

July 1940 to August 1945

GOVERNMENT

SECOND KONOE CABINET (22 July 1940—17 July 1941)

Premier	PRINCE KONOE FUMIMARO
Foreign Minister	MATSUOKA YŌSUKE
Finance Minister	KAWADA ISAO
War Minister	LIEUTENANT GENERAL TŌJŌ HIDEKI
Navy Minister	ADMIRAL YOSHIDA ZENGO
	ADMIRAL OIKAWA KOSHIRŌ (5 September 1940)
Chief Secretary	TOMITA KENJI

THIRD KONOE CABINET (18 July—16 October 1941)

Premier	PRINCE KONOE FUMIMARO
Foreign Minister	ADMIRAL (RET.) TOYODA TEIJIRŌ
Finance Minister	OGURA MASATSUNE
War Minister	LIEUTENANT GENERAL TŌJŌ HIDEKI
Navy Minister	ADMIRAL OIKAWA KOSHIRŌ
Chief Secretary	TOMITA KENJI

TŌJŌ CABINET (18 October 1941—18 July 1944)

Premier	GENERAL TŌJŌ HIDEKI
Foreign Minister	TŌGŌ SHIGENORI
	GENERAL TŌJŌ HIDEKI (1 September 1942)
	TANI MASAYUKI (17 September 1942)
	SHIGEMITSU MAMORU (20 April 1943)
Finance Minister	KAYA OKINORI
	ISHIWATA SŌTARŌ (2 February 1944)

343

Appendix "A"

War Minister   GENERAL TŌJŌ HIDEKI
Navy Minister   ADMIRAL SHIMADA SHIGETARŌ
                  ADMIRAL NOMURA NAOKUNI (17 July 1944)

Chief Secretary   HOSHINO NAOKI

KOISO CABINET (22 July 1944—5 April 1945)
Premier   GENERAL (RET.) KOISO KUNIAKI
Co-Premier   ADMIRAL YONAI MITSUMASA
Foreign Minister   SHIGEMITSU MAMORU
Finance Minister   ISHIWATA SŌTARŌ
                  TSUSHIMA JUICHI (21 February 1945)
War Minister   FIELD MARSHAL SUGIYAMA GEN
Navy Minister   ADMIRAL YONAI MITSUMASA

Chief Secretary   TANAKA TAKEO
                  HIROSE HISATADA (11 February 1945)
                  ISHIWATA SŌTARŌ (21 February 1945)

SUZUKI CABINET (7 April—15 August 1945)
Premier   ADMIRAL (RET.) BARON SUZUKI KANTARŌ
Foreign Minister   TŌGŌ SHIGENORI
Finance Minister   HIROSE TOYOSAKU
War Minister   GENERAL ANAMI KORECHIKA
Navy Minister   ADMIRAL YONAI MITSUMASA

Chief Secretary   SAKOMIZU HISATSUNE

HIGH COMMAND

Army

Chief of General Staff
                  FIELD MARSHAL PRINCE KAN-IN (13 December 1931)
                  FIELD MARSHAL SUGIYAMA GEN (3 October 1940)
                  GENERAL TŌJŌ HIDEKI (21 February 1944)
                  GENERAL UMEZU YOSHIJIRŌ (22 July 1944)
Vice-Chief of General Staff
                  LIEUTENANT GENERAL SAWADA SHIGERU (2 October 1939)

LIEUTENANT GENERAL TSUKADA KŌ (15 November 1940)

LIEUTENANT GENERAL TANABE MORITAKE (6 November 1941)

LIEUTENANT GENERAL HATA HIKOSABURŌ (8 April 1943)

GENERAL USHIROKU JUN (21 February 1944)

LIEUTENANT GENERAL KAWABE TORASHIRŌ (7 April 1945)

Director of Military Affairs Bureau

LIEUTENANT GENERAL MUTŌ AKIRA (30 September 1939)

LIEUTENANT GENERAL SATŌ KENRYŌ (20 April 1942)

LIEUTENANT GENERAL SANADA JŌICHIRŌ (14 December 1944)

LIEUTENANT GENERAL YOSHIZUMI MASAO (27 March 1945)

Navy

Chief of General Staff

ADMIRAL OF THE FLEET PRINCE FUSHIMI (2 February 1932)

ADMIRAL OF THE FLEET NAGANO OSAMI (9 April 1941)

ADMIRAL SHIMADA SHIGETARŌ (21 February 1944)

ADMIRAL OIKAWA KOSHIRŌ (2 August 1944)

ADMIRAL TOYODA SOEMU (29 May 1945)

Vice-Chief of General Staff

VICE-ADMIRAL KONDŌ NOBUTAKE (21 October 1939)

VICE-ADMIRAL ITŌ SEIICHI (1 September 1941)

VICE-ADMIRAL TSUKAHARA NISHIZŌ (1 March 1944)

VICE-ADMIRAL OZAWA JISABURŌ (18 November 1944)

VICE-ADMIRAL ŌNISHI TAKIJIRŌ (29 May 1945)

VICE-ADMIRAL TAKAYANAGI GIHACHI (20 August 1945)

Director of Naval Affairs Bureau

REAR ADMIRAL ABE KATSUO (18 October 1939)

VICE-ADMIRAL OKA TAKASUMI (15 October 1940)

VICE-ADMIRAL TADA TAKEO (18 July 1944)

VICE-ADMIRAL HOSHINA ZENSHIRŌ (15 May 1945)

APPENDIX "B"

JAPANESE-AMERICAN DRAFT-UNDERSTANDING

9 April 1941

THE GOVERNMENTS of the United States and of Japan accept joint responsibility for the initiation and conclusion of a general agreement disposing the resumption of our traditional friendly relations.

Without reference to specific causes of recent estrangement, it is the sincere desire of both Governments that the incidents which led to the deterioration of amicable sentiment among our peoples should be prevented from recurrence and corrected in their unforeseen and unfortunate consequences.

It is our present hope that, by a joint effort, our nations may establish a just Peace in the Pacific; and by the rapid consummation of an *entente cordiale*, arrest, if not dispel, the tragic confusion that now threatens to engulf civilization.

For such decisive action, protracted negotiations would seem ill-suited and weakening. We, therefore, suggest that adequate instrumentalities should be developed for the realization of a general agreement which would bind, meanwhile, both governments in honor and in act.

It is our belief that such an understanding should comprise only the pivotal issues of urgency and not the accessory concerns which could be deliberated at a Conference and appropriately confirmed by our respective Governments.

We presume to anticipate that our Governments could achieve harmonious relations if certain situations and attitudes were clarified or improved; to wit:

1. The concepts of the United States and of Japan respecting international relations and the character of nations.
2. The attitudes of both governments toward the European War.
3. The relations of both nations toward the China affair.
4. Naval, aerial and mercantile marine relations in the Pacific.
5. Commerce between both nations and their financial cooperation.

6. Economic activity of both nations in the Southwestern Pacific area.
7. The policies of both nations affecting political stabilization in the Pacific.

Accordingly, we have come to the following mutual understanding subject, of course, to modifications by the United States Government and subject to the official and final decision of the Government of Japan.

I. The Concepts of the United States and of Japan respecting International Relations and the Character of Nations

The Governments of the United States and of Japan might jointly acknowledge each other as equally sovereign states and contiguous Pacific powers.

Both Governments assert the unanimity of their national policies as directed toward the foundation of a lasting peace and the inauguration of a new era of respectful confidence and cooperation among our peoples.

Both Governments might declare that it is their traditional, and present, concept and conviction that nations and races compose, as members of a family, one household; each equally enjoying rights and admitting responsibilities with a mutuality of interests regulated by peaceful processes and directed to the pursuit of their moral and physical welfare, which they are bound to defend for themselves as they are bound not to destroy for others.

Both Governments are firmly determined that their respective traditional concepts on the character of nations and the underlying moral principles of social order and national life will continue to be preserved and never transformed by foreign ideas or ideologies contrary to those moral principles and concepts.

II. The Attitudes of both Governments toward the European War

The Government of Japan maintains that the purpose of its Axis Alliance was, and is, defensive and designed to prevent the extension of military grouping among nations not directly affected by the European War.

The Government of Japan, with no intention of evading its existing treaty obligation, desires to declare that its military obligation under the Axis Alliance comes into force only when one of the parties of the Alliance is aggressively attacked by a power not at present involved in the European War.

The Government of the United States maintains that its attitude toward the European War is, and will continue to be, determined by no aggressive alliance aimed to assist any one nation against another. The United States maintains that it is pledged to the hate of war, and accordingly, its attitude toward the European War is, and will continue to be, determined solely and exclusively by considerations of the protective defense of its own national welfare and security.

III. China Affairs

The President of the United States, if the following terms are approved by His Excellency and guaranteed by the Government of Japan, might request the Chiang-Kai-Chek [*sic*] regime to negotiate peace with Japan.

a. Independence of China

b. Withdrawal of Japanese troops from Chinese territory, in accordance with an agreement to be reached between Japan and China

c. No acquisition of Chinese territory

d. No imposition of indemnities

e. Resumption of the "Open Door;" the interpretation and application of which shall be agreed upon at some future, convenient time between the United States and Japan

f. Coalescence of the Governments of Chiang-Kai-Chek and of Wang-Ching-Wei

g. No large-scale or concentrated immigration of Japanese into Chinese territory

h. Recognition of Manchukuo.

With the acceptance by the Chiang-Kai-Chek regime of the aforementioned Presidential request, the Japanese Government shall commence direct peace negotiations with the newly coalesced Chinese Government, or constituent elements thereof.

The Government of Japan shall submit to the Chinese concrete terms of peace, within the limits of aforesaid general terms and along the line of neighborly friendship, joint defense against communistic activities and economic cooperation.

Should the Chiang-Kai-Chek regime reject the request of President Roosevelt, the United States Government shall discontinue assistance to the Chinese.

IV. Naval, Aerial and Mercantile Marine Relations in the Pacific

a. As both the Americans and the Japanese are desirous of maintaining the peace in the Pacific, they shall not resort to such disposition of their naval forces and aerial forces as to menace each other. Detailed, concrete agreement thereof shall be left for determination at the proposed joint Conference.

b. At the conclusion of the projected Conference, each nation might despatch a courtesy naval squadron to visit the country of the other and signalize the new era of Peace in the Pacific.

c. With the first ray of hope for the settlement of China affairs, the Japanese Government will agree, if desired, to use their good offices to release for contract by Americans certain percentage of their total tonnage of merchant vessels, chiefly for the Pacific service, so soon as they can be released from their present commitments. The amount of such tonnage shall be determined at the Conference.

V. Commerce between both Nations and their Financial Cooperation

When official approbation to the present understanding has been given by both Governments, the United States and Japan shall assure each other to mutually supply such commodities as are respectively available or required by either of them. Both governments further consent to take necessary steps to the resumption of normal trade relations as formerly established under the Treaty of Navigation and Commerce between the United States and Japan. If a new commercial treaty is desired by both governments, it could be elaborated at the proposed conference and concluded in accordance with usual procedure.

For the advancement of economic cooperation between both nations, it is suggested that the United States extend to Japan a gold credit in amounts sufficient to foster trade and industrial development directed to the betterment of Far Eastern economic conditions and to the sustained economic cooperation of the Governments of the United States and of Japan.

VI. Economic Activity of both Nations in the Southwestern Pacific Area

On the pledged basis of guarantee that Japanese activities in the Southwestern Pacific area shall be carried on by peaceful means, without resorting to arms, American cooperation and support shall be given in the production and procurement of natural resources (such as oil, rubber, tin, nickel) which Japan needs.

VII. *The Policies of both Nations affecting Political Stabilization in the Pacific*

    a. The Governments of the United States and of Japan will not acquiesce in the future transfer of territories or the relegation of existing States within the Far East and in the Southwestern Pacific area to any European Power.

    b. The Governments of the United States and of Japan jointly guarantee the independence of the Philippine Islands and will consider means to come to their assistance in the event of unprovoked aggression by any third Power.

    c. The Government of Japan requests the friendly and diplomatic assistance of the Government of the United States for the removal of Hongkong and Singapore as doorways to further political encroachment by the British in the Far East.

    d. Japanese Immigration to the United States and to the Southwestern Pacific area shall receive amicable consideration—on a basis of equality with other nationals and freedom from discrimination.

Conference

    a. It is suggested that a Conference between Delegates of the United States and of Japan be held at Honolulu and that this Conference be opened for the United States by President Roosevelt and for Japan by Prince Konoye. The delegates could number less than five each, exclusive of experts, clerks, etc.

    b. There shall be no foreign observers at the Conference.

    c. This Conference could be held as soon as possible (May 1941) after the present understanding has been reached.

    d. The agenda of the Conference would not include a reconsideration of the present understanding but would direct its efforts to the specification of the prearranged agenda and drafting of instruments to effectuate the understanding. The precise agenda could be determined upon by mutual agreement between both Governments.

Addendum

The present understanding shall be kept as a confidential memorandum between the Governments of the United States and of Japan.

The scope, character and timing of the announcement of this understanding will be agreed upon by both Governments.

APPENDIX "C"

DECISION OF THE
IMPERIAL CONFERENCE OF 2 JULY 1941

Outline of National Policy Attendant
upon the Changing Situation

I

POLICY

1. Regardless of changes in world conditions, Japan shall firmly adhere to the policy of establishment of the Greater East Asia Co-Prosperity Sphere, thereby contributing to maintenance of the peace of the world.

2. Japan shall continue to press forward with efforts for solution of the China Affair, and shall proceed with the southward movement to secure the basis for self-sufficiency and self-defense. The Northern problem will be dealt with in accordance with changes in the situation.

3. Japan shall overcome all obstacles to attainment of the foregoing objectives.

II

SUMMARY

1. In order to expedite the surrender of the Chiang regime, increased pressure from the Southern areas shall be applied. In accordance with the changes in the situation, the right of hostilities against the Chungking regime shall be resorted to at the opportune time, and enemy concessions in China shall be confiscated.

2. For the sake of her self-sufficiency and self-defense, Japan shall continue necessary diplomatic negotiations with nations concerned in the southern regions, and shall promote other necessary measures. For this purpose preparations shall be made for war against Britain and the United States, and various moves vis-à-vis Indochina and Thailand shall first be carried out in accordance with the "Outline of Measures toward French Indochina and Thailand" and "Concerning the Expediting of Measures

351

vis-à-vis the South," thereby strengthening our position for southward advance.

In order to achieve these purposes, Japan shall not decline war with Britain and America.

3. Though our position toward the Russo-German war shall be based on the spirit of the Tripartite Axis, we shall not intervene for the time being, but shall maintain an independent position while secretly completing military preparations against the U.S.S.R. Meanwhile, diplomatic negotiations shall of course be carried on with great caution.

Should the Russo-German war develop advantageously for Japan, she shall resort to arms for solution of the Northern problem, thereby establishing security in the North.

4. In the making of decisions on various measures, especially resort to arms, for execution of the preceding paragraph, maintenance of the basic position for war against Britain and the United States shall not be substantially prejudiced.

5. In accordance with the established policy, every effort, diplomatic and otherwise, shall be made to restrain the United States from entering the war. Should the United States nevertheless do so, Japan shall act in accordance with the Tripartite Pact; but the timing and method of resort to arms shall be independently decided.

6. The nation shall promptly be shifted to a complete and firm war footing. Special efforts shall be made to strengthen the national defense.

7. Concrete plans shall be separately decided.

APPENDIX "D"

DECISION OF THE
IMPERIAL CONFERENCE OF 6 SEPTEMBER 1941

Outline of Execution of National Policy

IN VIEW OF the current grave state of affairs, and especially of the offensive against Japan precipitated by the United States, Great Britain, the Netherlands and other countries, the situation of the U.S.S.R., and the resilience of our national strength, Japan will carry out the action vis-à-vis the South, provided for by the "Outline of National Policy Attendant upon the Changing Situation," as follows:

1. In order to insure her self-sufficiency and self-defense, Japan shall complete her preparations for war by the latter part of October, with the determination not to decline war with the United States (and Britain and the Netherlands).

2. Japan shall, in parallel with the above, endeavor to exhaust diplomatic measures to attain her demands vis-à-vis the United States and Britain.

The minimum demands to be attained in negotiations with the United States and Great Britain, together with the maximum concessions which Japan can make, are as stated in the Appendix.

3. Should there be no prospect, by early October, of attainment of our demands through the above negotiations, war against the United States (and Britain and the Netherlands) shall be forthwith determined upon.

Measures other than those concerning the South shall be carried out in accordance with the established national policy. In particular, efforts shall be made to avert the formation of a Russo-American combined front against Japan.

APPENDIX

Minimum Demands to be Attained and Maximum
Concessions which may be Made in Negotiations
with the United States (and Great Britain)

Appendix "D"

I

Minimum Demands to be Attained

1. Matters relating to the China Affair

The United States and Great Britain shall neither intervene in the China Affair nor disurb Japan's disposition of it.

  a. Japan's efforts to settle the China Affair on the basis of the Japan-China Treaty of Basic Relations and the Japan-Manchoukuo-China Joint Declaration shall not be obstructed.

  b. The Burma Road shall be closed, and neither military nor economic aid shall be given to the Chiang regime.

N.B.: The above does not derogate from Japan's position in Operation "N" [1] in connection with settlement of the China Affair. In particular, the stationing of troops in China, in accordance with agreement to be reached between Japan and China, shall be firmly insisted upon.

However, assurance may be given that Japan is prepared in principle to withdraw troops dispatched to China for carrying out the China Affair, other than those referred to in the preceding paragraph.

Assurance may also be given, with regard to the rights and interests in China of the United States and Great Britain, that Japan has no intention of restricting them, so far as those nations understand the new East Asia and act accordingly.

2. Matters Necessary for the Security of the National Defense

The United States and Great Britain shall not take such action in the Far East as to prejudice Japan's national defense.

  a. The special relations, based on the Japanese-French Agreement, between Japan and French Indochina shall be recognized.

  b. No military installations shall be established in Thailand, the Netherlands East Indies, China or the Soviet Far East.

  c. Military forces in the Far East will not be reinforced beyond their present levels.

3. Matters relating to Acquisition by Japan of Necessary Materials

The United States and Japan shall co-operate in obtaining materials necessary for Japan.

  a. They shall restore trade relations with Japan, and shall make available from the territories in the Southwest Pacific materials indispensable for her existence.

---

[1] "Operation Nomura," *i.e.*, the Japanese-American negotiations.

b. They shall ungrudgingly co-operate in Japan's economic collaboration with Thailand and the Netherlands East Indies.

II

Maximum Concessions which can be Made

Should the demands of Japan as stated in I be accepted:

1. Japan will make no military advance, with French Indochina as a base, into any neighboring area other than China.

2. Japan will undertake to withdraw her troops from French Indochina upon establishment of an equitable peace in the Far East.

3. Japan is prepared to guarantee the neutrality of the Philippines.

N.B.: (1) If inquiries are made concerning Japan's attitude toward the Tripartite Alliance, it should be affirmed that there will be no change in Japan's carrying out of her obligations under the Tripartite Pact. We should not, however, initiate discussion of either Japan's attitude toward the Tripartite Pact or that of the United States toward the European War.

(2) If inquiries are made concerning Japan's attitude toward the U.S.S.R., reply should be made that there is no intention on our side to resort to military action so long as the U.S.S.R. is faithful to the Neutrality Pact and refrains from taking action, such as menacing Japan and Manchoukuo, in conflict with the spirit of the Pact.

INDEX

357

Index

Index

Index

Index

370

Index

ABOUT THE TRANSLATORS

MR. TŌGŌ FUMIHIKO *has been a Japanese diplomat since his graduation from Tokyo University in 1939, and he is now a member of the Japanese Permanent Delegation at Geneva, Switzerland. In accordance with a Japanese custom, he was adopted as a son by Foreign Minister Tōgō when he married Ise, daughter of the former Foreign Minister and his German-born wife.*

MR. BEN BRUCE BLAKENEY *first went to Japan as an intelligence officer in the Air Force. He returned as defense counsel in the war-crimes trials which began in 1946. He defended, among others, Foreign Minister Tōgō, General Umezu, chief of the Army General Staff, and Admiral Toyoda, chief of the Naval General Staff and the first high-ranking officer to be acquitted. In 1949 he became lecturer in American law at Tokyo University, and he is also engaged in the general practice of law in Tokyo.*

A PAGE FROM THE ORIGINAL MANUSCRIPT